The Economic
Point of View

Studies in Economic Theory
Laurence S. Moss, Editor

The Economic Point of View

An Essay in the History of Economic Thought

By Israel M. Kirzner

Edited with an Introduction by
Laurence S. Moss

SHEED AND WARD, INC.
Subsidiary of Universal Press Syndicate
Kansas City

The Economic Point of View
Copyright © 1960 by the Institute for Humane Studies.
Introduction to the Second Edition
Copyright © 1976 by the Institute for Humane
Studies, Inc., Menlo Park, California

Library of Congress Cataloging in Publication Data

Kirzner, Israel M
    The economic point of view.

    (Studies in economic theory)
    Includes bibliographical references and indexes.
    1. Economics.   2. Economics—History.   I. Title.
II. Series.
HB71.K5   1975   330'.09   75-42449
ISBN 0-8362-0656-8
ISBN 0-8362-0657-6 pbk.

B'EZRAS HASHEM
TO OUR PARENTS

Foreword

The inauguration of a systematic science of economics, an achievement of the social philosophy of the Enlightenment that also begot the doctrine of popular sovereignty, was a challenge to the powers that be. Economics shows that there prevails in the succession and interdependence of the market phenomena an inescapable regularity that man must take into full account if he wants to attain ends aimed at. Even the most mighty government, operating with the utmost severity, cannot succeed in endeavors that are contrary to what has been called "economic law." It is obvious why despotic rulers as well as leaders of revolutionary masses disliked such doctrines. For them economics was the "dismal science" and they fought it indefatigably.

However, it was not the hostility of governments and powerful political parties that fomented the protracted discussions about the epistemological character and the logical method of economics in which the very existence and significance of this branch of knowledge were again and again questioned. What generated these debates was the vagueness that the early economists evinced in defining the field of their studies. It would be absurd to blame them for this want of clearness. They had sufficient reasons for concentrating upon those problems which they were trying to deal with and for neglecting others. What had stimulated their inquiry was definite issues of contemporary political controversies. Their great accomplishment was the discovery of the uniform order prevailing in the emergence of events previously considered chaotic. Only the later generations of economists were puzzled with the epistemological problems involved.

Doctor Kirzner's book provides a historical account of all the solutions suggested in this debate. It is a very valuable contribution to the history of ideas, describing the march of economics from a science of wealth to a science of human action. The author does not, in the fashion adopted by some recent histories of economic doctrines, indulge in value judgments and paradoxical observations. He prefers to follow the sober methods of the best historians of economic theories, Böhm-Bawerk and Edwin Cannan. Every economist—and for that matter everybody interested in problems of general epistemology—will read with great profit Doctor Kirzner's analyses, especially his treatment of the famous discussion between Benedetto Croce and Vilfredo Pareto or the critical examination of the ideas of Max Weber and Lionel Robbins.

Essays on the history of economic thought are to be appreciated not only purely as history. No less important is the fact that they enable us to re-examine the present state of economic theory in the light of all attempts earlier generations made for their solution. In comparing our point of view with past achievements and errors we may either detect flaws in our own theories or find new and better reasons for their confirmation. Doctor Kirzner's thoughtful essay is a real aid in such a re-examination and in this consists its great value.

LUDWIG VON MISES

Introduction to the Second Edition

The first edition of Israel M. Kirzner's *The Economic Point of View* was published in 1960. In the meantime, the dogmatic brand of positivism that advocated the banishment of all references to mental states from scientific explanations and their replacement by the "data of the senses" has been discredited. In addition, many contemporary philosophers concede the inherent rationality of human action, that is, man's capability of freely choosing among alternatives (as well as creatively discovering what these alternatives are); and further the indeterminateness of individual behavior on the basis of what has gone before. Yet despite these important concessions to the subjectivist position regarding methodological precepts consistent with sound scientific investigation, the full import of the teachings of Ludwig von Mises in *Human Action* and of Frank H. Knight in *On the History and Method of Economics* about the subjective character of economic phenomena either has not been fully digested by practicing economists or else has been received with great hostility by those anxious to submit their models to statistical testing.

As Kirzner's study makes clear, the subject matter of economics is human action, and a concern with the abstract character of action is what defines the economic point of view. Human action in contrast to, say, reflexive action is action directed toward goals and purposes. Furthermore, while such action often results in the measurable displacement of real world objects, the significance of such displacements cannot be adequately understood by merely correlating (or regressing) one displacement with (on) another. Economic explanations must either explicitly or implicitly make reference to individual purposes and plans; otherwise they ignore a realm of experience as real as the world of things. While modern philosophers of science often insist that to explain an event is to show that it is an instance of a scientific law, Kirzner would add this proviso: the general law must itself be explicable in terms of the purposes and plans of acting individuals. According to Kirzner, the entire science of economics is a subset of the broader (but less developed) discipline that Mises termed "praxeology," or the science of human action.

It took two hundred years for economists to discover that the subject matter of their discipline was none other than the structure of human action itself. Much of Kirzner's study is a historical survey of the various attempts economists have made to define the scope of their discipline. According to Kirzner, significant progress in this area began only in the second quarter of this century when Lionel Robbins, Mises, and Knight instituted a shift from a "search for a department of human affairs to which the adjective 'economic' applies, to a search for the appropriate aspect of affairs to which economic concepts are of relevance." Kirzner's study is controversial when he declares that, by insisting on the subjectivity of their discipline, Mises and Knight produced an advanced and more perfect understanding of what in fact constitutes economic knowledge.

Modern economists are generally quite comfortable with some variant of Robbins's definition of economics as a discipline concerned with the allocation of scarce means among alternative ends where the means themselves are capable of a variety of applications. What they are apparently less willing to do is go beyond Robbins and insist, after Mises, that the science must be founded on an analysis of the subjective categories of human action because these categories provide the only firm grounding for economic laws. Modern economists tend to consider economic laws useful, not because they are consistent with our understanding of human action, but because they help organize large bodies of business and government data. Often economists act as if the only importance of economic theory is the ease and elegance with which it helps shuffle and reshuffle large bodies of statistical data (an unfortunate consequence of the novelty and increased availability of high-speed computers).

In recent years the problem or 'grounding aggregate relationships on microeconomic foundations has attracted some attention among economists. This concern is certainly in the spirit of the program Mises and other members of the subjective school advocated many years ago. But it is also important to realize that aggregate relationships are themselves worthless if the statistical data on which they are based distort the underlying reality they are supposed to represent.

Consider, for example, the notion of "cost" and how it is often misnamed by economists. The cost of a specific action to a decision maker is the next best opportunity he gives up when he chooses that course of action over all others. The cost of a certain action is always related to another course of action that has not been taken. But if the other course of action has not been taken, then there is no record of it in the market. Thus, at best, what economists call the "cost of production," or the money outlay of a firm in producing an object, may represent the value of the next best application of these resources to the other market participants; but whether or not these expenses also measure the opportunity cost forgone by the firm's decision maker is another question. A firm may be making a money rate of return of 20 percent on its financial investment at one point in time and be quite satisfied. At another point in time a money return of 22 percent may not be enough to keep that firm in the industry if it discovers an opportunity for making greater profits still. Clearly the connection between recorded, or accounting, costs and those costs that influence human choice may be so tenuous that statistical laws founded on the former will reveal very little about human action itself.

In the last decade or so applied economics has become synonymous with trying to change the behavior or specific values of statistical aggregates. The important question of how these statistics are at all related to the qualitative choices made by acting individuals is treated as if it were unworthy of serious scholarly investigation or as if it were something better left to government accountants. Thus, where once the goal of a sound monetary policy was to guarantee a stable and secure currency, the modern concern is that of "stabilizing prices," which frequently means no more than keeping the consumer price index constant at some base-period value or else permitting departures from that base value according to some definite and predictable rule. Often a government policy designed to contribute to the fullest utilization of resources becomes bogged down to the point of an obsession with the behavior of the Bureau of Labor Statistics' estimate of unemployment. The fact that time spent unemployed may be used for an entirely different purpose in 1975 from that used in 1933 does not seem to bother many economists.

If, however, one considers the most important task of applied economics to be the discovery of the type of institutional structure that provides for the greatest coordination of individual plans and efforts, then the subjective character of the discipline is brought to the forefront. Here the goal of science is to aid men not in maximizing or minimizing some statistical average, but in eliminating or lessening the frustrations that occur when the plans of one individual come into conflict with those of another. For example, it is not the physical existence of capital on which the prosperity of society's members depends but rather the position these goods play in the plans of acting individuals. One need not go so far as some members of the subjectivist school and argue that statistical investigations are of absolutely no value in the derivation of economic laws. It is sufficient to insist that the meaning of such measurements be constantly checked against the underlying human plans and purposes that they allegedly represent.

Thus at the very heart of the science of economics is the idea that capital goods, consumer goods, costs of production, and the like take on economic significance, not because of their physical characteristics or the procedures of tax accounting, but because of the meaning their individual owners attach to them in the course of pursuing their ends. It is my hope that this new edition of Kirzner's study of *The Economic Point of View* will reacquaint economists with the subjective basis of their science and help to engender a more critical attitude toward modern-day research methods.

LAURENCE S. MOSS

Charlottesville, Virginia
October 1975

Author's Preface

The present essay is an attempt to explore with some thoroughness an extremely narrow area within the field of the history of economic thought. Although this area is narrow, it merits a scrutiny quite out of proportion to its extension, relating as it does to fundamental ideas around which the entire corpus of economic thought has revolved for some two centuries. It remains as true today as ever before that the direction taken by economic theory is in large measure determined by the "point of view" adopted by the economist as his special perspective. It is in this connection that the present study seeks to make its contribution, by setting up the problem in its proper context as a chapter in the history of ideas.

The nature of the subject matter, in this instance, has made thoroughness in its exploration a matter of extreme difficulty, exhaustiveness a sheer impossibility. In general my aim has been to provide a careful survey of the literature relevant to each of the ideas treated, while resolutely refusing to succumb to those imperious temptations which would have turned my book into an annotated bibliography. This has frequently moved me to refrain from mentioning works of considerable importance in order to avoid fruitless repetition of ideas already cited from other sources. Despite the self-restraint exercised in this regard, I have felt it wise to relegate all notes and references to the end of the book, in order to make for a smoother account in the body of the work.

My exploration of the subject dealt with in this book began several years ago while writing my doctoral dissertation under Professor Mises. Much of the material gathered in my work on that project has provided a useful foundation for the broader investigation undertaken in preparation for the present volume.

Grateful appreciation is here accorded for the assistance which enabled me to pursue my researches at that time, first as Volker Fellow, and then as an Earhart Fellow, at New York University.

My intellectual debt to the unique contributions made by Professor Mises to the epistemological problems discussed in my book is, I believe, sufficiently evident throughout the work itself. Here I take particular pleasure in recording the friendly patience and warm encouragement which he has shown me unstintingly throughout the project, as well as the inspiration which I have derived from his own enthusiasm and penetrating integrity of thought, as unfolded in countless discussions, both privately and in seminar.

I have benefited on numerous occasions from highly valuable discussions on various aspects of the study with my colleagues in the Department of Economics, School of Commerce, New York University. I am, in addition, particularly grateful to Dean T. L. Norton and Professor T. J. Anderson, Chairman of the Department, for making special arrangements to lighten my teaching duties during a part of the time spent in research on this project, as well as for their constant encouragement during its completion. Valuable assistance in connection with questions of style and clarity of expression has been gratefully received from Dr. Arthur Goddard. Responsibility for the shortcomings of the work is, of course, undividedly my own.

I have, finally, the pleasant if somewhat difficult task of acknowledging my wife's contribution, both tangible and intangible, to the emergence of the volume. My indebtedness in this regard (as well as the difficulty of its expression) is the deeper for the peculiar circumstance that the altogether indispensable nature of this contribution is itself in large measure to be ascribed to conditions rendering it at the same time exceptionally meritorious.

ISRAEL M. KIRZNER

New York, N. Y.
March, 1960

Acknowledgments

The author gratefully acknowledges his indebtedness to the courtesy of the following institutions, associations, and publishers:

The American Economic Association (for permission to quote from their publications, including the *Survey of Contemporary Economics*, 1949); George Allen and Unwin Ltd. (for permission to quote from N. Senior, *Outline of Political Economy*, and J. Bentham, *Economic Writings*, edited by Stark); Jonathan Cape Limited (for permission to quote from L. Mises, *Socialism*, and L. Robbins, *The Economic Causes of War*); Columbia University Press (for permission to quote from E.R.A. Seligman, *Economic Interpretation of History*, 1902, and from Political Science Quarterly, 1901); the editorial Board of *Economica* (for permission to quote from *Economica*, 1933, 1941); the editor of the *Economic Record* and the Melbourne University Press (for permission to quote from the *Economic Record*, No. 61, November, 1955); The Free Press (for permission to quote from *Max Weber on the Methodology of the Social Sciences*); Harper and Brothers (for permission to quote from F. H. Knight, *The Ethics of Competition*); Harvard University Press (for permission to quote from the *Quarterly Journal of Economics* and from H. Myint, *Theories of Welfare Economics*, 1948); William Hodge and Co. Ltd. (for permission to quote from Max Weber, *Theories of Social and Economic Organization*); Howard Allen, Inc. (for permission to quote from K. Boulding, *The Skills of the Economist*); Richard D. Irwin, Inc. (for permission to quote from T. Scitovsky, *Welfare and Competition*); Kelley and Millman, Inc. (for permission to quote from W. Mitchell, *The Backward Art of Spending Money*); Alfred A. Knopf, Inc. (for permission to quote from S. Patten, *Essays in Economic Theory*, edited by R. Tugwell); Longmans, Green and Co., Ltd. (for permission to quote from R. Hawtrey, *The Economic Problem*); The Macmillan Company, New York (for permission to quote from L. Haney, *History of Economic Thought*, 1949, F.S.C. Northrop, *Logic of the Sciences and*

Humanities, 1949, A. Marshall, *Principles of Economics,* 1920); Macmillan and Co. Ltd., London (for permission to quote from *Economic Journal, International Economic Papers,* and works by Croce, Hutchinson, Jevons, Macfie, Marshall, Robbins, and Pigou; for the Pigou works acknowledgment is gratefully extended also to the St. Martin's Press, Inc., New York); Oxford University Press and the Clarendon Press, Oxford (for permission to quote from the *Proceedings of the British Academy,* and from I. Little, *Critique of Welfare Economics);* Routledge and Kegan Paul Ltd. (for permission to quote from P. Wicksteed, *The Common Sense of Political Economy,* F. A. Hayek, *Road to Serfdom,* and G. Myrdal, *Value in Social Theory);* Staples Press (for permission to quote from E. Cannan, *Wealth,* E. Cannan, *Theories of Production and Distribution,* D. H. Robertson, *Economic Commentaries);* University of Chicago Press (for permission to quote from F. A. Hayek, *Road to Serfdom,* F. H. Knight, *History and Method of Economics,* and from the *Journal of Political Economy);* The Viking Press, Inc. (for permission to quote from T. Veblen, *The Theory of the Leisure Class, The Place of Science in Modern Civilization, Essays in Our Changing Order,* and W. Mitchell [editor], *What Veblen Taught);* Yale University Press (for permission to quote from L. Mises, *Human Action).*

Table of Contents

1

On Defining the Economic
Point of View

. . . What does the economist economize? " 'Tis love, 'tis love," said the Duchess, "that makes the world go round." "Somebody said," whispered Alice, "that it's done by everybody minding their own business." "Ah well," replied the Duchess, "it means much the same thing." Not perhaps quite *so* nearly the same thing as Alice's contemporaries thought. But if we economists mind our own business, and do that business well, we can, I believe, contribute mightily to the economizing, that is, to the full but thrifty utilization of that scarce resource Love—which *we* know, just as well as anybody else, to be the most precious thing in the world.

Sir Dennis H. Robertson

It is impossible to draw a clear-cut boundary around the sphere or domain of human action to be included in economic science.

Frank H. Knight

Social phenomena, like other matters of interest to be found in the real world, lend themselves to analysis by a number of disciplines. The same raw data may be capable of classification and explanation in a variety of ways, each of which complements the others and so contributes to the full grasp of the phenomena under consideration. In the interests of reaping the advantages attendant upon the division of labor, a sequence of events may be seen as reflecting the simultaneous operation of several distinct chains of cause and effect. Each of these chains may then

1

become the focus of inquiry, and it may enhance the advantages to be derived from the division of labor to be able to set forth in precisely what ways any one such causal chain constitutes a potentially fruitful theme for separate investigation.

Such a classification of the factors in the observed phenomena that require explanation will, of course, reflect the different points of view with which the observer approaches the data. In the final analysis, the definition of a particular field of investigation is tantamount to the exposition of the point of view chosen by the investigator.

With regard to economics and to the "economic point of view," many attempts, under a variety of guises, have been made to describe this peculiar field of investigation. Writers have defined the noun "economy"; they have expatiated on the precise demarcation of the scope of economics; they have indulged in lengthy disquisitions on the character of economic activity and on the nature of economic interpretation. They have discussed at length the relationship of the economist to the sociologist, the psychologist, the moralist, the technologist, and the jurist. And they have, in addition, engaged in heated and protracted controversies about the utility of these same definitions, disquisitions, and discussions.

They have, in short, made a large number of attempts to determine precisely the particular point of view of the economist, to dispute existing expositions of it, or to deny altogether to the economist the joy of having a distinct point of view. The sum total of this activity over the better part of two centuries is a vast and fascinating literature. The contemplation and subsequent digestion of this literature yields a series of formulations of the economic point of view that are astounding in their variety. The present essay attempts to survey the literature and to review in historical perspective this wide range of formulations. As a chapter in the history of ideas, this account of the constant search for the precise expression of the point of view of the economist focuses on the particular avenues by which it has been approached and on their remarkable heterogeneity.

Although the present account is historically oriented, we shall adopt the topical, rather than the chronological, approach. We shall not present the various formulations in the order in which they were successively proposed in the history of economic thought. Instead, we shall take up one by one the principal groups of definitions to be found in the literature and shall treat each of them separately as fully as possible. The part played by each group in the history of the problem will become apparent from the discussion of the definitions themselves. We shall discover, in fact, that at any one time a number of widely differing formulations have usually been current. It will be convenient, therefore, to devote to each of these groups of formulations a discussion of its development that will be complete in itself, without the distraction of noticing the simultaneous parallel developments of other definitions.

In this introductory chapter we shall attempt to bring our problem into perspective. It will be helpful in this connection to discuss the significance to be attached to the task of making explicit the nature of the economic point of view; to make clear which operation is, and which related operations are not, the objects of our interest; and to survey briefly the place that has been occupied in economic thought by the attempts to elucidate this economic point of view.

The Economic Point of View and the Scope of Economics

The formulation of the nature of the economic point of view is, of course, intimately related to discussions concerning the scope of economics. The problem of the scope of economics, however, has frequently involved questions with which this essay has nothing to do, and it is perhaps worthwhile to make this clear at the outset. Marshall once wrote to John Maynard Keynes: "It is true of almost every science that, the longer one studies it, the larger its scope seems to be: though in fact its scope may have remained almost unchanged. But the subject matter of economics grows apace . . ." [1]

This growth in the subject matter of economics of which Marshall writes is typical of those aspects of the question with which we are not concerned. A perusal of a list of courses offered

in the economics department of any university or a cursory examination of the catalogue of the economics room in a large library
will easily convince one of the luxuriance of this growth. It is
clear that "economics" covers a body of facts, figures, theories
and opinions embracing a vast range of phenomena related to
one another only in the most tenuous way—often merely by historical accident. At least one outside observer of the controversies concerning the scope of economics has hinted darkly that
they represent simply a way of claiming the exclusive right to
teach certain subject matter in the universities.[2] Dealing, over half
a century ago, with the "economic" interpretation of history,
Benedetto Croce wrote:

> When it is asserted, that in interpreting history we must look chiefly
> at the *economic factors,* we think at once of technical conditions, of
> the distribution of wealth, of classes and subclasses bound together
> by definite common interests, and so on. It is true these different
> representations cannot be reduced to a single concept, but no matter,
> there is no question of that; here we are in an entirely different
> *sphere* from that in which abstract questions are discussed.[3]

Discussions concerning the scope of economics frequently involve these "different representations" that cannot be reduced to
a single concept. Our own inquiry, on the other hand, concerns
that entirely different sphere in which abstract questions *are* discussed. And in this sphere it does indeed matter whether or not
the term "economic" is understood as being reducible to a single
concept; whether, in other words, it is understood as connoting a
distinct "point of view." [4]

Our problem, then, relates not to the scope of the subject
"economics," but to "economic theory." When we speak of the
point of view of the economist, we shall have him specifically in
mind, either as a theorist or as the applier of theory. For ordinary
purposes, as Cannan remarked,[5] it may well be true that economic
things can best be described as economic. The emergence of a
voluminous literature attempting to define the economic point of
view is not, however, to be dismissed as unfruitful pedantry; it is
rather the expression of concern with the epistemological character

of economic theory to an extent that goes far beyond that sufficient for ordinary purposes.[6]

The point can perhaps be expressed somewhat more succinctly by the use of the terminology of the logician. Definitions in general lend themselves fundamentally to classification as either nominal definitions or real definitions.[7] The former relate to "names" and attempt to interpret given symbols, verbal or otherwise. Real definitions, on the other hand, try to define "things," to expose in some way the "essence" and "nature" of the thing defined. The formulations of the economic point of view that are of interest to us in this essay do *not* content themselves with providing a translation of the word "economic"; they seek to reveal to us the "nature" of the *definiendum*—which in this case is a concept, a "point of view." The fascinating variety of these formulations reflects, as we shall see, the numerous, quite distinct operations that logicians have discovered to have been actually performed when men have set out to seek real definitions.

The Multitude of Economic Points of View

Certainly the most outstanding result of the urge to expound the nature of the economic point of view has been the number and the range of the definitions to which it has given rise. This startling multiplicity and variety of formulations was noticed long ago—at a time when their number was modest in comparison with the subsequent accumulations. And for over three-quarters of a century the depressing lack of unanimity among these formulations has led writers to doubt seriously whether they have any value at all.[8]

Economists have, for example, been well agreed among themselves that the operations of the merchant are of specific interest for the economic perspective on social phenomena; but at this point their unanimity abruptly breaks down. For some, the merchant is engaged in economic activity because he deals in material goods; for others, because his operations involve the use of money; for still others, because these operations hinge on acts of exchange. Some writers see the merchant as an economic agent because his activities are allegedly motivated by selfishness or marked by a peculiar shrewdness in calculating the pros and cons of his dealings. Others see his relevance for economics in that his wares are to some extent related to the maintenance of human life; others, in that they pertain to human "welfare." Still others classify mercantile pursuits as economic because they involve the judicious disposition of scarce means, while others again find their economic character in their reflection of human motives that permit of measurement. And the list could be still further extended.

The disquietude to which the contemplation of such an array of criteria gives rise is deepened by the realization that in most cases each of them represents a completely different opinion concerning the function of economic analysis. Nor is our equanimity restored by observing the diversity of ways in which the problem of definition is approached. Probably the most significant differences are not those among the specific definitions arrived at, but the disagreements among writers concerning the kind of entity that they are seeking to define and the very direction in which they are to begin their search. Definitions of economic science have time and again required preliminary discussions revolving around the question whether the discipline concerned a kind of object, a kind of activity, a kind of man, or a kind of satisfaction or welfare.

The natural consequence of this state of affairs has been to stimulate frequent soul-searching among economists about the fundamental purpose of defining the economic point of view, as well as a salutary awareness of the real complexity of the problem. The fact that so many different starting points to a territory of knowledge are conceivable is a sign of the intricacy with which the purely economic must be intertwined with other phenomena. And it raises serious questions regarding the very concept of a specifically economic point of view and the usefulness of its precise formulation through rigorous definition.

The Controversy Over the Utility of Definition

As we shall discover, a number of sharply contradictory opinions have been expressed on the usefulness of undertaking the careful definition of the economic point of view or of the nature of the subject matter of economic theory. To those who have considered such a task as significant, its fulfilment represents in itself a distinct scientific achievement. On the other hand, many writers have been at pains to disassociate themselves from an undertaking whose accomplishment seems, in their opinion, to possess no scientific value in itself nor to promise any fruitful results for further work. This book will deal in some detail with many more or less careful attempts at such a definition; and it is only proper to pause to consider the question whether these attempts were potentially fruitful or were by their very character necessarily doomed to be wordy disquisitions, fertile in nothing but the stimulation of sterile controversies.

Among those considering any search for a precise definition of the economic point of view to be a barren enterprise, we find Pareto, Myrdal, and Hutchison.[9] Pareto denied that there is objectively an economic phenomenon and considered it therefore "a waste of time to investigate what it may be," since only a man-made distinction is in question. Myrdal, writing some thirty years later, voiced a closely similar view. A definition of economics can only be a search for arbitrarily drawn boundary lines. "Economics," in Myrdal's view, is the only term regarding the precise definition of which the economist need not be concerned; nothing in economic science depends upon it. Hutchison has flatly declared that "the actual assignment of a definition to the word 'Economics' does not appear to solve, or even help in the solution of, any useful scientific problem whatsoever." These pronouncements seem typical of what one writer has noticed as a widespread impression that the discussions concerning the nature and scope of economics "are merely an endless and useless logomachy." [10]

But the contrary opinion has been repeatedly expounded. The very voluminous literature on defining economic theory, including the works of the most illustrious masters of the science, constitutes in itself a formidable monument to this position.[11] Robbins especially has several times vigorously denied that it is a waste of time to attempt a precise delimitation of the field. It is, on the contrary, a "waste of time not to do so." [12] The science has developed to the point where further progress can take place only if the objective is clearly indicated; where problems are suggested only by "gaps in the unity of theory." Knight has referred to the delimitation of the nature and content of value theory as "perhaps the ultimate conceptual problem in economics." [13] Macfie, among others, has pointed out the harm that can be done by a lack of a clear-cut definition; more especially he has stressed the distortion that a faulty definition could introduce into the character of the science.[14]

For the appreciation of the historical trend to the investigation of which this essay is devoted, it is important to understand the nature of this sharp divergence of views concerning the usefulness of a precise definition of the economic point of view. It is possible to interpret the disagreement as merely the expression of different attitudes towards the utility of expending energy in discussing the nature of economics, as compared with that of the effort devoted to the actual increase of our stock of economic knowledge. Numerous justifications for merely perfunctory attempts to provide a definition of the economic point of view do, in fact, stress the great difficulty of the undertaking, in conjunction with its alleged lack of importance for the work of the economist.[15] The disagreement might thus be understood as simply reflecting differing estimates of the worthwhileness of the alternatives costs involved in achieving intellectual tidiness in the systematic exposition of the science. But such an interpretation would be a superficial one and would ignore the most significant aspect of the controversy.

An Interpretation of the Controversy

The writers who have denied the fruitfulness of the precise delimitation of the scope of economic theory must be considered as constituting a group whose views, in effect, make up yet another "definition" of the economic point of view—one that altogether denies any such concept. The notion of a peculiarly economic point of view has been variously defined in terms of a large number of different criteria. The subsequent chapters of this essay set forth the more important of these formulations. Certainly it is of moment that there is place found for yet a further attitude towards the notion of a uniquely economic perspective— an attitude that completely fails to recognize any such unique point of view. The disagreement concerning the usefulness of defining economics is thus reducible to a far more interesting controversy: one that deals with what, in fact, is meant at all by defining economics; a controversy concerning the very existence of that economic point of view which we are asked to define.

The issue may be seen most clearly in the question with which one writer found himself faced before embarking on the search for a definition of the economic principle. He asked himself whether economics is "a pie which every economist can . . . make up with his own 'recipe,' or is it a given pie . . . which is basically made up of well-defined and hardly changeable ingredients? In other words, is economics what the economist is prepared to let it be, or does economics have a 'nature' of its own . . . ?" [16] Once it is denied that economics has a "nature" of its own, once it is declared that no recipe for a uniquely economic pie, in fact, exists, then, of course, any lengthy search for such a recipe must seem a waste of time. And, similarly, the determination of the particular recipe that may, quite arbitrarily, have been used by some or many economists to make up their own pie then becomes a quite uninteresting undertaking.

If, however, it is maintained that economics *has* a nature of its own, then it may clearly seem of the highest interest to bring to light the precise character of this economic point of view. Moreover, once the existence of a *given* recipe has been discovered, and the conviction has been acquired that economics is *not* a pie to be made up at will, then definition becomes important for yet another reason. It becomes of the first moment to expose the specific character of economics, if only to convince the doubtful of the existence of this uniquely economic point of view that they are so much inclined to deny. The search for the precise nature of economic theory becomes of importance simply because it offers proof that economics *has* a "nature of its own."

Definitions, as we have seen, may be either real definitions **or** nominal definitions. Now, a nominal definition may be given to a term even though one is convinced that no real "thing" in the world in fact corresponds to what the term signifies. But one can embark on a search for a real definition only if it is recognized that the term to be defined actually represents a thing or a concept the essence or nature of which can be set forth. If it is denied that the subject of economic theory displays any essential unity that might be worthy of precise characterization in a definition, then it is clear that any definition of the discipline must remain merely nominal. And if it is believed that economists have been arbitrary in their selection of their problems, then there can be little value in the formulation of the nominal definition of economics.

On the other hand, the discovery in economics of an entity of which a real definition may be advanced promises an interesting range of investigation. It has been demonstrated that when men have attempted to obtain real definitions, they have in many cases proceeded to engage in a wide variety of operations.[17] In some cases a search for a real definition of X has meant the search for the *key* to X, for a single fact from which all the facts of X can be deduced. In other cases the search for real definitions has meant the search for "abstractions," i.e., the "becoming aware for the first time of a new general element in one's experience and giving it a name." In still other cases real definition has concealed the attempt to *analyze* an abstraction. (A school child in learning that the circle is the locus of all points in a plane equidistant from a given point has learned the analysis of a previously known abstraction, the circle.)

It is not difficult to understand that when writers concerning the scope of economic theory believe themselves to have discovered the "key" with which to explain all departments of economic life, they may feel pardonably complacent about the usefulness of the "definition" in which their discovery is crystallized. It is still more understandable that economists should stress the usefulness of definition when their own formulation of the nature of economics reveals to the world their awareness of a new general element in their experience. Croce provides perhaps the best example of this situation. He *was* aware of a new general element in his experience of human affairs. This element was not moral, it was not technical, nor did it coincide with any other already-named abstractions. In his formulations, Croce made a vigorous attempt to present this abstraction to the attention of the world by ascribing to it the word "economic."

When definition entails, in addition, the task of *analyzing* this newly presented abstraction, that operation becomes more than ever meritorious. If in the effort to provide an adequate definition of economics, an attempt is made to analyze the concept of economy, for example, one necessarily becomes involved in a problem of economic science itself. It was here that Croce could most effectively criticize Pareto's view that the cutting off of that slice of phenomena which is to constitute the field of economics is a quite simple and arbitrary affair.

You talk of *cutting away a slice* from a concrete phenomenon, and examining this by itself, but I enquire how you manage to cut away that slice? For it is no question here of a piece of bread or cheese into which we can actually put the knife, but a series of representations which we have in our consciousness, and into which we can insert nothing except the light of our mental analysis. In order to cut off your slice you would thus have to carry out a logical analysis . . .[18]

When the nature of economics is defined in this way, by the analysis of a unique general element in our consciousness to which only the term "economy" corresponds, then it must seem very obvious indeed that faulty definitions can seriously distort the character of the science. And when the analysis of this element has been made possible only by virtue of familiarity with the substantive content of the science itself, then its formulation into a definition can clearly take on the character of a positive scientific contribution. It is in this sense that Hayek, in a somewhat different context, was able to write:

It is one of the causes of the unique position of economics that the existence of a definite object of its investigation can be realized only after a prolonged study, and it is, therefore, not surprising that people who have never really studied economic theory will necessarily be doubtful of the legitimacy of its existence . . .[19]

From this perspective it will be useful to survey rapidly in the next few pages the historical trend in the attention that economists have paid to the definition of their subject. This will make clear what they have, at various times, looked for in such a definition. Our survey will thus provide a useful introduction to the more detailed discussions in the subsequent body of the essay.

The Economists and Their Definitions: the Classical Economists

Modern investigations into classical economic thought are gradually providing us with a more coherent picture of the intellectual scenery in early nineteenth-century political economy. Among the more important contributions in this direction is the final interment of the idea that there was ever a happy unanimity of opinion, a generally accepted body of theory in the propagation of which the classical economists were a united band of enthusiastic missionaries. Similarly the notion, once widespread, that the classical economists were as a body unconcerned with the methodological foundations of their work is rapidly disappearing from discussions of the subject.[20]

It seems worthwhile to dispel the rather common impression that the classical economists were generally unconcerned with attaining and enunciating a precise definition of the subject of their inquries.[21] This is by no means the case. It is true that J. S. Mill, writing in 1836,[22] felt obliged to apologize for the lack of a definition of political economy "framed on strictly logical principles," by explaining that the definition of any science "has almost invariably not preceded, but followed, the creation of the science itself." But many economists had already felt the need to delineate the boundaries of their inquiries. And while it is true that the classical economists were generally in broad agreement concerning what it was that they were talking about, they were by no means agreed about how to demarcate this area of their investigations or even how to conceive the unity and logical nature of their field.

The early economists, in fact, when offering definitions of their science, were often far more earnestly concerned with expressing its true essence and nature than were many of their successors. Although the latter, as Mill asserted, may have been better equipped for this task, they had far less occasion to engage in it. For the thinkers of the late eighteenth and early nineteenth centuries, there was a real need for a mode of definition that could justify the conception of a new and separate science. While their definitions might only imperfectly indicate the actual character of their inquiries, they still had to demonstrate the peculiarity in subject matter or method of investigation that prevented economics from being subsumed under some wider, extant discipline.

Classical writers could express themselves about the nature of the economic in two distinct ways. They could define the subject known as political economy. Or, having defined political economy as the science of wealth, they could proceed to set forth the nature of that wealth with which it was maintained that economics is concerned. Each of these approaches was freely used both before and after Mill's own elaborate attempt to define political economy.

Yet it is true that after 1830 a trend toward more sophistication in definition is undeniably visible. Methodological self-examination became a fairly fashionable undertaking. It was in this period that many of the assumptions hitherto implicitly accepted by economists were first brought to light, and most of the important issues that were to be the subject of methodological controversy over the succeeding century were first given explicit statement. As far as the question of the scope of economics was concerned, discussions treated it as a problem in its own right rather than as one merely introductory to a more important topic. Senior, J. S. Mill, and later Cairnes all devoted careful attention to definition, and so also did many lesser-known economists. At a meeting of the Political Economy Club of London in 1835 the question of the scope of the discipline was put up for discussion. (In 1861 Senior proposed a similar question for debate at the club.) [23]

Moreover this period reflected a significant advance in the actual approach taken to the task of setting forth the nature of the economic. As will be seen in the subsequent chapters of this essay, writers after 1830 began to rebel against the more extremely objective view of it as the science of wealth that the earlier classical economists had generally held. To several writers after 1830 it was becoming increasingly evident that what they were investigating was not so much a set of objective phenomena whose common denominator was wealth as the phenomena resulting from the wealth-oriented actions of *men*. What the fundamental characteristic of such actions was, and what the precise balance to be maintained in political economy between the facts of human nature and those of the external world should be, were the subjects of lively discussion. But the first step had been taken along the road toward emancipating economics from its ties to wealth and material welfare.[24]

The Economic Point of View: the Background of the "Methodenstreit"

After 1870, attempts to define the nature of the economic were definitely colored by the intellectual background of the period. In Germany, Austria, and England economists were paying a good deal of attention indeed to the necessity for reconstructing economics "from the ground up." This necessity was proclaimed by both groups that were in reaction against the hitherto dominant classical economics. Those following Roscher, Hildebrand, and Knies in their revolt against the abstract reasoning of Ricardian-type economics, as well as those who with Menger and Jevons were dissatisfied with the objectivism of the classical economists—all were imbued with the desire to make over the entire discipline. Inevitably this desire was accompanied by a flourishing self-consciousness on the part of economists in regard to the status of their discipline as a science, its relation to kindred branches of learning, and, in general, its objectives and the kind of knowledge it might be expected to furnish. Together with their researches into economic problems proper, the leaders of both new schools of economic thought felt called upon to still both their own misgivings and those of the public at large concerning the nature and significance of a subject whose methods of approach, after a century of study, its own students were branding as unsound.

It is true, of course, that these discussions came to hinge on the narrower problem of method rather than on that of scope. Even definitions of economics were required, during this period, to embrace statements concerning the purpose and the method of the discipline as well as the character of its subject matter.[25] But the methodological points that were at issue in the *Methodenstreit* did have a direct bearing on the conceptions that were formed of the character of economic phenomena. At the risk of some excusable simplification, the controversy over method could, indeed, be described quite clearly in terms of the different conceptions of the phenomena purportedly investigated by economics. According to the Historical School, economics seeks to describe the phenomena of the real, empirical economic world as it unfolds in its setting of time and space. According to the "theoretical," "abstract" school of thought, on the other hand, the task of economics is not—or, rather, cannot be—to explain "individual" (or particular) economic phenomena, but only to discover the regularities, the "general" chains of cause and effect, that *underlie* the innumerably various forms that present themselves in economic history.[26]

Although this statement of the disagreement does not, of course, point to any simple parallel disagreement concerning the nature of the economic, it does throw light on the background against which discussions about the character of economic phenomena were carried on in the last quarter of the nineteenth century. During this period we find, especially in the German literature, a concern with the correct characterization of economic phenomena that went far beyond previous investigations. It may safely be said that almost all the numerous criteria that have, during the history of economics, been used to define the economic aspect of affairs were in some way mentioned already in the formidable German literature of these decades. Even some definitions that were clearly discussed only in the twentieth century were at least vaguely envisaged during these years. Dietzel and Neumann in particular demonstrated considerable insight in their work in this area. Under the influence of Menger and his followers, writers of this period devoted careful attention to the scarcity criterion and to the operation of the "economic principle." On the other hand, economists of the Historical School tended to stress the social character of economic phenomena. Both groups still clung to the idea that wealth stands at the core of economic affairs, but frequently the retention of conventional phraseology merely concealed a far more advanced and sensitive grasp of the real nature of economic phenomena.

In England at this time, despite its own form of the *Methoden-streit,* far less advance was to be seen in formulations of the scope of the discipline. Jevons had kept his economics closely tied to hedonism, and he was followed in this by Edgeworth. Marshall devoted part of his inaugural Cambridge lecture in 1885 to the problem, with interesting results. Several of the methodological rebels were intent on denying economics a separate status apart from sociology. There was even a proposal put forward in the British Association for the Advancement of Science during the late seventies to abolish the very existence of a separate economic section of the association. J. N. Keynes contributed to the judicious resolution of the methodological issues, but did little to advance the conception of the character of the economic point of view. It was not until the appearance of Wicksteed's brilliant work in this field in 1910 that we find a contribution comparable in exhaustiveness and refinement to several of the German discussions.

Meanwhile in other countries economists were giving the problem careful attention. In the United States literature a number of useful pronouncements are to be found concerning the importance of a correct definition, as well as several highly refined and well-reasoned substantive formulations.[27] In France [28] and Italy too, parallel advances are to be found in the literature. In 1883 Supino published the first book devoted to an account of the existing definitions of economics.[29] Pantaleoni, Pareto, and

Croce devoted considerable space to the question of definition, and the famous correspondence at the turn of the century between the two last-named writers contains considerable material that is of particular value for any history of this question.

Twentieth-Century Economic Points of View

Fraser has classified definitions of economics into Type A definitions and Type B definitions.[30] Type A definitions consider economics as investigating a particular *department* of affairs, while Type B definitions see it as concerned with a particular *aspect* of affairs in general. The specific department singled out by Type A definitions has usually been wealth or material welfare. The aspect referred to in Type B definitions is the constraint that social phenomena uniformly reveal in the necessity to reconcile numerous conflicting ends under the shadow of an inescapable scarcity of means.

During the twentieth century two distinct trends are visible in the definitions of the economic point of view. On the one hand, a transition from Type A to Type B definitions has been vigorously carried forward. On the other hand, there has been a pronounced movement toward the denial of any distinctly economic point of view whatsoever, and the consequent conviction that all attempts to present such a point of view with clarity must be a waste of time.

It will be seen in subsequent chapters that the classification of definitions of the economic point of view into Types A and B is far from an exhaustive one. The voluminous literature since the turn of the century dealing with the problem of definition reveals, indeed, the entire range of formulations that are discussed in this essay. Nevertheless, it remains true that the most outstanding development in the history of the problem is the switch from the search for a department of human affairs to which the adjective "economic" applies, to the search for the appropriate *aspect* of affairs in which economic concepts are of relevance. (It should be noticed that almost all the numerous formulations of the specific point of view of economic science are considered by their authors, not as describing a new science, but as offering a more consistent characterization of the existing discipline.) [31] The emergence of the Type B definitions is reflected in a considerable body of literature on the continent as well as in the English-speaking countries. Type A definitions are treated in the second chapter of this essay, and the transition to Type B definitions is traced in the sixth chapter. Type B definitions are associated especially with the name of Professor Robbins, whose work of 1930 has had an outstandingly stimulating effect on all subsequent discussions.

The final chapter of this essay traces the further development, in recent decades, of this trend away from the association of economics with specific "ends" or a specific department of human affairs. In this development the work of Robbins has been consistently pursued to what appears to the writer to be the most adequate solution of the problem. The developments described in this final chapter are made up of the contributions of several eminent economists, including Mises and Knight. These writers in no way constitute a "school," and although in this essay the developments of the final chapter are described as "praxeological" (following Mises' terminology), it is not to be understood that all the writers cited in that chapter fully subscribe to what is here called the praxeological outlook. It is maintained, however, that the consistent and refined development of the ideas first brought to a focus in the Type B definition constitutes a distinct contribution to the history of the problem. The path-breaking work of Mises in this regard has a significance that, in the writer's opinion, has not been sufficiently recognized because it has not yet been brought into historical perspective.

The movement from Type A definitions toward Type B definitions and finally to the praxeological position runs, of course, in a direction diametrically opposed to that taken by writers who disparage painstaking definitions of economics altogether. What is common to all these writers is, as was noticed earlier in this chapter, that they deny the existence of any given "pie" that could constitute economics. There *is* no specifically economic point of view, and economic science does not investigate any uniquely separate group of phenomena, or phenomena in general from any uniquely economic aspect. The consistent development of the Type B definition and of praxeological ideas represents the completest denial of this view. Both these conceptions of economics have been able to focus attention, with a clarity never hitherto attained, on an element in our experience that corresponds to nothing else in our consciousness. This element in our experience conforms precisely to the foundation that is discovered to be rigorously necessary and sufficient for the construction of economic theory as it has developed during the past two centuries.

The body of this essay consists of the study of the many alternative formulations of this economic point of view, which make up the trend culminating in the insights of the final chapters.

2

The Science of Wealth and Welfare

This fatal word "material" is probably more responsible for the ignorant slanders on the "dismal science" than any other economic description . . .

Alec L. Macfie

Political Economy is a science in the same sense in which Astronomy, Dynamics, Chemistry, Physiology are sciences. Its subject-matter is different; it deals with the phenomena of wealth, while they deal with the phenomena of the physical universe.

J. E. Cairnes

. . . In becoming consciously a science of human behavior economics will lay less stress upon wealth and more stress upon welfare.

Wesley C. Mitchell

It is almost as difficult to define the boundaries of welfare economics as it is to define economics itself.

Kenneth E. Boulding

We take up first of all the class of writers for whom the specifically economic point of view is in some way necessarily associated with wealth or with welfare. It seems fair to consider this view before examining the many other opinions extant in the literature, simply because its supporters (those espousing what Fraser calls the Type A viewpoint) [1] were for a long time

20

the ones most frequently to be found in discussions on the subject. And it is a matter of no little significance that it was one form of this view, viz., the description of the economic side of affairs exclusively in terms of *wealth,* that the earliest classical economists almost invariably adopted. In the course of our discussion it will become apparent that a number of quite different conceptions of economic phenomena at various times found expression in the definitions that simply spoke of wealth or welfare as being the central focus of economic interest. Yet despite the variety of these conceptions they all admit of being broadly grouped together. Those writers who speak of the production of wealth and the distribution of wealth or of some special type of human welfare as being the peculiar interest of the economist share a common outlook on the subject. No matter how widely their opinions on the nature of wealth or welfare may diverge, what is common to all these writers is that they see the distinctive peculiarity of economic phenomena in the class of *objects* around which they especially revolve or in the specific human *condition* that they are thought especially to affect. The criterion used by the student of economic phenomena to mark out the scope of his subject is the fact that it is concerned with a special class of *objects* or a special type of human *condition.* The botanist studies the phenomena of plant life, the astronomer studies celestial phenomena, the philologist studies a specific "object," viz., languages—and the economist quite analogously occupies himself with the study of wealth or welfare. The conditions governing the production of wealth or the enhancement of economic welfare, the effects of given events on the exchange and the distribution of wealth—all these are "economic" phenomena because they have to do with wealth or welfare.

We shall see that many writers of this opinion still further narrowed down the concept of wealth to the idea of *material wealth,* and many of those stressing *welfare* qualified the term by singling out the *material* welfare of mankind. These developments meant that more than ever economics has to do with a particular *class of objects* as its special province of study. And we shall be concerned in this chapter to explain the emergence of this general outlook on the nature of economics simultaneously with the emergence of the science of economics itself. We shall also be concerned to trace the various forms that this general outlook has taken in response to developments within the science of economics and to discover some of the implications of this outlook.

The Emergence of Political Economy as the Science of Wealth

The writers on economics at the time of the emergence of the subject as a serious discipline in its own right, where they made any attempt at all to outline the scope of their inquiries, did so quite as a matter of course by reference to "wealth" as its subject matter. By the latter half of the eighteenth century, thinkers in England, France, and Italy were coming to recognize that the subject of the mass of writings and speculations dealing with commerce, industry, foreign trade, money, interest, taxation, and the like constitutes a distinct theme of inquiry. Hitherto these speculations (such as those of the mercantilist writers and of those whom Schumpeter has called the consultant administrators and pamphleteers) had been isolated inquiries seeking to explain specific phenomena of the real world. Where inquiries on these and kindred subjects had been incorporated into more general systems, they appeared as unmistakably subsidiary material introduced to round out treatises whose subjects were juristic, political, or moral.

With the recognition of the fundamental unity of the principles underlying these scattered inquiries and of their analytical independence of juristic, political, and moral systems, economics, or political economy, emerged as a distinct discipline. Works appeared attempting to deal with economic phenomena *in general,* and these works typically identified their subject matter as being "wealth."

It is worthy of notice that the existence in "wealth" of a subject matter ripe for independent investigation seems to have been assumed with little discussion. The conception of wealth as being a distinct phenomenon with its own peculiar scholarly interest was *not* a creation of the classical economists.[2] Adam Smith, who defines political economy as treating of the "nature and causes of the wealth of nations,"[3] freely applies the term to denote the area of concern of mercantile policy-makers of a century earlier.[4] What converted scattered scraps of knowledge on the subject of "wealth" into an integrated system of ideas was simply the discovery of the regularity of the phenomena of wealth as determined in the market. Newly discovered, seemingly inexorable "laws" governing the wealth of nations turned this "wealth," already the center of many isolated investigations, into the subject matter of a new science.

That this new science was considered, not as explaining the operation of a specific type of social organization or the results of a certain kind of human behavior or any of the various other matters that economists have at times believed it to be their principal concern to explain, but as primarily explaining the phenomena of wealth, is a circumstance that deserves some closer attention. It seems appropriate to glance briefly at the background against which economic thought developed, in order to throw some light on this interesting circumstance before we trace the later history of this idea on economic affairs.

In later chapters there will come under discussion a number of possibly more sophisticated conceptions of that economic point of view from which the economist scrutinizes the world. In the course of these discussions, the failure of the classical economists to perceive the unity of their subject to be implied in such conceptions will be more fully understood as stemming at least in part from their freedom from those influences that were operative in the emergence of the later views. At this point four positive elements in the background of early economic thought and its surrounding *Zeitgeist* may be distinguished as possible catalysts in the precipitation of wealth as the recognized subject matter of a distinct discipline.

1) Later methodologists were to devote considerable effort to the problem whether to treat political economy as a positive *science* or as an *art*, whether to cast its teachings in the indicative

or the imperative moods. There can be little doubt that the founders of economics felt themselves to be expounding an art. According to Adam Smith, political economy "proposes to enrich both the people and the sovereign." [5] A recent writer has characterized the classical economists as a school of economic and social reform.[6] The roots of this attitude toward their teachings are not hard to find. Economics, as we have seen, developed, in part at least, from the work of mercantilist writers, the "consultant administrators and pamphleteers." This class of writers was quite simply interested in practical results. Any scientific work that came from their hands must quite naturally be considered the by-product, rather than the attained goal, of their endeavors. The growing application, in the eighteenth century, of sober and sound analysis to the questions that these earlier writers had discussed did not involve any change in this attitude. Hence, the conception that Smith, the economist, had of his subject was not much removed from that of Steuart, the mercantilist, to whom "oeconomy . . . is the art of providing for all the wants . . ." and to whom the "principal object" of his inquiry was "to secure a certain fund of subsistence for all the inhabitants." [7]

It is not difficult to see that this attitude toward the utility of economic inquiries necessarily carried with it the elevation of wealth into an object of scientific study. An investigation that sets out to find the means of enriching the people and the sovereign, if it discovers laws governing the attainment of this objective, may not unnaturally presume to have discovered the laws of wealth. If we grant the assumption that the goal of economics is to make the nation wealthy, a goal to which a fairly well-understood meaning was attached, then it follows that economists must be considered, both by themselves and by the public, as expounding the principles of wealth—understood in the same sense—and its acquisition by the nation. How a nation wrests wealth from niggardly nature, how this wealth is distributed and exchanged within the nation—all these inquiries focus the attention on that which now becomes an *object* of scientific scrutiny. The general objectivism of the classical school in its substantive economic doctrines here finds its counterpart in that school's very conception of its task: an economist investigates the phenomena of a special class of objects that together comprise wealth.

2) Another force in the eighteenth-century environment that must have helped to set up wealth as the subject matter of a separate discipline seems to have been the intellectual interest in private property. Despite the variety of meanings that we shall find to have been attached to the term "wealth" by classical economists, almost all these meanings find some common ground with a definition of wealth as consisting in the objects of ownership. Throughout the seventeenth and eighteenth centuries a peculiar attraction seems to have resided in inquiries into the legal and moral bases of the institution of private property. Grotius had discussed the matter from a juristic standpoint. With Hobbes the inquiry into the nature and origins of private property became merged with his theories on the origins of the organization of society under the sovereignty of the state. Locke saw the origin of and justification for private property in natural law. These speculations and theories affected much of the thought of the leading writers throughout the eighteenth century. Discussions of civil justice must turn on the acceptance and justification of property rights; discussions of the legitimacy of slavery must involve the question of the admissible extent of property rights; the movements in France and America towards democracy were generally accompanied by specific attention to private property. For many years democracy was to mean democracy for the property owners. Godwin's call for the abolition of private property once again drew attention to the foundation of the entire institution.[8]

Myrdal has attempted to show that it was the heritage of the ideas of the natural-law philosophers regarding property rights that accounts for the classical, and especially the Ricardian, theories of value.[9] For the purposes of the present study the relevance of this observation seems sufficiently obvious. The isolation from the other ends of human action of that end represented by property on the one hand reflected, and on the other hand itself strengthened, the artificial line drawn between the study of the phenomena connected with property and the study of human action in general. The focusing of the attention of jurists, philosophers, and moralists on the institution of property cannot but have helped in keeping wealth in a compartment all its own. Moreover, the fundamental defect of classical economics, its lack of appreciation of the subjective nature of its phenomena, may perhaps be partly due to the fact that serious thought had for a long time been devoted to property and wealth in inquiries to which, indeed, this subjective element bore little direct relevance.

3) Yet another element in the environment of early scientific economics must be briefly alluded to in connection with the emergence of wealth as an object of intellectual interest. This is the approach of the moral philosophers of the period to the problems of the relation of the individual to society, and especially of the egoistic and altruistic motives. The birth of political economy may be regarded as a reflection of the confluence at this time of two streams of thought, ethics and politics. Ethics discussed the meaning of good and bad, the source of the sense of moral obligation. Politics explored the origins of society, the most desirable form of its organization, and the rights of the individual in relation to the state. In a society whose economy was becoming more and more dependent on the division of labor, it was natural for the ethics of the individual to become increasingly involved with his relation to society as a whole. The discovery of market regularities, predicated on individual avarice, in the phenomena of the wealth of nations meant in itself a unified application of ethical and political doctrines.[10]

The controversy stirred up during the eighteenth century by Mandeville's *Fable of the Bees* was typical of the problem to which the thinkers of the time sought the solution. Mandeville's provocative conclusion was "that what we call evil in this world, . . . is the grand principle that makes us sociable creatures, the solid basis, the life and support of all trades and employments . . ." [11] His critics, including both Hume and Smith, used all manners of approach to dispute his conclusions. Closely allied to this problem was that recognized by Mandeville's paradox, the venerable feud in human nature between the forces of self-interest and the forces of altruism. Whether or not the urge in a human being to benefit others than himself is a real one or merely the illusory reflection of a selfish desire to relieve one's own pain incurred by another's misery was a question well to the fore during this period. Hobbes had been the first of modern philosophers to expound his theory of egoism. Eighteenth-century philosophers, including Butler, Hume, and Smith generally rejected Hobbes' egoism and postulated a real distinction between selfishness and altruism.

This reaction against extreme egoism and especially against the effect on the nation's welfare ascribed to egoism seems to be at least partly responsible for the division of the field of human action into two independent classes, the one class of acts being induced by purely egoistic motives, the other class being constituted of acts in which the motivating forces are the altruistic and "higher" impulses. And it is not difficult to see how the acts induced by selfishness could be easily confused with acts aimed at fulfilling material desires. Careful thinking had demonstrated the existence of regularities in the phenomena of wealth. The identification of the study of these regularities with the study of material or other wealth thus obviously provided the new science with an appropriate and distinct niche within the structure of knowledge as conceived by the eighteenth-century thinkers.

4) One final strand in the web of eighteenth-century thought onto which a science of wealth was to be woven must be noticed. This is the position occupied by the natural sciences, and their relation to and influence upon the social sciences. In general the eighteenth-century view has been characterized as "anthropological and subjectivist," in contrast to the "cosmological and objectivist view which the nineteenth century had of the world." [12] Nevertheless, the position of the nineteenth century had its roots in ideas that go back well into the eighteenth century and earlier.

The tremendous advances in the natural sciences, especially mathematics and astronomy, associated with such names as Newton, Clairault, Euler, and d'Alembert, were radically transforming the intellectual atmosphere in which the eighteenth-century philosophers thought and taught. The reaction against airy metaphysical speculation set in motion by Hume and the other British empiricists, and the quasi-positivist philosophy of the French Encyclopedists, with its anathematization of all forms of anthropomorphism and animism, were all part of the environment in which economic science emerged.

It is not to be wondered at, then, that the enthusiasm engendered by the signal successes of the objective and impersonal methods of the physical sciences should have left its mark on the earliest researches of the classical economists. It has been well remarked that some of the founders of abstract economic theory in the eighteenth century were at the same time the founders of the positivism that was later to be deployed against that abstract economics.[13]

Differences of opinion may legitimately exist concerning the weight to be assigned to utterances by the moral philosophers that seem to illustrate the all-pervasive Newtonian influence.[14] But these references are persistent. Hutcheson and Hume, Helvetius and Beccaria expressed the desire to treat the data of ethics analogously to the data of experimental physics, or they made analogies between the force of self-interest and the force of gravity.[15] The simplification in the conception of the cosmos to which the physical sciences owed their characteristic fascination—i.e., the reduction of seemingly heterogeneous phenomena to a system governed by a few fundamental laws—seems to have perceptibly colored the thinking of the founders of economics. The extent of the gap between the conception of a science embracing the totality of action, on the one hand, and the conception of a science of wealth, on the other, owes something, it would appear, to the ease with which the latter could be incorporated into a structure of universal knowledge in which the physical sciences occupied so conspicuous a position. According to the English individualists, social phenomena spring, not from the interaction of individual subjective preference systems, but from the interaction of individuals under an impersonal pervasive force of self-interest in relation to objective, material wealth.

The Science of Material Wealth

Our account of the history of the point of view that sees economic affairs as essentially concerned with a special class of objects, i.e., with wealth, finds a convenient point of departure in an early and long-lived form of this idea, which confined economics to the consideration of *material* wealth.

From the beginning alternative suggestions were made by the economists themselves about what should and what should not be included under the heading of wealth even when the latter was universally regarded as the subject matter of economics. Indeed, many writers, in their definition of political economy, expressly included in its scope the exposition of "the nature" of wealth. Smith, Lauderdale, Malthus, and Senior all felt the elucidation of this question to be part of their task. As has been the lot of other problems taken up by economists, this question was treated in a variety of ways. As early as 1810 the French economist Ganilh cited eight distinct definitions of "wealth" by economists; Senior, writing on terms "peculiarly liable to be used ambiguously" in economics, somewhat despairingly quotes seven different definitions, besides his own contribution.

Of these controversies over the meaning of the term "wealth" probably the best known was that concerning its restriction exclusively to material goods. It must be remembered that the issue was not between a "materialistic" economics and one that embraced the catallactic consequences of man's "higher" interests and desires. The fact is that the classical economists were little concerned about why an item of wealth was desired. To invest an object with the quality of wealth (apart from other specific conditions, such as scarcity, that may have been required), it sufficed that it was desired. The issue between definitions of "wealth" formulated in material terms and those that extended the concept to include the immaterial was purely one of convenience in analysis. Both sides of the controversy had the same objectivistic outlook on wealth; neither side laid stress on the character of economic *behavior*. Malthus clearly states his reason for recognizing only material goods as wealth:

If we wish to attain anything like precision in our inquiries, when we treat of wealth, we must narrow the field of inquiry, and draw some line, which will leave us only those objects, the increase or decrease of which is capable of being estimated with more accuracy.[16]

The discussion concerning material vs. immaterial wealth began with Adam Smith's distinction between productive and unproductive labor. While not as limiting as the physiocrats' concept of the "sterile" classes, Smith's dichotomy put material wealth, the production of which was his criterion of productive labor, on a different level from immaterial wealth.[17] On the Continent, the French writers after Smith, following Say's leadership, generally rejected this artificial line of demarcation. In England Lauderdale defined individual wealth as consisting in "all that man desires as useful or delightful to him; which exists in scarcity." [18] This definition was quoted again and again by later writers and was in most cases criticized as too vague.[19] Such a criticism is illuminating in its revelation of classical economic conceptions. Thus Malthus:

This definition obviously includes everything, whether material or intellectual, whether tangible or otherwise, which contributes to the advantage or pleasure of mankind, and of course, includes the benefits and gratifications derived from religion, from music, dancing, acting, and similar sources. But an inquiry into the nature and causes of these kinds of wealth would evidently extend beyond the bounds of any single science. . . .[20]

For Malthus there was evidently no single bond in logic that could place these benefits and gratifications in a single discipline. McCulloch's comments are even more revealing:

. . . if political economy were to embrace a discussion of the production and distribution of all that is useful and agreeable, it would include within itself every other science . . . Good health is useful and delightful, and therefore, on this hypothesis, the science of wealth ought to comprehend the science of medicine; civil and religious liberty are highly useful, and therefore the science of wealth must comprehend the science of politics . . ." [21]

It would be difficult to discover a more damaging statement indicative of the kind of thinking exemplified by the less enlightened classical economists. Ricardo, to whom political economy meant only the *distribution,* not the production, of wealth, would never have excluded good health from economics on the ground that it involved the science of medicine. If the production of health involves medical science, the production of cement just as much involves chemistry, and the production of wheat, biology. According to McCulloch, wealth was clearly a distinct objective entity, the production of which involved the science of political economy. To draw the line so as to exclude from its purview such inconvenient studies as medicine and politics, McCulloch included only material goods in his technical definition of wealth. Apparently it was believed that certain general laws governing the physical production of material commodities could be abstracted from the several sciences concretely concerned with the production of each specific good. These laws, however, did not admit of further generalization so as to comprise the production of such immaterial goods as health or good government. The only sciences that were relevant to the latter were those of medicine and politics.

The striking feature of this discussion concerning Lauderdale's definition is that the criticisms levelled against it could easily have led to a *less* limited view of economic phenomena. It was clearly seen that the extension of the concept of wealth to include everything that is desired would mean the abandonment of the effort to arrive at any scientific laws involving objective wealth. But what was overlooked was that the very broadest conceptions of wealth involved an essential unity, from which a less limited political economy might take its point of departure.

However, the exclusive stress on *material* wealth was motivated by other considerations, besides those expressed by McCulloch. There appears to be a significant degree of correlation between the restriction of wealth to commodities and the restriction of the scope of political economy to the *distribution* of wealth, leaving out its production, exchange, and consumption. Ricardo and Read provide excellent examples of this. Both conceived of wealth exclusively as material goods.[22] And both emphatically limited political economy to the treatment of the *distribution* of wealth. Alike in his *Principles* and in his correspondence with Malthus, Ricardo had stressed this limitation of the scope of economics.[23] Read ("an acute but neglected writer," [24] and one of the economists rediscovered by Seligman) treated economics as "an investigation concerning the right to wealth," teaching what the rights and duties of men in society are with regard to property.[25] Read may be considered to have invested with normative and ethical significance Ricardo's conception of a science of the distribution of wealth. According to Ricardo, economics shows how wealth is distributed among the factors of production; according to Read, economics, in so doing, is at the same time laying down the law of the natural rights of the factors of production to their several shares.

There is every reason why economists concerned purely with the distributive aspects of economics should tend to concentrate on the tangible "pie" from which each of the factors of production is to receive a slice proportioned according to the laws of political economy. Students of "production" may find it difficult to exclude the production of any "utility," whether or not embodied in a material good. But the laws of distribution can clearly afford to be confined (and with so much more elegant definiteness) to the long-run tendencies in the division of tangible wealth. Where, as with Read, the laws of distribution are the handmaidens of the laws of private property, the convenience and reasonableness of a restriction of wealth to material, alienable goods must have appeared irresistible.

The Science of Subsistence

Thus far the account of what the economic point of view has meant to economists has treated of the classical conception of it as a science of wealth, with special reference to the restriction of the latter concept to that of material goods. The account of the gradual advance of economics from a science of wealth to one of welfare will be resumed later in the chapter, with special attention to those elements of the earlier "material" conception of wealth that continued to be retained. At this point a discussion is in order of a special case of this "material" approach to economics, which seems to have held a fascination for a number of economists over an extended period of time, viz., the view that saw economics as essentially concerned with the goods necessary to ensure the *physical subsistence* of mankind.

This view seems to be the most extreme form of the materialistic outlook on economic affairs. The distinctive feature of all conceptions of economics as a science of wealth or of material goods, as against alternative conceptions of the discipline, consists in their identification of economics with some special *end* of human action. Not all action is subject to economic law, but only such action as is directed towards a more or less well-defined class of objects, viz., wealth or material goods. Most of the definitions advanced during the greater part of the nineteenth century can be considered as variants of this view. The earlier ones saw economics as concerned with the results achieved with regard to these ends themselves, its enquiries being directed at describing the phenomena of this desired wealth. The later, less objectivistic definitions looked at economics, as will be seen in subsequent chapters, as a description of man in one department of his activities—that directed towards, or pertaining to, the desired wealth.

When economics is narrowed down still further by restricting it to the study of the goods necessary for human survival, the relevant range of human ends is contracted to the point where the term "end" begins to lose its meaning. No matter how objective a view one had of the wealth around which political economy was supposed to revolve, it was extremely difficult to close one's eyes to the fact that wealth is wealth only because it is desired by human beings, i.e., that it is an end of human endeavor. But when the only parts of wealth permitted to come into consideration are biological necessities, then it is dangerously tempting to consider these necessities as not being the ends of human desire at all. Instead of being goods brought under the play of market forces by being the goals of human aspirations, these necessities gain their economic relevance purely objectively, by being the physiologically determined causes of quasi-biological tropisms. And this, indeed, is the direction towards which a number of "subsistence" definitions of economic phenomena have tended.

There had been discussions for a long time concerning the question whether wealth should properly include luxuries as well as "necessaries." [26] Steuart had seen the goal of his subject as being "to secure a certain fund of subsistence for all the inhabitants." [27] It is noteworthy that during the period of the classical economists most writers did not embrace this "subsistence" approach. As a matter of fact several writers explicitly took a view diametrically opposed to the "subsistence" criterion. So far from confining wealth to necessities, these writers defined wealth as *excluding* necessaries.[28] Wealth was the *surplus,* often the surplus after all expenditures. Political economy was exclusively the science of great *riches,* of luxury phenomena. (Both Bentham and Malthus found it necessary to reject this view of economics and attempted to make it absolutely clear that *their* political economy was concerned with the poverty of nations quite as much as with their wealth.) [29]

Despite the general absence of the subsistence view in classical economics, there appears to be at least one sturdy offspring of the classical school to which this view is central. This is to be seen in the work of the Marxist writers in developing the thesis of the economic, or materialist, interpretation of history. The significance of the materialist interpretation in Marxist thought lies, of course, in its consequences for the "noneconomic" aspects of history. For the purposes of the present account, however, the Marx-Engels approach to history yields a fresh view of the scope of economic affairs. Superficially one might be content to explain the fact that Marx and his followers equated the "economic" with the "materialist" interpretation of history as deriving merely from the classical economists' stress on material wealth. An examination of Marx's writings, however, reveals his conception of political economy to have been even narrower. Professor Knight seems to have put his finger on the essential point when he writes: "The socialistic popularisers of [the economic interpretation of history] have leaned toward the narrower and more definite . . . conception of downright necessities." [30]

This view of the economic interpretation of history seems to be expressed in Marx's own writings. In a note in which he compares his conception of history to the doctrines of Darwin, Marx writes: "Technology discloses man's mode of dealing with Nature—the process of production by which he sustains his life, and thereby lays bare the mode of formation of his social relations, and of the mental conceptions that flow from them." [31] In the passage that Kautsky considered the classic formulation of the economic interpretation, Marx explains:

In the social production which men carry on they enter into definite relations; these relations of production correspond to a definite stage of development of their material powers of production . . . The mode of production in material life determines the general character of the social, political, and spiritual processes of life.[32]

It is of interest to note that the words which in this extract (from Stone's translation of Marx's preface to his *Critique of Political Economy*) are rendered ". . . in the social production which men carry on . . ." are in the German original: . . . *in der gesellschaftlichen Produktion ihres Lebens* . . . Other translators of Marx have rendered this phrase: ". . . in the social production of their every-day existence" [33] and ". . . in the social production of their subsistence. . ." [34]

Engels too made this subsistence approach very clear. "According to the materialist conception," he wrote, "the decisive factor in history, is, in the last resort, the production and reproduction of immediate life." [35] And again, "We understand by the economic relations, which we regard as the determining basis of the history of society, the methods by which the members of a given society produce their means of support . . ." [36]

Clearly, then, there emerges from the various formulations of the materialist interpretation of history a conception of economic affairs that centers about biological survival. Not the provision of wealth, but the provision of bare life is the realm of economics. Nor is it that life referred to in Ruskin's phrase, "There is no wealth but life" (in which life includes "all its powers of love, of joy, and of admiration"), but the elemental existence that is the subject of biology. Not "wants," in the sense of the reflections of standards of ultimate values, but rather the inexorable, objective requisites of survival—"needs"—are the data of economics.

In such a scheme, in which the relationship between ends and means as arranged by rational action is completely obliterated, economics and economic affairs clearly take their place as part of biology. Kautsky is easily understood when he insists that the materialist conception of history does not postulate the dominance of economic *motives*. We must, we are told, sharply distinguish between economic *motives* and economic *conditions*. It is only the latter that are assigned the decisive role in the Marxist scheme of history.[37]

It is not clear whether economists in general were greatly influenced by this idea. The literature yields very scanty traces of any school of economic thought that placed human survival at the center of their subject.[38] Yet it is of interest to notice passages in American economic and sociological literature at the turn of the century that do have a pronounced relevance to this general conception of the economic domain. It is, perhaps, not a complete surprise to find that it is Veblen who seems to approach most closely to the "biological" outlook on economics. Veblen explicitly points out that in the earlier stages of industry the "struggle for wealth" meant "a struggle for subsistence." [39] He considered the essence of the physiocratic system to consist in the fact that it saw "economic reality" in "the increase of nutritive material." [40] Again and again in his writings the phrase "the material means of life" is used as the criterion for distinguishing economic activity. "In economics, the subject of inquiry is the conduct of man in his dealings with the material means of life." This is a typical Veblenian sentence in this respect.[41]

We must probably see in this Veblenian tendency to identify

economics with the maintenance of life a reflection of a fashionable pastime of applying biological analogies to the phenomena of the social sciences. The terminology of biologists seems to have strengthened this tendency. Franklin Giddings drew attention to the different meanings that the word "economy" had for economists and for biologists. Inherent in the economists' use of the term is the presumption of "a conscious being, endowed with the capacity for pain and for pleasure, to plan and direct the economy and to profit by it." The biologists, on the other hand, use "the highly general notion of economy as any system of activities and relations which furthered the well-being of any class or species of living things." It is this concept that produces such phrases as "the economy of the animal kingdom" and the "economy of nature." "In these notions there is no implication of consciousness, of pleasure or of pain, and no presumption of intelligent planning or management on the part of the organisms that are benefited by their economy. The thought is altogether objective." [42]

The same explicit warning against the biological view of economic affairs was sounded by Sherwood.

In applying the physical formulae of evolution to psychical phenomena, sociologists are guilty of unscientific procedure . . . The physical formulae of evolution are statements of unexplained fortuitous change. The "fitness" which survives is an unforeseen fitness, an adjustment wrought out in consequence of the struggle. Psychical activities, on the contrary, are essentially teleological. They are directed to ends. The "fitness" in social adjustments is foreseeable, prearranged. Further than that, this fitness is nothing other than "utility" to the individual.[43]

This statement formulates the issue precisely. The imposition of "subsistence" as the goal of economic activity sets up a value involving among all others the least troublesome subjective differences between individuals. The only area of choice left to human intelligence is in the means objectively best suited to attain this one end. Once man's power to select his own ends is prescinded from economics, the subject is at once reduced to an only slightly more involved version of biology.

The Science of Wealth Retained

Meanwhile, side by side with this subsistence approach to economics, which it had fostered, the concept of wealth—and even of material wealth—continued to provide a convenient, if facile, criterion for defining the domain of the economic long after the close of the classical period. Mill, Senior, and Cairnes debated whether economics was a physical or a mental science. But Cairnes, famous as the last of the economists of stature to adhere to the general classical tradition, could write in 1875: ". . . neither mental nor physical nature forms the *subject matter* of the investigation of the political economist . . . The subject matter . . . is wealth." [44] And again, even more clearly: "Political Economy is a science in the same sense in which Astronomy, Dynamics, Chemistry, Physiology are sciences. Its subject matter is different; it deals with the phenomena of wealth, while they deal with the phenomena of the physical universe." [45]

Bonamy Price, even while describing the confusion regarding the definition of economics, was still able to declare: "All are agreed that it is concerned with wealth." [46] It is true that many of the pronouncements referring to wealth as the key concept were modified so as to conform more or less closely with more sophisticated views. Especially in a number of German definitions after 1870, the vital role played by acting, choosing man in all the phenomena connected with wealth was well recognized, and yet this did not prevent these definitions from assigning the key position to *Güter* (often *Sachgüter*).[47]

From both of the opposing sides in the *Methodenstreit* came statements tying the economic world to material goods. In so far as this criterion appeared in the works of economists of the Historical School, the matter admits of some explanation. In later chapters it will be seen that the earliest rebellion against the conception of economics as a science of wealth came as a result of the analysis of actual human behavior and the hypothetical isolation of a specific pattern of behavior in economic affairs. This diverted attention from the wealth itself towards the activity of the wealth-seeker. Such a way out from the limited conception of economics as a science of wealth was obviously closed to the Historical School. It was, after all, the very postulation of such hypothetical patterns of behavior on the part of "economic man" that had initially aroused the protests of the adherents of the Historical School and later became the butt of the ridicule expressed by those of their successors who went to the greatest extremes. The urge to restrict economics arbitrarily to material goods and to see the essential character of economic phenomena in their relationship to these objects may therefore well have been stronger for the adherents of the Historical School. So long as action is to be considered only in its empirical totality, any attempt at an *analytical* separation of economic phenomena from the rest is ruled out from the start.

In England a similar tendency is noticeable in the writings of proponents of the historical method during the small-scale British counterpart of the *Methodenstreit*. Such prominent writers as Cliffe Leslie and John K. Ingram found themselves embracing definitions of economics that were closer to those of the earlier classical writers than to those, say, of Mill, against whose then dominant type of economics they were now in rebellion. These writers, insisting on the scientific excommunication of *homo oeconomicus* and pouring scorn on the abstract constructions of earlier economists, were advocating the new science of sociology. While not going so far as Comte, who had flatly denied the existence of a separate field for economic inquiry, they stressed the futility of seeking laws in economics apart from the laws of society as a whole. "The study of wealth cannot be isolated . . . from the other social phenomena. There is, in fact, properly speaking, but one great science of sociology . . ." The laws of economics "must be sought in the great science of Society." [48]

All this meant only one thing. If any separate field is to be recognized for economics, it must be the result of viewing a class of objects constituting wealth as forming a distinct category whose conditions represent a legitimately separate area of knowledge. This knowledge, of course, can only be tapped from the larger Science of Society. "Political Economy is thus a department of the science of society which selects a special class of social phenomena for special investigation." By this "special class of social phenomena" there is no doubt that Leslie means the phenomena of wealth.[49]

What gives unusual interest to the German literature on "material goods" is the fact that goods and material goods are stressed even by the writers who gave the most careful and explicit attention to the problems of defining economics and economic activity. Writing in the eighties and nineties of the last century, Dietzel dealt exhaustively with the various criteria offered for use in definitions of economics. Most of the ideas to be incorporated in the more careful attempts at definition in recent decades seem to have been anticipated either directly in Dietzel's own writings or by the writers whom he cites. Dietzel came close to recognizing the universality of the category of human action and yet clung tenaciously to the objectivistic outlook on economics throughout his writings.[50] Characteristic is his remark that it is not method, but rather the *object,* that provides the criterion for distinguishing the activities that are the subject matter of economics.[51]

A similar situation to that in Britain and Germany prevailed in the United States and France during the same period. Again we find the traditional retention of the wealth formula often merely as a cover for a less limited conception of the scope and character of the science. And yet economists seem to have felt that it was their preoccupation with wealth that made their discipline in any way a development from, or a successor to, classical political economy. In one of Ely's earlier writings, in which he subjected classical political economy to severe criticism, he could yet find some merit in the older economics. "It separated the phenomena of wealth from other social phenomena for special and separate study." [52] For the eminent Belgian economist, de Laveleye, and for many French writers, the *définition habituelle* of their subject was unquestionably that which ran in terms of *richesses,* often with explicit limitation to material goods.[53]

The decades after 1870 were full of change for economics in many directions. The numerous alternative definitions to be considered in subsequent chapters may almost all be traced to the ferment of economic ideas that were revolutionizing economic theory at this time. Again and again it will be found that the application of methodological self-consciousness and precision to fundamental questions of economic epistemology began in earnest during the *Methodenstreit* of the eighties. The discussion in the foregoing pages demonstrates the persistence, in the face of these developments, of the older conception of economic affairs. Side by side with the newer views to be noticed later, definitions of economics as a science of wealth or of material wealth continued to occupy a central place in economic thought.

Man Against Nature

It is convenient here to notice a point of view that enjoyed the endorsement of a number of writers. They see economics and economic activities as consisting in the constant struggle on the part of man to subdue nature to his own ends. This creates a line of cleavage between two categories of resources. On the one hand, we have the human agent with all his powers of brain and brawn, emotions and skills. These resources he marshals to attack those of the external physical world which he turns to his own purposes. The interaction between man and his physical environment is the area of economic activity.

The earliest writer to have explicitly applied such a distinction to economic phenomena at all seems to have been the German economist (who wrote his book in French while at the Russian court in St. Petersburg) Storch.[54] Writing in 1815, Storch emphatically rejected the prevalent viewpoint, which confined political economy to wealth. Not the wealth of nations, but the "prosperity" of nations, should be the subject of political economy. By prosperity Storch included all "civilization," and in this connection he spoke of "inner goods" such as health, strength, reason, knowledge. These inner goods stand in contradistinction to wealth, which is comprised of "outer goods." Storch includes both inner and outer goods in his political economy, but his division between the two categories of goods shows what he understood to be meant by an exclusive science of wealth.[55]

The eminent British historian Lecky appears to have considered this distinction between "inner" and "outer" resources as of great importance. Writing in one of his earlier works, Lecky seems to feel the arbitrary nature of the conception of a science dealing with the phenomena of wealth. He considers political economy as an expression of what he calls the "industrial" philosophy, which he contrasts with the "ascetic" point of view. The latter philosophy acknowledges happiness as a condition of the mind and seeks to attain it by acting directly on the mind through diminishing the desires. The industrial philosophy seeks happiness, not by diminishing desires, but by acting on surrounding circumstances in order to fulfil the desires. This conception of economics clearly shifts the emphasis from material wealth as such and sees economic activity as the attempt to fulfil desires by altering the configuration of the external world.[56]

Among economists such a view seems to have found especial favor in Germany. Albert Schäffle, one of the earliest to stress the fundamental role of man in economic phenomena, appears to have consistently gone out of his way to avoid characterizing economics as concerned with "goods." The key word in Schäffle's many writings on the nature of the economy is the *Aussenwelt*—i.e., the external physical world.[57] Schäffle's avoidance of the criterion of goods in favor of a definition formulated in terms of the "external world" is best interpreted as a conscious attempt to draw attention to human activity directed at want-satisfaction. Not goods, but man's struggle and conquest of the external world is the subject matter of economics.

Other and later German writers referred to the "external world" in their writings, but often merely as an alternative expression for "goods." Mangoldt, Cohn, Sax, and several other writers may be mentioned in this connection.[58]

A fundamentally similar attitude to that of Lecky and Schäffle is evidenced about the turn of the century by the American Tuttle. Tuttle speaks of the "fundamental and universal economic principle"—a phrase that he uses in a sense quite different from the usual one. "Three primary facts," he writes,

lie at the basis of all economic phenomena: namely, man, man's environment—the outside world, nature—and the dependence of man upon nature. Man has . . . an economic relation to his material environment . . . a relation which may very properly be called the weal-relation. This weal-relation . . . is the fundamental and universal economic principle . . .[59]

Here again the economic relationship is conceived as one involving man and his surroundings. This view of the matter bears the clear imprint of the definition of economic phenomena in terms of material wealth. From the external world man creates the goods with which to satisfy his wants. To effect the production of these goods, man applies his own human resources to the external world. The changes that acting man imposes on the outer world both affect and are affected by the changes that are constantly taking place "within" man himself. Envisaging economic activity in this light, as the interaction of man—with all his shifting desires and human resources—and external nature, Tuttle offers a definition in consonance with the more popular conceptions, formulated in terms of wealth, and at the same time suggestive of the place of acting man in the phenomena of economic life.

From Wealth to Welfare

The period in which economic affairs were chiefly considered as being concerned with a class of objects known as wealth coincided roughly with the nineteenth century. Only since the turn of the century have economists been increasingly inclined to consider the scope of their subject in less objective terms. Yet most of the newer views on the question of definition had already found some expression in the writings of the more thoughtful students of economic methodology well before the present century. These murmurings of dissatisfaction with the traditional wealth-bound conception of economics may most illuminatingly be interpreted as the reflection of the more general revolt against the classical system that came to a head in the last quarter of the century.

This general revolt found expression in various ways. In the domain of formal reasoning, the development of the theory of marginal utility in the seventies by Jevons, Menger, and Walras marked the shift of attention from objective cost to subjective utility. In discussions concerning the nature and scope of economics, the change showed itself in the increasing awareness that this subject has as much to do with man as it has with wealth. Well before 1870 there were already many signs in England of the recognition of the humanistic character of economics.[60] Schäffle in Germany and Droz in France had insisted on placing the role of man in economics higher than that of goods.[61] Ely described the development of economics as occurring in three steps:

Writers of the first class regard political economy as a science which has to do with external valuable things or economic goods—that is, with wealth . . . ; writers of the second class, as the science which has to do with economic goods in their relation to man; writers of the third class, as the science which has to do with man in his relations to economic goods.[62]

All this made necessary a search for some new criterion for determining the scope of economics. If economics has to do with goods, then its scope is as clear as is permitted by the definition of the word "goods." But if it is urged that economics is primarily concerned with man, then there is an obvious need to make clear precisely which aspect of the study of man economic theory is concerned with. The subsequent chapters of this book deal with some of the different approaches that have been made toward the solution of this problem. At this point in the chapter describing the conception of economics as a science of wealth, attention must be drawn to one of the most popular of these approaches, viz., the view that sees economics as dealing with the phenomena connected with economic *welfare*.

This view of economics had, in fact, the most persuasive claim to qualify as the natural successor to the earlier definition of it as a science of wealth. Wealth promotes the economic welfare of man. If exclusive attention to the objects of wealth was to be declared scientifically inexpedient, then the problem could be avoided by shifting attention from the goods themselves to the welfare to which they minister. Instead of studying the effects of various measures on the wealth of a nation, economic analysis may be viewed as going a step further and studying the welfare of the nation as affected by these measures.

Such a conception of economics provided a framework into which the received body of doctrine could be fitted without excessive strain, while at the same time it reflected the new recognition of the subjective basis of market phenomena. The shift to this fresh conception seemed merely a broadening of the scope of the subject from one narrowly concerned with goods to one concerned with happiness.[63] Cannan, writing at the beginning of this century on developments since the appearance of Mill's *Principles,* saw this broadening as the work of the theory of marginal utility:

Whatever definition of economics may be adopted, it is clear that the conception of its subject has become wider than it was . . . The economist of today recognizes that he has to do with man in relation to one particular kind of human welfare. . . . Ever since Jevons . . . it would be impossible for any economist of the present day to repeat Malthus' remark that Adam Smith mixes the nature and causes of the wealth of nations with the causes which affect the happiness and comfort of the lower orders of society.[64]

From the point of view of the long-run developments in the definition of economic phenomena, this broadening of the economics of wealth into the economics of welfare does not mark so radical a change as that marked by the appearance of any of a number of later conceptions to be taken up in subsequent chapters. In fact, as against the other definitions of economics, both the wealth and the welfare formulations contain much in common; many of the features found to be objectionable in the wealth criterion appear unchanged in its welfare counterpart.

Both formulations are "classificatory" and "departmental" rather than "analytical." [65] Both see economics as studying *something* that is produced, whether goods or happiness, rather than a certain type of *activity*.[66] Especially where economic welfare is understood as meaning *material* welfare, the concept of welfare evinced a strong bond of continuity with that of material wealth.

Nevertheless, as the neoclassical expression of the classical wealth-oriented definition of economics, the welfare and utility criterion did call for a conscious alteration of focus in the contemplation of economic phenomena. This point of view, while it became popular only after the introduction of marginal utility economics, had its forerunners as far back as the classical economists. One of Adam Smith's successors, Dugald Stewart, considered political economy as dealing with "the happiness and improvement of political society." [67] The position of Henri Storch has already been noticed in this chapter. He broadened economics so as to deal, not with the wealth of nations, but with the "prosperity" of nations—a concept that included "civilization" as well as wealth. John Stuart Mill, when he came to consider the question of defining economics, criticized Say for having a similarly wide conception of political economy. Sismondi's emphasis on happiness and consumption in economics [68] and Lauderdale's all-embracing definitions of wealth place their conception of economics in the same group.

The more general movement towards the idea of economics as a science of welfare rather than of wealth that accompanied the reaction against the classical school is evidenced in the literature in a number of directions. Cliffe Leslie, who was to become the vigorous proponent of historical consciousness in British economics, had a hand in this development. Writing as early as 1862 in a frequently cited essay, *The Love of Money*, Leslie attacked the notion that the pursuit of wealth represented a self-contained human motive. The love of money means completely different things to different people. To the scholar it may mean the love of books; to the toper it may mean love of liquor. There is nothing unique in the motives that lead men to seek monetary gain; they are as heterogeneous as are human tastes themselves. Later arguments like these were to lead Leslie and others to denounce the classical economists for their postulation of the possibility of valid laws of *wealth* apart from the "laws of society." Yet the impact of these ideas undermining the concept of a unique category of wealth through reference to the heterogeneity of the demand side of economics undoubtedly contributed toward a better grasp of the nature of economic theory. For example, it was the increased attention to the demand factor that made it possible for Jevons to "take utility . . . as the subject matter of economics," or for an American writer to declare that all definitions of economics reduce to "the science of enjoyment or . . . the science of the means of enjoyment." [69]

In France a long tradition of stress on utility lent force to the growing dissatisfaction with the definitions of economics formulated in terms of wealth.[70] Welfare, utility, ophelimity—these were the terms around which expositions of economic doctrines revolved. The "ethical neutrality" with which these terms were explicitly invested even further removed the newer views from the wealth-bound conception of the subject, while it at the same time provided the bridge across which economics could, if desired, pass in order to become a science of conduct or a logic of pure choice.

By the early years of the present century, the idea that economics is essentially concerned with welfare, or at least with material well-being, was probably the view most generally accepted among the English economists. Both Marshall and Cannan introduced widely used textbooks, running to many editions, with definitions formulated in terms of material welfare.[71] Marshall, it is true, had made it clear that it is only an accident that economics is concerned with material wealth and that its "true philosophic *raison d'être* must be sought elsewhere." [72] Cannan, however, held the criterion of material welfare to be the real distinguishing feature of economics. When Robbins, in attacking this proposition, took Cannan's enunciations of it as his principal target, Cannan gladly took up the cudgels in its defense.[73] In America economists representing such different outlooks as Fetter and Mitchell both called for a shift in interest away from wealth itself towards the human welfare with which it is related; both saw a need for such a shift in the very conception of the nature of economic science.[74]

Of course, the identification of economics with the study of economic welfare raised fundamental questions about the justifiability and validity of propositions concerning changes in social welfare. It is under the shadow of this thorny problem, involving the admissibility of interpersonal comparisons of welfare and the legitimacy of possible ethical assumptions, that welfare economists in recent decades have been consciously working.[75] Sir Dennis Robertson cites the contention that the implications of envy make it uncertain that welfare would be increased even if everyone had more of every commodity. Robertson's characteristic reply to this possibility would certainly have won Cannan's concurrence:

How much better, surely, to assert as a plain matter of fact that *economic* welfare undoubtedly *will* be increased in this event; and *then* to call in the Archbishop of Canterbury to smack people over the head if they are stupid enough to allow the increased happiness which might be derived from this plain fact to be eroded by the gnawings of the green-eyed monster; and I cannot at present persuade myself that such a common-sense distinction between the economic and the not is fatally undermined by the fact that the Archbishop draws a salary and that his gaiters embody scarce resources which might have been devoted to an alternative use.[76]

Robertson's words gives added salience to the difficulty that the advance from wealth to welfare brought in its train. If economics is concerned with a part of welfare, how is this part to be identified? The "material wealth" criterion embraced by Cannan provided an answer to this question by retaining a direct bond to the discarded conception of economics as a science of wealth. The objections which might be raised against such a criterion, and which Robertson here brushes aside, are clearly in large measure those that can be levelled at the type of definition treated generally in the present chapter.

The Science of the Lower Side of Human Nature

This chapter on the definitions of economics as a science of wealth cannot close without taking account of the stigma which has persistently clung to economics, and for which these definitions of the subject in terms of wealth must bear a major share of responsibility. Well over a century ago, Bailey discussed the popular view that economics is "a mean, degrading, sordid inquiry." [77] Economists have shrugged off somewhat uneasily Carlyle's contemptuous description of their subject as a "pig-science." But economists themselves, especially by conceiving of their subject as a science of wealth, have clearly laid themselves open to such criticisms. From the start an economics centered around wealth had to contend with a climate of opinion in which the so-called "economic virtues" had long been held in moral disrepute.[78]

By the close of the main period of classical economics, leading writers on the subject found it necessary again and again to defend the ethical standing of their discipline against its detractors.[79] Economists of the 1830's and 1840's refuted the criticisms levelled against their moral status with indignation, with ridicule, or with disdain. The unworthiness of political economy in public opinion stemmed directly from its explicit preoccupation with so degrading a subject matter as wealth. All the depravities that moralists throughout the centuries have ascribed to wealth became naturally attached to the science of wealth.

The defenses raised by some of the economic apologists against those strictures are revealing. A popular argument that was used did not attempt to deny the possible immoral associations of wealth. But then, the argument ran, political economy must be studied all the more diligently in order to know how to *avoid* wealth! [80]

Nevertheless, despite rather extensive apologetics on the part of these writers, the observer may be excused if he gains the impression that many economists themselves were not altogether convinced by these discussions. If they did not consider their subject as actually a degraded one, they very certainly did consider it as concerned chiefly with the lower and seamier side of human nature. R. Jennings, one of the "precursors" of subjectivism in economics, painted a highly repulsive picture of the motives with which economics is concerned. Writing in 1855, he announced that "Political Economy treats only of those human susceptibilities and appetences which are similar or analogous to those . . . in the brute creation; . . . it never attempts to enter those higher paths of human conduct which are guided by morality, or by religion." [81]

Among later writers, especially those who favored the hedonistic view of economics, a similar opinion prevailed. Economists displayed a sense of moral inferiority towards the votaries of the "higher," less mundane branches of knowledge. Bagehot speaks of other studies "which are much higher, for they are concerned with things much nobler than wealth or money." [82] Jevons wrote: "My present purpose is accomplished in . . . assigning a proper place to the pleasures and pains with which the Economist deals. It is the lowest rank of feelings which we treat . . ." Edgeworth considered economics as "dealing with the lower elements of human nature." [83] It comes as no surprise to find Jevons hopefully writing that he does "not despair" of "tracing the action of the postulates of political economy" among dogs and other more intelligent animals.[84]

The whole literature on the "lower" side of human nature with which economics was held to be concerned provides a commentary on the wealth-bound conception of the subject.[85] The foremost characteristic of this type of definition is that it associates economic activity with a specific type of *ends*. Of the many goals of human endeavor, one, that known as wealth, is singled out as the subject of economics. Grant that wealth ministers, or at least ministers chiefly, to physical wants, and the sordidness of economic phenomena is well established. It was only in the twentieth century that the need for the ethical insulation of economics became widely recognized, so that the identification of the subject with any one type of *end* has receded from fashion.

3

The Science of Avarice; Getting the Most for the Least

In the past economists have often been attacked on the grounds that their theories only applied to selfish people; such attacks were brushed aside as absurd. But they were not absurd . . .

I. M. D. Little

The bottle of medicine for a dying child, or of wine for himself; the tools for his trade; the supplies for a home for the aged, bought as a contribution to the home from a future inmate—all are bought with the same end of getting the most for the least, whatever the motive for the purchase may be.

J. Viner

In the present chapter a number of types of definitions are grouped together by virtue of their possession of either of two special characteristics. These definitions either see economic activity as being essentially motivated by pecuniary self-interest or they see it as conforming to a pattern of behavior prescribed by the so-called "economic principle." These two points of view and the postulation of a common starting point for both require some elaboration.

The Science of Avarice

As is well known, for a long time it was widely held that economists were able to study human action solely by subjecting

51

themselves to the self-imposed limitation of considering only selfishly inspired behavior. On the strength of this popular opinion, economists came to be pilloried as viciously unrealistic or as having gotten themselves into "an entirely damned state of soul." [1] In a well-known passage the historian Buckle accounts for the difference in tone between Adam Smith's *Theory of Moral Sentiments* and his *Wealth of Nations* by the hypothesis that in the latter Smith assumes only selfish motives, while altruistic motives find a place in the earlier work.[2]

For many years now, economists have been at pains to disassociate themselves from this view of economic activity. The latter is seen as reflecting all motives, altruistic as well as selfish. This contention, together with the broadening effect it possessed on the scope of economic analysis, is one of the basic undercurrents guiding the development of definitions of economics. At this point it is sufficient to observe that the connection between economics and selfishness was for a long time widely assumed. This assumption served as the foundation for a separate conception of the nature of economics, viz., as the science of the operation of self-interest in human activity.

Of course, much of the stress on selfishness which was ascribed to economists, or which was admitted by economists, did not involve the explicit definition of the subject in these terms. Selfishness was often merely a convenient assumption by means of which the analysis of the data could extract rather definite results. The essential character of economics may have been seen, for example, to concern material goods, and the postulation of selfishness was in such a case only an incidental simplification, made to assist the theorist, of the real economic phenomena. The discussion in the previous chapter, as a case in point, revealed the conception of economic affairs held by the classical economists to have been predominantly bound to a class of objects called "wealth." How far the classical economists did, in fact, exclude from their consideration all human motives other than self-interest is a matter of controversy that need not detain us here. But to the degree that selfishness *was* assumed by Smith, Ricardo and their followers, it certainly did *not* constitute the essence of the phenomena that they undertook to investigate.

Indeed, the possibility of carving out a segment of activity governed by self-interest as a distinct subject of study could offer itself only to economists who recognized the hypothetical character of such an assumption. If a *homo oeconomicus* endowed with only one aspect of human nature, viz., that of greed, is postulated, then it is possible to see the whole body of economic theory as the extended exposition of the consequences of this greed. The knowledge that real men are actuated by other motives besides greed makes feasible the conceptual isolation of that aspect of human activity from which these other motives have been prescinded. But it is precisely this possibility that was not open to the earlier classical economists. In so far as these writers assumed the impulse to economic activity to arise from selfishness, they considered their assumptions to conform closely to the facts of the real world. "It is," Ricardo wrote in a well-known passage, "self-interest which regulates all the speculations of trade . . ." Because they believed the pursuit of wealth to be characterized by self-interest, and because they conceived of economics as studying the phenomena of wealth, the classical writers made use of the concept of selfishness in their analysis. But this selfishness was only incidental to the real object of study. In no way did economics, as they conceived it, revolve exclusively around that aspect of man's nature inspired by selfishness.

In fact it may fairly be argued that the stress that came to be laid on the hypothetical isolation of self-regarding activity provided the earliest major advance in the conception of the essence of economic affairs over that of the classical economists. The earlier classical writers had set up an objective subject matter for study, viz., wealth. The writers of the 1830's, outstanding among whom were J. S. Mill and S. Bailey, found themselves rebelling against this position. It was becoming increasingly evident that what economists were investigating was not the objective phenomena of wealth, but rather the wealth-oriented actions of *man*. This step forward was taken most clearly and influentially in

Mill's essay *On the Definition of Political Economy; and on the Method of Investigation Proper to It.*[3]

The popular definition of the subject in terms of the production, distribution, and consumption of wealth provided Mill with a convenient point of departure. But the production of wealth, it is evident, involves a complete range of the sciences, including agriculture, physiology, chemistry, geology, etc., all of which cannot possibly be meant to be included under political economy.[4] Nor is Mill satisfied to consider the subject as consisting of the general laws common to the production of *all* kinds of wealth. "The real distinction between Political Economy and physical science must be sought in something deeper than the nature of the subject matter. . . ." It is to be found in the distinction between "physical and moral science."

The laws of the production of . . . wealth are the subject matter both of Political Economy and of almost all the physical sciences. Such, however, of these laws as are purely laws of matter, belong to physical science, and to that exclusively. Such of them as are laws of the human mind and no other, belong to Political Economy, which finally sums up the result of both combined.[5]

For "the purposes of the philosopher," Mill presses on with still further refinement and rigor of definition. Political economy does not treat of the whole of man's nature;

. . . it is concerned with him solely as a being who desires to possess wealth . . . It makes entire abstraction of every other human passion or motive; except . . . aversion to labor, and desire of the present enjoyment of costly indulgences . . .[6]

In his final and most carefully formulated definition, the "laws of society" rather than those of wealth are set aside for investigation. Political economy is the science

which traces the laws of such of the phenomena of society as arise from the combined operations of mankind for the production of wealth, in so far as those phenomena are not modified by the pursuit of any other object.[7]

This conception of the nature of economics is thus closely bound up with the appearance on the literary horizon of that ill-fated creature, the notorious "economic man." [8] Mill sets up a being from whom he abstracts every human passion other than that for the pursuit of wealth. The laws of economics express the consequences of the interplay in society of the activities of economic men. In his *Logic,* Mill seems even more insistent on defining political economy as the study of the operation of human wealth-seeking activities rather than of the phenomena of wealth itself.[9]

The construction of a model of a human agent endowed solely with the passion for wealth carried with it, of course, the implication of the paramountcy of self-interest. Not all economists, to be sure, were prepared to exclude altruistic motives. Both Whately and Senior, for example, pointed out that wealth may be sought in order to be used for charitable purposes.[10] But the tradition that was initiated by the emergence of *homo oeconomicus* was certainly responsible for the economists' continued retention of explicit assumptions concerning the selfish motivation of the activities they investigated. Writers such as Bagehot, Lowe, Cunningham, and Edgeworth, who more or less openly held self-interest to be "the first principle of pure economics," were simply carrying on the received tradition.[11]

The elevation of pecuniary self-interest into the carefully selected criterion for distinguishing activity capable of economic analysis marked a significant advance over the earlier classical position. Even granting that economic man was a monstrous caricature, he was yet a being who acted, and it was his actions that were the object of study. The earlier writers had taken wealth as their subject matter; to the economists after the 1830's wealth was important merely as the object that aroused the particular kind of human behavior in which the economist was interested. Considerable effort has been devoted to the finding of traces of subjectivistic thinking in economics prior to 1870. A fair body of literature during this period has been brought to light in which may be seen the beginning of the reaction against the objective value theories of the classical school.[12] It is tempting to see a significant parallel to this reaction against classical objectivism in the shift in outlook on the nature of economics from the conception of it as a science of wealth to the view that regarded it as the study of the man in quest of wealth. To Ricardo, who "stopped at the valuations of the market and did not press through to the valuations of the individual," political economy was perfectly acceptable when conceived as an investigation into an aspect of the phenomena of wealth, with the relevant factors of human nature relegated completely to the background. To a Bailey or a Senior, whose outlook on value was further advanced, such a view must necessarily seem inadequate.

Yet in spite of the progress represented by the conception of economic activity as motivated essentially by pecuniary self-interest, this view still, of course, bears obvious signs of its close relationship to the earlier definitions of economics as the science of wealth. In fact, economics as the science of avarice is most illuminatingly understood as the link between economics as the science of wealth and the more sophisticated conceptions of the subject that have emerged in recent decades. The concept of wealth involved the postulation of some common quality in the objects constituting wealth—a quality that was generally identified as "material" or as catering to the "lower" needs of man. These objects themselves were the focus of economic attention. By shifting this focus of attention away from wealth itself and towards acting man in his quest for wealth, Mill and Bailey were still obliged to assign a significant role to wealth. And the qualities common to the objects constituting wealth became perhaps even more pivotal to economic analysis, since it was attraction towards these qualities that kindled and conditioned the avarice of economic man.

But the break with the earlier definitions formulated in terms of wealth, however slight it may seem, was enough to point the way to the complete extrusion of that clumsy and misleading concept from economics. Once economics was conceived as involving a certain pattern of *behavior*, or even a uniquely motivated kind of behavior, then the bonds that attached it to the class of objects constituting wealth could easily be broken. Although it was wealth that was the initial structural unit in the formation of the pattern of behavior of wealth-seeking man, this goal could soon be discarded as scaffolding unnecessary to the completed structure. The behavior of wealth-seeking man was found to be sufficiently distinctive, but at the same time sufficiently universal, in pattern to warrant a separate treatment in its own right. Economics could then be identified, not in terms of wealth, nor even in terms of men-in-quest-of-wealth, but in terms of a unique pattern of human behavior: *the getting of the most for the least.*

The Economic Principle

This pattern of behavior came to be variously known as conforming to the "economic principle," as obeying the "law of least means," the "maximization principle," and the like. One of the earliest formulations of the principle, which displays its close kinship with the classical science of wealth, is that of Senior, when he asserts, as the first of the four elementary propositions of political economy, that "every man desires to obtain additional wealth with as little sacrifice as possible." [13] In this early form, the economic principle is hardly distinguishable, indeed, from pecuniary self-interest. It is this type of proposition that Henry George had in mind when he complained many years later that "for the principle that men always satisfy their desires with the least exertion, there has been substituted, from the time that political economy began to claim the attention of thoughtful men, the principle of human selfishness." [14]

The conception of economics in terms of the principle of maximization, whether expressed in terms of selfishness or not, was, in fact, in the direct line of development that was initiated by the explicit delineation of the character of economic man. Its relationship to the view of economic activity that sees it as motivated by pecuniary self-interest parallels that which the concept of welfare bore to the early formulations of economics, discussed in the previous chapter, as the science of wealth. Just as welfare had come to be regarded as the central point of economic interest instead of the objects (i.e., the wealth) considered as necessary for the enjoyment of welfare; so, quite analogously, the idea of behavior patterned on the principle of maximization—i.e., the abstract urge to get more for less—replaced the conception of selfish wealth-oriented activity as central to economic affairs, even though it was greed for wealth that was at first thought to be the sole stimulant to this pattern of conduct.

Although a number of early expressions of the importance of the so-called economic principle appear in the literature, it was not until the last quarter of the nineteenth century that there was any extensive discussion of its significance for the conception of the nature of economic inquiry. Besides Senior, the German economist Hermann had seen the maximization of want-satisfaction as the key concept in economic activity.[15] Much of the later discussion in Germany seems to have taken Hermann's idea as a starting point.

Curiously enough, although it was in England that the pecuniary self-interest conception of economics came into prominence, the maximization criterion did not gain much popularity in British economic literature after the 1870's. One finds few statements of the principle and no real debate as to its significance until Wicksteed's masterly work in 1910. Perhaps the clearest expression, in decidedly hedonistic terms, was that of Jevons, who described the "object" of economics as being "to maximize happiness by purchasing pleasure, as it were, at the lowest cost of pain." [16]

But in Germany and in the United States the fundamental economic principle was accorded quite extensive and sensitive treatment. The debate in Germany over the status to be assigned to the economic principle is the clearest evidence of the advance in the conception of economics in the last quarter of the century. Regardless of the opinions expressed on both sides, the fact that such a controversy did occur is a sign of the sophistication with which economists were now examining their subject matter. Whether to consider the principle as the *defining* criterion of economic phenomena or as merely a convenient tool in the analysis of an independently recognized economic activity was a problem that the classical economists were precluded from considering. It was necessary for the economist first to recognize that he is concerned with a species of activity rather than with a species of object before he could begin to debate the role of the economic principle in understanding such activity—whether as an explanatory aid or as a defining characteristic.

The debate in Germany was largely confined to economists who were not afraid of "abstractions" or of theory. Economists of the Historical School, who were pouring scorn on the abstractions of the theorists employing the economic principle as a fundamental hypothesis, could, of course, hardly consider the use of this principle as a possible means of definition. Among the economists who did find a place in these discussions were such prominent figures as Schäffle,[17] Wagner, Neumann, and Dietzel. Wagner seems to have undergone a change of outlook on the problem during the thirteen years between the publication of the second and the third editions of his basic textbook. In 1879 he had carefully defined *Wirtschaft* in terms of the economic principle, which he characterized clearly as prescribing the maximization of want-satisfaction with a minimum of sacrifice. In the 1892 edition this passage is replaced by a conventional definition of *Wirtschaft* in terms of the production of goods.[18]

In the interval between the two editions of Wagner's book Dietzel and Neumann had objected strongly to the use of the economic principle as the defining characteristic of economic activity. Fully aware of the crucial importance of the principle for economic theory, and displaying a sensitive understanding of its meaning, both these writers rejected the use of the principle as the criterion of the economic on similar grounds. Both pointed out that the economic principle describes the pattern of human activity in general and appears in areas of behavior with which the economist has never been concerned.[19] Both failed to consider the possibility that this very fact might signify the real homogeneity of all human action, including the "economic," and might thus render artificial any rigid demarcation of the domain of economics.[20]

In the United States too the use of the maximization formula as a definition for economics met with the objection that the principle had wide application far beyond the boundaries of that science. Hadley had described the material out of which the science of economics is built as being, not material goods, but a few simple laws of human nature, "the chief of which is that men strive to obtain the maximum of satisfaction with the minimum of sacrifice." [21] But Hawley pointed out that if economics is defined in terms of actions involving the balancing of pros and cons, then it becomes "the Science of Motive in general, which it certainly is not." [22] It is of some interest to notice that Davenport, on the other hand, when declaring that the "economic problem can . . . be stated as the minimizing of sacrifice," was rather pleased to find this formula "equally well-adapted to the non-economic facts of life. . . ." [23]

The "Economic Impulse"

These discussions of the significance, for the understanding of economic phenomena, of such concepts as the pursuit of wealth or the maximization of want-satisfaction invite a brief digression on the idea of a specifically economic motive or impulse. It is clear that the meaning, if any, that is to be attached to such an expression depends on the view taken of economic activity generally. For example, if the view mentioned in the previous chapter is accepted, according to which economic activity is concerned with the sustenance of human life, then the urge for self-preservation may fairly be understood as the economic impulse.[24]

What makes the question of the meaning of the economic motive especially relevant to the present chapter is that the developments that have been discussed in the conception of economic activity point for the first time to the possibility that no such economic drive may in fact exist. So long as an objective entity—viz., wealth or economic welfare—is singled out as the phenomenon of interest to the economist, as it was in the definitions considered in the previous chapter, then, of course, the concept of an economic motive is meaningful in terms of a drive towards this objective entity. And when economics is understood, as it has been in definitions considered in the present chapter, as examining the phenomena that are attendant upon the activities of man in so far as he is in pursuit of a definite end, viz., wealth, then the economic impulse emerges as the very focus of the economists' interest. But when the pattern of human activity aimed at maximizing want-satisfaction is made central to economics and the idea of wealth is quietly discarded, then the nature of any economic motive becomes highly problematical.[25]

The specificity of any one human drive depends on the uniqueness of the end that stimulates and activates it. The most conspicuous feature of the earlier definitions of economics was their identification of the subject with an allegedly unique category of ends, viz., wealth. And it was this association that gave plausibility to the concept of an economic motive. With the recognition that the ends embodied in wealth are as heterogeneous as human wants themselves, the significance of the concept of wealth as a criterion for defining the nature of economic activity declined. Thus, with the progress seen in the present chapter from an economics analyzing human avarice towards an economics analyzing the maximization pattern of human behavior, the notion of a specifically economic impulse fell under a shadow.

In a later chapter it will be seen that a large group of economists who, with Robbins, see the essence of economic activity in the economizing of scarce means consider a major contribution of this conception of economics to be its explosion of the notion of specifically "economic" ends and motives. The idea of an economic motive still has, to be sure, considerable popularity. One recent writer has seen in "acquisitive drives" one of the really significant aspects of behavior in modern economy.[26] But the difficulties surrounding the singling out of wealth as a distinct end of human activity were exposed already in the middle of the last century. We have noticed in the previous chapter that Cliffe Leslie, in an influential essay, vigorously attacked the idea of wealth as a unique end. Leslie's criticisms were aimed at the classical conception of the character of economic activity, especially as embodied in the construction of an economic man. Leslie's recognition of the multiplicity of motives actuating the quest for wealth impelled him to urge upon economists a more historically oriented and less abstract and deductive methodology. A similar impulse lies behind a remark of Roscher, one of the leaders of the "older" German Historical School in economics. Roscher describes the change in economics since the era of the classical economists as consisting in the investigation of man in the economic sphere of life, instead of the earlier analysis of economic man.[27]

Thus, the attack on the isolation of any specifically economic motive came from both directions. On the one hand, the theorists were finding it unnecessary to invest wealth with any special role; it was sufficient for analysis to introduce a specific type of human behavior aiming at maximization. On the other hand, the historically-minded economists, interested in the "full reality" of economic phenomena, were finding that it was a misleading oversimplification to see the motive of economic activity in the desire for wealth and were probing into the many and diverse impulses that together constitute the pursuit of wealth.

The most decisive rejection of the notion of any economic motive was contained in Wicksteed's writings. He terms the concept "a false category" and "one of the most dangerous and indeed disastrous confusions that obstruct the progress of Economics." The desire for wealth reflects "all the motives and passions that actuate the human breast"; and if, by way of precaution, altruistic motives are excluded by the economist in his study, only self-regarding activity being recognized, then clearly the desire to possess wealth is no longer being treated as the "motive" at all.[28]

There is one possibility of salvaging the economic motive that remains to be considered. Even when the essence of economic activity is seen in the special maximization pattern of behavior, i.e., in the activity of securing "the most for the least," it remains a question whether such behavior may not still be regarded as an end in itself in spite of the multiplicity of ends that this type of activity may promote. The rejection of the idea of a specifically economic motive, once the paramount position is given to a "most-for-the-least" pattern of behavior, stems primarily from the fact that this pattern of behavior occurs in areas in which radically different types of motives are at work. It is for this reason that, as we have seen, many writers have sought some other criterion for the delimitation of the economic domain.[29] The very fact that the distinctive feature of behavior characterized by maximization consists in its neutrality in regard to motives prevented its wide acceptance as a criterion for economics. The possibility now to be considered is that, despite its neutrality in regard to the motives actuating it, the very activity of maximization carves out a separate niche for itself in human affairs because it satisfies a self-sufficient human urge.

This possibility does not seem to have occurred to any of the nineteenth-century writers who discussed the maximization principle. But several more recent writers have laid stress on this newly isolated "end," especially in connection with the means-ends conception of economics that, as will be seen in a later chapter, was developed from the "most-for-the-least" approach. Viner seems to have this idea in view when he declares the ends of economic man to be simple enough for inductive investigation:

The bottle of medicine for a dying child, or of wine for himself; the tools for his trade; the supplies for a home for the aged, bought as a contribution to the home from a future inmate—all are bought with the same end of getting the most for the least, whatever the motive for the purchase may be.[30]

More recently a passage from Boulding typifies the use of this idea as a means of contrasting "the cold, calculating type of behavior" of economic man with the warmth and impulsiveness of romantic, heroic, and visionary natures.[31] Clearly this type of contrast tends to run counter to the opinion, previously cited, that the calculation-conscious behavior characteristic of maximization is relevant to all departments of human affairs. This, however, involves the entire problem of the place of the assumption of rationality in economic theory, which belongs in a different chapter. At this point the relevant concept is not the plausibility of that assumption, but rather the recognition, in the activity of getting the most for the least, of an element that makes activity tend to be worthwhile for its own sake, regardless of the further ends that it may serve.

This recognition has been most vigorously accorded in the writings of Macfie. In a book devoted to the isolation and scrutiny of this element in economic activity, Macfie has elevated "economy" into a value with intrinsic appeal to the human capacity for reverence.[32] Such a position, if accepted, would clear the way for the retention of the maximization principle in the definition of economic activity. As Macfie himself stresses, any such recognition of the value-laden qualities of economy would, by attaching a specific end to economic activity, convert economics once again into an "ethical" discipline, which it had escaped being when previously defined in terms of the maximization principle. In any survey of what has been understood by the term "economic impulse," Macfie's contribution has earned a distinguished place.

Selfishness and "Non-Tuism"

In a chapter which has dealt with the view that economic activity is essentially self-centered and egoistically motivated, space must be found for the novel idea of the economic relationship that Wicksteed substituted in place of the controversial concept of egoism. We have noticed Wicksteed's vigorous rejection of the notion that economic activity is exclusively self-regarding. Robbins has commented:

Before Wicksteed wrote, it was still possible for intelligent men to give countenance to the belief that the whole structure of Economics depends upon the assumption of a world of economic men, each actuated by egocentric or hedonistic motives. For anyone who has read the *Common Sense,* the expression of such a view is no longer consistent with intellectual honesty. Wicksteed shattered this misconception once and for all.[33]

In its place Wicksteed defined the economic relationship in terms of "non-tuism." This innovation seems to have attracted far less attention than Wicksteed's other contributions to the definition of economics.[34] "Non-tuism" is closely connected with the concept of exchange as the core of the economic relationship, but it is itself the actual criterion. The economic relationship is entered into by two parties each of whom is intent on the furtherance of his own (not necessarily selfish) purposes, *not those of the other*. Wicksteed illustrates this from the case of trustees.

Trustees who have no personal interest whatever in the administration of the estates to which they give time and thought will often drive harder bargains—that is to say, will more rigidly exclude all thought or consideration of the advantage of the person with whom they are dealing—in their capacity as trustees than they would do in their private capacity . . . the reason why . . . there is no room for "you" in my consideration is just because "I" am myself already excluded from my own consideration.[35]

Wicksteed's major contribution to the characterization of the scope of economics lies in his thorough and exhaustive analysis of the process of economizing. He realizes, however, that the principles of this process are not peculiar to economics but "are laws of life itself." He seeks to isolate within the realm governed by these laws an area in which a peculiarly "economic" relationship is at work. This area is characterized by "non-tuism":

. . . in our industrial relations the thing we are doing is indeed an end, but it is some one else's end, not ours; and as far as the relation is really economic, the significance *to us* of what we are doing is measured not by its importance to the man for whom it is done, but by the degree to which it furthers our own ends.[36]

The existence of such a separate area is made possible by specialization, the division of labor and exchange, but its essence is seen in the lack of regard for the interest of the man with whom one is dealing.

Of course, to postulate such a lack of regard for the interest of others in economic activity involved Wicksteed in the question of the morality of such activity. Egoism is morally reprehensible, but has economics really escaped the castigation of the moralists by throwing in its lot with the "non-tuists" rather than with the egoists? Wicksteed's answer is that immorality is not *necessarily* present in "non-tuistic" behavior, as the person with whom we have entered into economic relations "may be one of the last whom we are bound to consider." [37]

Few writers have followed Wicksteed in viewing "non-tuistic" behavior as a separate category.[38] The case for Wicksteed's boundary line seems to be built mainly on the conventions of demand-supply analysis. In conventional theory it is convenient and customary to group together all the factors affecting the demand side of the market separately from those underlying supply. While the earlier writers had thought this practice to be justified only on the assumption of self-regarding behavior on the part of both buyers and sellers, Wicksteed has shown that this is not the case. All motives, including the most idealistic and altruistic, could underlie either the demand or the profit-seeking motivating the production of the supply. But if the distinction between buyer and seller is to be preserved at all, Wicksteed felt it necessary to assume purely "non-tuistic" behavior on the part of each. Departure from such "non-tuism" was to be regarded as a well-recognized empirical fact, but one causing a divergence between the results of economic theory and the facts of the real world. The core of the economic relationship, for Wicksteed as well as for the economists who considered egoism as the mainspring of economic activity, lies in the pursuit of one's own purposes. Wicksteed's rejection of egoism allowed him to include under "one's own purposes" every conceivable interest *except* the interest in the person with whom one is dealing.

There is undoubtedly an element of artificiality, albeit ingenious artificiality, in this exception. If "one's own purposes" are wide enough to include concern for the support of charitable institutions, they are surely able to include an interest in the welfare of the person with whom one is dealing. Despite the skillfulness and persuasive beauty of Wicksteed's prose, it remains difficult to see the boundary line as other than the result of a quite arbitrary piece of surgery on the whole of commercial activity. While theorists have been both openly and tacitly employing such surgery on business behavior in order to simplify their analysis, few have followed Wicksteed in elevating what survives their excision into a separate category of economic behavior or in treating it as the sign of a separate economic relationship.

Economics and Mechanics

One further aspect of the class of definitions of economics dealt with in this chapter remains to be discussed. Both the conception of economic activity as the pecuniary operations of self-centered economic man and its conception as the process of getting the most for the least facilitate the analysis of such activity by (the same) mathematical methods. In the previous chapter mention was made of a number of passages in the writings of eighteenth-century thinkers in which the force of self-interest in human affairs was likened to the force of gravitation in the physical world. Economists of the nineteenth century who stressed self-interest or the maximization principle in economic affairs were in a position to pursue this analogy far more thoroughly. Thus, Senior, who, as we have seen, stressed the maximization of wealth as an essential element in economic activity, describes this element, like "gravitation . . . in Physics," as "the ultimate fact beyond which reasoning cannot go, and of which almost every other proposition is merely an illustration." [39]

For the earlier classical economists, who thought of economics as concerned with wealth understood in a more or less material sense, self-interest was an impersonal force that extracted this wealth from the factors of production and propelled it through the distributive channels of the economy. The greater stress laid by later writers on the force of self-interest itself as the core of economics and the consequent emphasis on maximization-patterns of behavior tended to enhance the attraction of the analogy to mechanics. Jevons' "mechanics of utility and self-interest" and the "Economic Calculus" of Edgeworth, which investigates the equilibrium of a system of hedonic forces each tending to maximum individual utility, are typical examples. It seems no accident that both Jevons and Edgeworth were early users of mathematical methods in economics. The emphasis that both writers laid on self-interest goes hand in hand with a desire to turn economics into a "science" like mechanics. This required the postulation of a pervading force manipulating "wealth" into various configurations susceptible of analysis through the use of maximization formulae from the calculus. Self-interest was seized upon with avidity from the classical system as providing just such a plausible "force."

In Italy Pantaleoni (who has been compared to Edgeworth in a number of respects) stressed both the maximization principle in economic activity and the mathematical exposition of the theorems of economics. "Economic problems, in a broad sense, are, e.g., those which constitute the mathematical doctrine known by the generic term: *de maximis et minimis . . .*" [40] "Economics," in its broadest sense, meant for Pantaleoni making the most of limited means in any and every connection. In order to delineate the scope of "economic science," Pantaleoni finds it necessary to limit himself to the consideration of "wealth," hedonism, and egoism.[41] Pantaleoni's countryman, Benedetto Croce, was later to criticize him for this,[42] vigorously asserting the freedom of the economic act from hedonistic or egoistic elements. But according to Pantaleoni, just as to Edgeworth, economic science described the maximization of pleasure, and the phenomena of the market adjust themselves, as it were automatically, under the play of the force tending in that direction.

This mechanical conception of economic phenomena clearly relegated man, the source of economic activity, to the background. It is somewhat ironical that the construction of the concept of a self-centered economic man, a development that led to an increase in the attention paid to the role of the human agent, should have tended to lead to a position in which the objective phenomena of economic life can be viewed as if they occurred automatically. Certainly the most extreme result of the mechanical view of economics in this respect is to be seen in Schumpeter's early conception of economic science. In his first book, *Das Wesen und der Hauptinhalt der theoretischen Nationalökonomie* (1908), Schumpeter made an attempt to place economics on a definitive scientific basis, to rear an edifice of impregnable logic grounded on foundations free of the shifting sands of metaphysical speculation. This he was able to do only by directing attention to "goods," which were to be viewed as if undergoing operations that are *not* the results of human action.[43]

Schumpeter's position seems in many respects like something of a return to classical ideas. Whereas his immediate predecessors had been gradually advancing towards the conception of economics as precisely an aspect of human behavior, Schumpeter found it necessary to carefully exclude human activity from economic investigation. Schumpeter's view of economics was a conscious effort to see economic affairs from the point of view of mechanics. In mechanics we start with given masses located in a given spatial configuration and attempt to determine the changes in mass and in configuration at future points in time. In economics, Schumpeter explains, we have "economic quantities" of goods undergoing mutually determined changes that admit of being expressed by means of mathematical functions. It is these objective, measurable things possessed by men that make up the Schumpeterian economic system. It is the existence of these functional relationships between all these quantities that makes economic science possible. Indeed, it is these relationships themselves that constitute the whole of the subject matter of that science.[44]

Although Schumpeter's lack of interest in the behavior of men and his stress on the impersonal changes in "quantities of goods" are reminiscent of the classical approach, his economics is far from identical with their science of wealth. Schumpeter does not recognize "wealth" as constituting in itself a subject of investigation by virtue of its character as wealth, but simply postulates the presence of mathematical interdependence between the quantities of various "goods" possessed by members of the *Volkswirtschaft*. It is the exposition of this mutual dependence of goods, rather than the investigation of goods or wealth as such, that constitutes the sum and substance of Schumpeter's economics.

Yet the absence of man from Schumpeter's economics remains a classical feature. This effort to exempt, or rather interdict, the economist, *qua* economist, from investigating the behavior of man as an economic agent stems from, or at least runs parallel to, Schumpeter's dream of replacing the concept of causality or purpose in economics by the type of relationship expressed by the mathematical function.[45] Here Schumpeter's enthusiasm for the mathematical method in economics and for the physical sciences generally [46] is undoubtedly responsible for his explicit rejection of teleology as in any way essential to the conception of economic phenomena. The category of purpose has no place in a positivist system from which all but functional relationships have been carefully exorcised.

A criticism that Croce addressed to Pareto (whose position bears a number of points of resemblance to that of Schumpeter) [47] would probably have been applicable to Schumpeter as well. While recognizing the service that mathematicians have rendered economics by "reviving in it the dignity of abstract analysis, darkened . . . by the mass of anecdotes of the Historical School," Croce complains that they have introduced their own professional prejudices into economics. They take up with regard to economics "which is the science of *man*, of a form of the conscious activity of man," the same attitude that they "rightly take up in relation to the empirical natural sciences." [48] The roots of the mechanical conception of economics against which Croce was crusading go back as far as the ascendency of self-interest in economics and its translation into the maximization-pattern of behavior in a form amenable to mathematical treatment. The mechanical conception of economics may thus fairly be regarded as an outgrowth of the conceptions of economics dealt with in this chapter.

4

Economics, the Market, and Society

The definition to which economic writers have yielded a more general assent than to any other . . . is "the science of exchanges."
                                                    A. S. Bolles (1878)

. . . that definition of Political Economy which calls it the science of exchanges, is absurd.
                                                    Franklin H. Giddings (1887)

The present chapter groups together definitions that see economic affairs as in one way or another necessarily connected with the act of *exchange* as a social phenomenon. Two groups of these definitions may be distinguished. The one explicitly raises exchange to the first place in economics, regarding the very notion of a distinct economic sphere as revolving around a more or less carefully defined concept of exchange. The other definitions do not stress the phenomenon of exchange itself, but focus attention on such ideas as the market, the economic system, and the "economy" as an aspect of the larger concept of society. These ideas, too, depend in the last analysis on a fusion of individual activities into a social "system" through some form of the exchange relationship. Both groups of definitions provide a fresh and distinctive outlook on economic phenomena, which at the same time reveals a number of points of contact with many of the alternative conceptions.

71

Economics and Catallactics

The importance of exchange to economics was recognized very early in the development of the science. In France the physiocrats had stressed exchange and had required ability to be exchanged as a condition for the wealth with which political economy is concerned. Among the classical economists there was some debate as to whether the possibility of exchange was either a sufficient or a necessary condition for wealth. James Mill and McCulloch were among those requiring exchangeability as a condition. But Malthus pointed out that many things outside the scope of political economy may be the objects of exchange. "It has been said . . . that the liberties of England were chiefly obtained by successive purchases from the crown." [1] A number of the classical definitions of economics in terms of wealth included the exchange of wealth as a department of the subject together with its production, distribution, and consumption. One French writer had even written: "Society is purely and solely a continual series of exchanges . . . *commerce is the whole of society*." [2]

But during the early classical period there was no attempt to take this phenomenon of exchange and make it the very core of economics. Political economy was the science of wealth. The fact that wealth is exchanged may have been recognized as of the first importance for a science of wealth, but this recognition did not of itself convert political economy into the science of exchanges.

The first attempt to reconsider the scope of political economy in favor of the exchange criterion was the basis for Archbishop Whately's suggestion in 1831 to rename the entire subject. "The name I should have preferred as the most descriptive . . . is that of CATALLACTICS, or the 'Science of Exchanges.'" Whatley's outlook is perhaps best seen in his definition of man as "an animal that makes exchanges." [3] Whately joined Senior in denying the applicability of political economy to the activities of isolated man. "Robinson Crusoe is in a position of which Political Economy takes no cognizance." [4] It was no longer sufficient to characterize political economy as concerned with the phenomena of wealth or even with the wealth that is involved in exchanges. The catallactic view of economic affairs saw their unity solely in the act of exchange and conceived of political economy as expounding the principles governing these interpersonal exchanges.

Whately's opinions on the scope of the subject seem to have aroused some interest at the time. At Dublin Whately had endowed a chair in political economy.[5] At least two of the holders of the Whately professorship followed the catallactic view of their subject. But besides the enthusiasm of these followers and acceptance by several minor writers,[6] Whately's proposal, where noticed, was rejected as unjustifiably narrowing the scope of the subject.[7] It was not until several decades after the publication of Whately's book that Macleod seized on the view of economics as the science of exchanges and enthusiastically launched the idea in his crusade to revolutionize the entire subject.[8] However, Macleod's unfortunate propensity for expressing his often good ideas in an apparently bombastic fashion prevented his work from making any appreciable impression on the general economic thought of his time.

The substitution, in definitions of political economy, of a verbal noun ("exchange") instead of the classical noun ("wealth") was, of course, of considerable significance. The subject matter of the science was now uniquely characterized, not by the objective nature of the goods-phenomena that it investigates, but by the character of the *operations* involved in the appearance of these phenomena. Nevertheless, the break from the classical conception of economics as a science of wealth that was involved in Whately's proposal was not so complete as might at first glance be imagined. That which is exchanged in Whately's Catallactics is still the same "wealth" with which the political economy of a McCulloch is concerned. The views of those who held that economics is a science of exchanges, in fact, provide another interesting example of definitions that, while themselves closely related to the older wealth-bound formulations, point to a complete emancipation from these bonds. An arresting illustration of this is furnished in the writings of Lawson.

Lawson, one of the Dublin professors, devoted his first lecture in 1844 to problems of the scope and methodology of his subject. The object of political economy is "to investigate and trace to general laws the different phenomena of the commercial or exchanging system . . ." This is clearly in the Whately tradition. But even more noteworthy is Lawson's declaration that political economy is a science that has man as its subject matter and "views him in connexion with his fellow-man, having reference solely to those relations which are the consequences of a particular act, to which his nature leads him, namely, the act of making exchange." [9] What Lawson has put before us is no less than a completely original "economic man," fully capable of bearing comparison with his more familiar cousin, the economic man created by J. S. Mill. Mill's creature was a being bereft of all passions other than avarice. Mill's economics was a body of principles governing the consequences of avaricious behavior. Lawson's economic man, on the other hand, is a far less repulsive caricature. His obsession is merely to engage in the act of exchange "to which his nature leads him," and the task of Lawson's political economy is to investigate the consequences of this human urge —an impulse that Adam Smith had long ago made famous as the "propensity to truck, barter, and exchange one thing for another." [10]

The separation of acts of exchange and their identification with a distinct human urge made the division between economic and other human affairs a far less painful operation for Lawson than it had been for Mill. The consequences of the propensity to truck may be isolated simply by considering only the results of acts of exchange. There is no need to call upon controversial operations of "abstraction" and "hypothesis" as is necessary when one attempts to segregate the consequences of human pecuniary self-interest. Clearly the catallactic view could facilitate the conversion of political economy from a science of wealth into a science of man.

And yet Lawson himself in his second lecture gave a definition of his subject almost identical with the earlier formulations in terms of wealth.[11] The contradiction between the first and the second lectures seems capable of resolution only on the assumption that Lawson himself was willing enough to follow Whately in terminology but was not prepared to admit that this difference meant any substantive alteration in outlook.

Several decades later the American Perry warmly endorsed the catallactic view of Whately and Macleod precisely because it offered an escape from the idea of wealth. In order to avoid the difficulty involved in giving an adequate definition of the concept of wealth as the core of political economy, Perry turned to the conception of that discipline as a science of exchanges.[12] We have already noticed a trend in economic thought, towards the latter part of the nineteenth century, that favored the abandonment of wealth as the focus of economics and its replacement by such ideas as welfare and the maximization-pattern of behavior. This trend was now reinforced by Perry's proposal to reject the concept of wealth altogether in favor of the idea of exchange, thus taking the catallactic idea a step beyond Lawson. It may be remarked that Perry's suggestion was not generally accepted by American economists of his time. Walker pointed out that until one knows precisely *what* is being exchanged, little meaning is conveyed by defining economics as the science of exchanges. If, on the other hand, one admits that it is wealth that is being exchanged, then, of course, one immediately renounces any claim to the excision of that troublesome concept.[13] The definition of economics in terms of exchange has not gotten rid of the notion of wealth; it has simply swept it under the rug. Henry George wrote of Perry's discarding the noun wealth: "Without the clog of an object-noun political economy . . . has plunged out of existence . . ." It is true that one American writer asserted that economists yielded the definition of economics as the science of exchanges "a more general assent than to any other." [14] But more typical of general opinion was probably the blunt declaration made to the American Economic Association in 1887 that "that definition of Political Economy which calls it the science of exchanges, is absurd." [15]

Despite the alleged absurdity of this definition, it has always retained some measure of popularity. Several twentieth-century economists who devoted careful attention to the problem of defining their subject and weighed the merits of several more sophisti-cated formulations still preferred the exchange criterion.[16] But the selection of exchange to serve as the core of economics may yet reflect any one of a number of points of view. This is so because the exchange concept itself reflects several related, but distinct, aspects of economic activity, each of which deserves to be kept in clear focus.

Exchange and the Propensity to Truck

The first aspect of the exchange phenomenon that deserves attention is the status of the act of exchange as an element in the activity of an individual. Adam Smith saw exchange as the result of a human propensity to barter. Whately defined man as an animal that exchanges. Now, human beings engage in barter be-cause they hope to improve their positions by exchanging. The act of exchange is thus no different in this respect from all human actions that are undertaken in the hope of improving one's posi-tion. Of course, the act of exchange involves the cooperation of another person, but some further property is needed to distinguish exchange from other forms of cooperation or from the act of bestowing a gift upon one's fellow man. It is here that the concept of exchange becomes entangled with ideas of sacrifice, of the mutual coincidence of interests, and the like.

In a number of the definitions of the economic that are couched in terms of exchange, the aspect that is stressed is the fact that exchange involves a *quid pro quo*. In an atmosphere in which economics and self-interest were linked together, the most char-acteristic feature of exchange is that it provides a new means of getting something for oneself. It is this aspect of commercial behavior that aroused the ire and moral indignation of Ruskin against the "cash-payment relation" between man and man. Ex-change suggests the habit of helping one's neighbor only on the condition that one will be more than repaid in return.

If this aspect of exchange is implicit in the notion of a science of exchanges, then there appears good reason to reject Walker's contention that in the absence of a clear conception of what is being exchanged a science of exchanges has no meaning. Perry, against whom Walker was arguing, did, in fact, in one connection define economics as concerned with actions done by one person to another for the sake of receiving something in return.[17] Clearly this points to the real meaning behind Perry's exchange formulation. There is no urgent need to introduce any concept of wealth to make precise the definition of economic activity as that which is directed to another person for the sake of obtaining something in return.

In this form, the conception of economic activity as exchange is closely parallel to the "non-tuism" that was noticed in the previous chapter. Wicksteed's definition of the economic relationship in terms of a lack of regard for the interests of the person with whom one is dealing was given alternative expression as the "relationship into which men spontaneously enter, when they find that they can best further their own purposes by approaching them indirectly"; and as involving man in the search for "some one else to whose purposes he can directly devote his powers or lend his resources . . ." "The industrial world is a spontaneous organization for transmuting what every man has into what he desires . . ." [18] Exchange in this context is the device whereby a man can get the things he wants by giving up to another the things he has. The entire realm of economic affairs, in this form of the catallactic view, is a vast net of relationships in which this device is being put to work. Several other American writers at the turn of the century seem to have in mind this aspect of exchange as a means of enticing one's fellow man to provide one with the goods one desires.[19] The "propensity to truck" must be understood as the faculty that men possess of recognizing situations in which the device of exchange, understood in this sense, would prove profitable.

Exchange and the Division of Labor

However, the significance of an economics defined as a science of exchanges may be seen, not in the nature of the act of exchange itself, but in its wide consequences. The market may be viewed, not as an institution facilitating the indirect fulfilment of individual desires (in Wicksteed's sense of disregarding the competitive interests of other people), but on the contrary, as an institution through which individuals may *cooperate* to satisfy their wants at higher general levels of satisfaction. As Smith pointed out, each individual, by indulging his propensity to truck, unconsciously helps society as a whole to benefit through the increased division of labor. The "general opulence" associated with specialization is a consequence of this propensity to truck and may arise without any knowledge on the part of the barterers of the "extensive utility" that they promote.

This idea is, of course, related to Smith's "invisible hand," which directs each member of the economic community to produce that which is most urgently required by the consumers. Looking at the market, the observer recognizes that the benefits of the division of labor in increasing the nation's output would, at least in principle, be obtained if the producers and consumers could be induced to specialize by any means whatsoever. A system in which productive effort was inspired by the hope of being accorded public honor, such as Marshall has imagined,[20] or by the communistic ideal, in which the sole incentive is the desire to promote social welfare, or by a system of police compulsion, can be imagined as directing individual effort into channels sufficiently specialized to increase the total product far beyond what could be achieved by a primitive autarky. The exchange system embodied in the market is only one of several conceivably efficient mechanisms to attain this end; and its distinctive feature in Smith's view is that this "end" need never be consciously aimed at by any participant in the market.

This remarkable property of the exchange system may thus well be seen as the central thread uniting all economic endeavor. Since of all the possible devices capable of attaining economic specialization only the market system can evolve spontaneously, and it alone is compatible with conventional notions regarding private property rights, the act of exchange emerges as the key to all social cooperation. There seem grounds for suggesting that the early proponents of catallactics did, in fact, have this aspect of exchange in mind. Whately was not thinking of the act of exchange as merely an expression of a more sophisticated avarice. The unwillingness to accord Crusoe the edification of being made the subject of economic analysis was simply the expression of the belief that political economy was primarily interested in the exciting new vistas of social cooperation made possible by the division of labor that was being encouraged by the rise of modern capitalism. Whately's interest in man as an exchanging animal arises from the tendency of individuals to become *associated* through acts of exchange and thus to pool their human and acquired resources for the ultimate benefit of all. It is of some interest to note that two eminent sociologists, Gabriel Tarde and Max Weber, saw this aspect of exchange as the central feature of economic life.[21] The charge raised against the catallactic definitions that they have failed to eliminate the concept of wealth from their subject undoubtedly has some validity on such an interpretation. The recognition, in the existence of a system of exchange, of a factor favorable to the expansion of total production does presuppose concepts of measurements that, again, imply some form of the idea of wealth.

The "Purely Formal" Concept of Exchange

The catallactic view of economic affairs may be interpreted to refer to yet another aspect of exchange. Like that discussed in the preceeding paragraphs, this view ignores exchange as a peculiarly motivated human *act* and focuses attention on the consequences of the act. But instead of gaining its significance from the advantages arising from the social cooperation involved in exchange, the idea of exchange is now to be assigned importance as the means whereby "economic quantities" are changed. An exchange of goods alters the configuration of goods in the economy. An exchange of productive resources alters the arrangement of those factors of production. If the exclusive object of interest is the transfer of the goods themselves, then exchange is significant merely as involving the simultaneous variation of several sets of "economic quantities." A purchase of a consumer good has resulted in a reduction both in the inventory of the seller and the cash holdings of the purchaser. The act of exchange is the event that has altered these economic quantities and has generated the ratio of their variations, viz., the phenomenon of *price*.

The most ambitious attempt to expound this conception of exchange is contained in Schumpeter's 1908 definition of the scope of economics in terms of the exchange relationship.[22] His concept of economy is coincident with this concept of exchange. Perhaps the most arresting and widely discussed implication of Schumpeter's concept of exchange is its application to the Crusoe economy. If an act of exchange is significant only as the simultaneous alteration in stocks of goods, then the idea of exchange may easily be extended to the activity of a single individual. When Crusoe shoots game, in Schumpeter's example, he is merely exchanging shot and energy for food. This use of the idea of exchange has been considered by critics as an arbitrary and unfruitful piece of mental gymnastics, but has, at the same time, earned grudging respect as "never to be forgotten subtlety." [23]

Schumpeter's outlook is, of course, consistent with his wish to ignore human behavior as a factor in economics. Leaving human behavior to the psychologists, the economist is merely to examine the *results* of behavior in terms of related variations in the quantities of goods and prices. From a less positivistic point of view, Schumpeter's extension of exchange to the isolated economy may, in fact, be seen, not as an extension, but as a restriction, of the interpersonal concept of exchange. With the recognition of the purposive element in human action, exchange is simply the sacrifice of the satisfaction of lesser, for the sake of satisfying more urgent, needs. Interpersonal exchange is significant as reflecting the possibility of simultaneous actions on the part of two purposeful human beings, each intent on attaining that position which he prefers among all the alternatives open to him. And, of course, this element of exchange can be pointed out in the isolated economy as well. It requires neither special subtlety nor mental gymnastics to see that Crusoe is exchanging one satisfaction for another whenever he forgoes the first in order to secure the second. In the words of Seligman, "Crusoe exchanges in his mind apples and nuts in estimating their value to him." [24] But when Schumpeter considers Crusoe to exchange, not by forgoing one pleasure for the sake of another, but because the quantities of the various resources at his command undergo simultaneous variation, then he has effectively robbed the concept of exchange of all but its barest externals. There is little real difference, on this view, between the case where A exchanges his horse for B's cow and the case where A's horse and B's cow have exchanged places and refuse to budge. Nothing is added to the exposition of related variations of economic quantities by explaining that these variations constitute *Tausch*. Something of this seems to have been felt by Schumpeter himself in writing that his conception of all activity as exchange is "purely formal." [25] The Schumpeterian exchange relationship is best understood when it is denoted by the alternative term that Schumpeter uses for it, "price." [26] Price to Schumpeter meant simply a parameter governing the simultaneous variations in the quantities of goods. The *Tausch*-relation meant nothing more. The definition of economics in terms of Schumpeter's exchange relationship merely conveyed in different terms his "mechanical" definition of the subject noticed in an earlier chapter, centering around changes in "economic quantities."

Exchange and the Economic System

The final aspect of exchange that may make it of significance for defining the scope of economics is its importance in the visualization of an economic *system*. It is primarily this aspect that is concerned in the second group of definitions mentioned at the beginning of the chapter, which use the idea of an economic *system* or organization as their criterion. The recognition that, expressed in the anarchy of numberless, seemingly haphazard transactions of economic life, there is a system that relates apparently disconnected actions and organizes them to achieve social "ends" is an achievement of economic science. But the discovery of the existence of such a system clears the way for a fresh conception of the nature of economic science itself. The existence of a system offers a new *object* for investigation, viz., the system itself. The system may concern wealth, the selfish behavior, or the propensity to truck, of a variety of economic men; but it does provide an independently unique phenomenon in its organization, its structure, and its operation.

The system has been described variously as the exchange system, the price system, the market, and so on. These terms reflect possibly varying outlooks on the character of the system, but all of them imply the phenomenon of exchange. The description of the subject matter of economics as exchanges may thus imply the entire *system* of exchanges. In the words of one writer: "Economics studies the market as political science studies the state. Appreciation of this analysis seems to me to be fundamental to the catallactic point of view." [27] Undoubtedly this aspect of exchange is akin to that described in a previous section, in which exchanges secure the advantages of specialization and the division of labor, but the two are quite distinct. There the act of exchange was seen as bringing to a focus the possibilities for mutual benefit that are opened up for men by the division of labor, and the aggregate of all such acts of exchange measured the maximum of specialization and effective social cooperation attained. Here the relevant aspect is the relationship between all the acts of exchange themselves, the structural pattern of these acts, and the way in which they all together succeed in "delivering the goods." [28]

When the success of the system in achieving generally prized results is not considered, then a description of the system reduces to a positive statement of the functional relationships among the sets of variables within it. And the *totality* of these relationships may have no special interest independently of the various sets of relationships themselves. This is the standpoint of Schumpeter's definition in terms of exchange and the other "mechanical" formulations discussed in this and the previous chapter. But if the whole body of interrelationships is considered in its unity, and the existence of such a unity is considered significant in itself, then the idea of a system may assume a prominent place in economics.

Bastiat is an example of an economist who, stressing the exchange point of view, did see the prime interest of his subject as existing in the exposition of such a system. And it seems likely that at least part of the criticism aimed at his work arises from a misunderstanding of Bastiat's self-assigned scope of investigation. Bastiat is often characterized as a shallow optimist content to bestow lyric praise on the laissez-faire economy. Cairnes attacked Bastiat as unscientific. Bastiat, Cairnes complained, considers it his task as an economist, not only to discuss the phenomena of wealth in a laissez-faire economy, but also to demonstrate that this system is the optimum one.[29] This, Cairnes declares, is to assert that the results of political economy are a foregone conclusion, and if this is the case, then it is not a science at all, because "science has no foregone conclusions." By attempting to justify rather than explain the facts of wealth, Bastiat is departing from the impartiality of science.

Cairnes' insistence on the disinterested character of scientific inquiry in general, and of economics in particular, is a classic statement of a jealously guarded tenet of scientific economics. Bastiat's enthusiasm for the innate harmonies of a free economy did produce passages in his writings that are vulnerable to the type of criticism levelled by Cairnes. Nevertheless, it seems that Bastiat's conception of his subject was sufficiently different from that of Cairnes to exculpate him from at least part of the blame imputed to him in the latter's reproaches. Bastiat was impressed by the comparative smoothness with which the tremendously complicated machinery of economic endeavor succeeded in fulfilling the wants of consumers. His classic passages in the opening chapter of *Harmonies économiques*,[30] in which he describes how a humble carpenter is served, in exchange for his skilled labor, with commodities brought from the four corners of the earth and how each day the great city of Paris is provided with colossal quantities of food and other articles, have been echoed in subsequent economics textbooks again and again. One would be closing one's eyes to the light, Bastiat observes, if one failed to recognize that all this is the product of a "prodigiously ingenious mechanism." "This mechanism is the object of study of political economy."

Clearly, then, Bastiat felt some justification for assuming beforehand that the system to be studied by political economy was one that worked. After all, it was this successful operation of the system—a success that Bastiat felt to be grounded on observation—that was the *object* of the study. For Cairnes, who considered economics a dispassionate study of the phenomena of wealth, any predilections towards one system in particular must be unscientific. For Bastiat, what invited explanation was precisely the large degree of efficiency empirically evinced by the system, a phenomenon of which the recognition hardly deserves the suspect position of a "foregone conclusion."

Be this as it may, Bastiat is typical of a fairly numerous group of writers stressing the *organization* of the economy as the focus of economic attention and seeing the significance of exchange primarily in this connection. Two eminent twentieth-century economists may be cited as examples of the popularity of this view. Hawtrey writes:

. . . when the perfect cooperation which would be the ideal of reason is denied us, we turn back to . . . the whole apparatus of human motives, instinctive, habitual, or other. If each member of society can be induced or impelled to do his allotted task by associating it with some motive that appears to him adequate, then he need never know how he is contributing to the real end, and need not even be aware of the end at all. It is this problem of organization that we shall call the Economic Problem. It is in fact the real subject matter of political economy.[31]

And Hayek writes:

. . . the spontaneous interplay of the actions of individuals may produce . . . an organism in which every part performs a necessary function for the continuance of the whole, without any human mind having devised it. . . . The recognition of the existence of this organism is the recognition that there is a subject matter for economics. It is one of the causes of the unique position of economics that the existence of a definite object of its investigation can be realized only after a prolonged study . . .[32]

Economics, the Economy, and the "Volkswirtschaft"

This line of thought leads directly to the role played in discussions of the scope of economic inquiry by the idea of the *Volkswirtschaft*. The word seems almost by philological accident to have given rise to features in German-language definitions that are absent in English-language discussions of the subject. Numerous disquisitions on the *Wesen* of the *Volkswirtschaft* evince conceptions ranging from the more holistic views of some of the economists of the Historical School and advocates of *Sozialpolitik*, in which the *Volkswirtschaft* is considered as an organic whole, to views that see it merely as an agglomeration of separately operating individual "economies." [33]

It is significant that the existence in the German language of a single word to represent compactly so complex a conception has had considerable bearing on the direction taken by definitions of economic affairs. Many writers defined their subject directly in terms of the study of the *Volkswirtschaft* (hence *Volkswirtschaftslehre*). Thus, such a definition immediately places the accent on the *social* character of economic activity. The absence for a long time in English of a word corresponding to *Volkswirtschaft* meant that English definitions of the subject were not prone to be thus influenced.[34] The current use of the term "the economy," itself a reflection of the interest in macroeconomic "aggregates," is too recent and too specialized to have had much influence on English definitions. When Schmoller used the term "political economy" as the equivalent of *Volkswirtschaft*, the *grossen gesellschaftlichen Körper*, he was coining what must at that time have been a new meaning for "political economy." [35]

Moreover the use of the term *Volkswirtschaft* seems to have had more than coincidental connection with a conception of economic phenomena in which *temporal* relationships, and historical significance generally, were stressed. The term carried with it, especially to the writers who stressed the organic unity of the whole, the same implications of continued identity over time as are associated with terms such as the State or the Nation (terms cited by Schmoller, for example, as analogous to the *Volkswirtschaft*).[36] To the endowment of the economy with an only arbitrarily divisible extension along the time dimension is certainly in some degree to be ascribed the well-known description of economics by Mangoldt as the "philosophy of economic history" and the similar view of Roscher [37] and other economists of the Historical School. Conceived as possessing in this way a kind of fluid unity in its extension over both space and time, the idea of the *Volkswirtschaft* could lay claim to a distinct entity (distinct, e.g., from the "body politic") only by virtue of its more conspicuous and enduring function of providing for the material needs of the nation.

It was noticed in the previous chapter that German economists paid considerable attention to the maximization principle. This interest sometimes ran into sharp conflict with the notion of economics as the study of the *Volkswirtschaft*. One writer typically dismissed these discussions of the "economic principle" by declaring that the task of economics is not to investigate the effects of *Wirtschaftlichkeit,* but to understand the workings of the *Volkswirtschaft.*[38] In the twentieth century Amonn, who stresses the *social* character of economic phenomena probably more than any other writer, has sharply criticized attempts to define the scope of economic science in terms of such concepts as individual acts of economizing. Attempts to build up the notion of a *Volkswirtschaft* from the elements of individual economic behavior are foredoomed to failure.[39] It is from the *social* relationships involved in economic activity that such activity derives its distinctive character. This point gave rise to vigorous disagreement from those who attempted to construct the *Volkswirtschaft* out of the *Wirtschaft.*[40]

Also associated with the idea of the *Volkswirtschaft* are those definitions of economics that are couched exclusively in terms of national aggregates. To this class belong, for example, the views of economists from the time of the classical school who saw their subject as concerned with *national,* not individual, wealth.[41] Discussion of "social goals" as something apart from individual motives, to which the economy as a whole is conceived as striving, are also related to the idea of the *Volkswirtschaft*. Both the writings of R. Stolzmann and Othmar Spann are relevant in this regard.[42]

Economy and Society

Many of the ideas mentioned in the preceding sections of this chapter have a bearing on the relationships that have at various times been held to exist between economics and the social sciences generally. The structures of interpersonal patterns of contact that the economist studies in his analysis of the market may, of course, be of interest to the sociologist or the social psychologist from a totally different aspect. And writers who identified the specifically economic aspect of phenomena with the social quality inherent in exchange, the market, and the like, found themselves influenced more or less deeply by their ideas on the nature and methodology of the social sciences as a group.

The social character of the phenomena studied by the economist was recognized early in the history of the discipline. In his definition of political economy J. S. Mill had stressed this aspect to a degree that seems to have escaped later writers.[43] Nevertheless, it is true that the emergence of sociological thought in the second half of the nineteenth century brought with it a vastly increased awareness of the contribution that economics can make to the systematic study of society. This in turn made for a "sociological" attitude towards the study of economics itself, which manifested itself in a variety of forms.

At the extreme was the opinion first propounded by Comte, and taken up by later writers, that it was futile to seek for laws in economics apart from the laws of society as a whole. To Comte the recognition of economic affairs as part of the phenomena of society meant that an economic analysis of society that leaves out intellectual, moral, and political factors must be a "metaphysical" subject, created by an "irrational" separation.[44] Later writers, especially those of the Historical School, held essentially similar views. In England Ingram and Leslie were stressing the need for turning to the "great science of society" for any valid economic knowledge.[45]

Carried to the extreme position held by Comte, these ideas

meant, not that the social character of economic affairs made possible a fresh means of definition, but that the awareness of this social character led to the denial that there are any specifically economic affairs whatsoever. Phenomena of wealth might indeed be distinguished. But once it is insisted that the derivation of the laws of wealth requires analysis of intellectual, moral, and political factors, then it is at once contended that no specifically economic point of view can be scientifically illuminating at all.

However, awareness of the sociological importance of economics did not, of course, always involve its submersion in a broadly understood sociology.[46] Any number of writers at the turn of the century could be cited who diligently pursued the study of economics, but who were fully conscious of its status among the social sciences. Confining our attention strictly to that aspect of the sociological outlook on economics which affected the conception of the nature of the economic point of view, we notice several strands of thought that run through the literature during the present century.

At one level, we observe again Amonn's insistence on the futility of the search for the nature of economic science in any concepts built on individual activity. There does exist a given pie that the economist studies, but its essence is the structure of the societal relationships that make up economic affairs as we know them in the world and as they have been traditionally studied by the economists from Ricardo on. To attempt to analyze economic affairs by referring them back to the individual is to abstract from their very essence.[47] From the point of view of the scope of this essay, this view is primarily of importance as constituting a rejection of the formulations of the economic point of view that we take up in the final chapters. The emphasis on the social aspect has, however, been used by one or two writers to distinguish economics from technology.[48]

In a somewhat different context, the recognition that economic affairs refer to the actions of men, not in isolation from one another, but within a societal framework, has affected the conception of the economic point of view in respect of the *goals* of economic activity. Anderson, Haney, Parsons, and Macfie may be taken as examples of the many writers during the past half century who show this influence.[49] The stress, at this level of discourse, is not on the social patterns of relationships that emerge during the course of economic activity. Rather, these writers tend to emphasize the fact that the values and motives that affect and inspire economic activity are overwhelmingly conditioned by society as a whole. Whatever the role of individual activity, it is pointed out that values are socially determined and are the product of forces whose explanation must be sought in sociology or social psychology. This trend of thought, too, seems to be significant to our own problem chiefly in its implied rejection of the "atomistically individualistic" conceptions of the economic point of view treated in later chapters.

Finally, in this necessarily brief and fragmentary survey of the sociologically conditioned conception of the economic point of view, we must notice the attempts to "locate" economics within the more general expanse of sociological theory. These attempts have generally been made by writers who were primarily interested in the study of society and intent on defining precisely the nature of the economic point of view, not for its own sake, but in order to have more clearly in focus the separate facets that together make up the complete sociological perspective. Thus, Pareto conceived of economics as an integral part of sociology and believed that the distinctively economic point of view is obtained by a conscious restriction of attention to certain "variables." [50] A complete sociological theory would entail consideration of all the variables that affect action in society. Economics obtains its separate status by deliberate "abstraction" from the "noneconomic" variables and thus becomes a hypothetical subdiscipline within the all-embracing theory of society. The particular criteria that are to determine the "economic" or "noneconomic" nature of any one variable are not here of chief interest. (In fact they reflect the points of view discussed in several of the chapters in this book.) What is of moment is the idea that an economic point of view is possible only as a first and crude abstraction from a more comprehensive and complex theoretical system, viz., the theory of society.

Professor Parsons, who in his earlier writings had embraced

this conceptual framework for the "location" of economics, has more recently espoused a somewhat different idea.[51] The new view sees the "economy" as a subsystem of society. The theory of social systems in general will apply to the economy as a special case. The basic variables operative in the economy, (as well as in all special-case subsystems of society) are the *same* variables as govern the theory of social systems generally. The economy is that subsystem of society which is distinguished by its *adaptive* function, i.e., that function of any social system which relates to its control of the environment for the purpose of attaining goals.

This view of the matter places the economic point of view even more firmly in a position subordinate to general sociological theory. Economic theory becomes a special case of sociological theory and is conceived, indeed, as providing a mirror that reflects, *mutatis mutandis*, the propositions of such a theory. The more interesting and important implications of this approach for economics reach beyond the scope of this enquiry. For us it is sufficient to have noticed yet another conception of the economic point of view, one that shares with those noticed in this section the characteristic of leaning heavily on the social aspect of economic affairs, and thus indirectly on the ideas of exchange discussed at length at the beginning of this chapter.

Money, Wealth, and Exchanges

The most obvious form in which money presents itself as relevant to a definition of economics is in its relationship to wealth. For the most general and powerful form in which wealth appears is in that of ready cash. Money, as the medium of exchange possessing the property of being able to command goods when and where they are needed, is, in general, one of the most desirable forms in which to store wealth. And, of course, the emergence of certain metals as popularly accepted media of exchange was in part the consequence of their suitability for being stored over periods of time without loss of general appeal.

Adam Smith, in his exposition of the nature and causes of the wealth of nations, had found it necessary to point out that the accumulation of a national stock of gold does not, of itself, secure national prosperity. There has, of course, been controversy about whether or not Smith was unjust to the mercantilists in ascribing to them this identification of national wealth with gold.[1] It is, in any event, true that the early definitions of political economy in terms of wealth were not confined to, and did not even particularly stress, the monetary form of wealth. On the contrary, writers tended rather to emphasize that money in itself lacks many of the characteristics of wealth. The problems of production and distribution in which the classical writers were interested pertained to the goods that directly satisfied human wants or to the productive factors for such goods. The pronounced disregard for the purely monetary effects on the economy, which is a characteristic of classical economics, helped to keep interest from focusing on the medium of exchange.

Nevertheless, there were soon several economists who wrote in terms that made wealth tantamount to money. "Political Economy," wrote the French Dupuit in 1844, "being concerned only with wealth, can take account of the intensity of a wish only through its monetary expression."[2] Bagehot, who defined political economy as the "science of business," wrote that "as far as people are what we now always call 'men of business,' money, the thing

they look for and the thing they want, is their sole object . . ." ³
The passage by Robert Lowe (Viscount Sherbrooke) in which he
justifies the possibility of a science of economics is famous: "In
love or war or politics, or religion, or morals it is impossible to
foretell how mankind will act . . . But once place a man's ear
within the ring of pounds, shillings, and pence, and his conduct
can be counted on to the greatest nicety." ⁴ When Cliffe Leslie
wished to attack the notion of a single wealth-seeking motive in
human beings, he did so, as we have seen, in an essay entitled *The
Love of Money* (1862) and quite obviously assumes that by ex-
posing the nonexistence of such a homogeneous love of money he
is demolishing the economic man, in whose breast nothing is im-
planted but the desire for wealth.

In itself there is perhaps not much significance to be attached
to this identification of wealth with money. In the earlier formulations in which an objective wealth was the focus of attention, we
have seen this identification to have been lacking. The stress on
the monetary form of wealth appears in the writings of those who
give paramount importance to an economic man, intent on the
accumulation of wealth. Since in a market economy the drive for
wealth is most easily fulfilled by translation into a drive for money,
there is little difference whether one describes economic man by
reference to a passion for wealth or to a passion for money.

What these citations do suggest, however, is a tacit assumption
that exchange is essential to actual economic affairs. And this
circumstance suggests a fresh link between definitions of economics in terms of exchange and the endowment of economic man
with an exclusively pecuniary self-interest. Bagehot's definition
of economics as the "science of business" shows the connection
quite clearly.⁵ Bagehot had been impressed by the criticisms of
classical political economy made by the historically-minded economists. He acknowledged the "relativity" of economics with respect to time and place and wished to salvage economic theory by
restricting its scope to the "business world," where its assumptions
of self-interest, rationality, and the like were reasonably fulfilled.
The degree to which the self-interest assumed by the economist is
actually at work in the business world, and certainly the treating

of this assumption as the unifying thread of economic theory, postulated the introduction of a sharp division into the whole of human action separating the activities of men in their capacity as consumers, on the one hand, from their activities in the capacity of business-type producers, on the other. Of course, what motivates the earning of income is hope of the pleasures to be purchased by spending it, but it was believed that only in their capacity as "men of business," as income-earners, does the behavior of men admit of economic "laws." Only in this sphere of activity could it be seriously maintained that pecuniary self-interest is the exclusive passion. In this context the desire for wealth becomes crystallized very definitely into a desire for money, the form in which men of business earn income.

This obviously arbitrary and artificial division is made possible only by the existence of indirect exchange. The fact that the division of labor in a modern economy is made feasible solely by the intervention of a medium of exchange between producer and consumer is responsible for the conception of a distinct area of activity in which men do act as businessmen. From this point of view, exchange, or even more accurately exchange for money, becomes a criterion of economic activity in an entirely novel sense. Economic analysis must be confined to activity revolving around monetary exchange, because only in such activity can an exclusively pecuniary self-interest be reasonably postulated. When men act in spending their income, economic analysis is admittedly baffled by the multiplicity of motives actuating their spending habits. But in so far as men do engage in a separate kind of activity in securing a money income, their actions are susceptible of analysis. Because men do not directly secure the innumerable and heterogeneous goods they desire, but first channel their demand for these goods into a demand for a *single* good, money, economics can proceed to analyze man's business behavior in terms of a single motive, viz., the desire for money, or in terms of the maximization of this single good.[6]

No doubt this conception of economic activity involves some circularity. We must confine economic analysis to human action only in so far as it has a single object in view, the maximization of money income, and we proceed to postulate an "economic" area of "business" defined in terms of such a single object of desire. The justification for such a procedure is the sharp distinction made possible, as we have seen, by the existence of a monetary bridge that both accentuates and spans the gulf between earning income and buying goods. There *is*, in fact, a twofold aspect to men's lives. Men do mark off part of their time for the earning of income and part for the enjoyment of income, however hazy the line of demarcation may be. And it is a fact that economic analysis has historically dealt predominantly with the first of these areas. Definitions of economics in terms of money are thus different from definitions of it in terms of wealth. The criterion of money fences off the area of income-earning and makes it a field fruitful for economic analysis.

The long-range trend in the conception of economic activity has consistently been to broaden its scope to cover *all* human action. Not a part of human activity, but an aspect of its entire range is selected as relevant to economics. The definition in terms of money in the sense here outlined is a special case of the older type of definition that marked off a part of the activity of men for economic analysis, postulating in the area so circumscribed a homogeneous mass of phenomena that did not occur elsewhere. It is of interest that even with the more recent "broad" definitions of economics, which recognize the essential homogeneity of *all* human action, the applicability of economic analysis is still overwhelmingly to be seen in the "business" or "money" sector of action. For this reason it is apparently still tempting to suppose that there is a clear-cut division between man's money-making activities and the rest.[7]

Money as the Measuring Rod

A definition of economic activity in terms of money that involves more sophisticated (and perhaps more controversial) considerations is that which sees money as a *measuring rod*. Economic analysis is concerned with that part of human activity, with that area of human welfare, which can be measured by the yardstick of money. The literature citing this definition reveals some confusion as to its origin. Usually this formulation of economics is ascribed to Pigou. In fact, Pigou seems to have simply taken over this definition from Marshall without much ado. It was Marshall who first most thoroughly expounded the conception of economics in terms of the money measure, and this despite the fact that his conception of economics is almost always presented by exclusive citation of the opening references in his *Principles* to "the ordinary business of life" and the "material requisites of well-being." [8]

Marshall developed his thesis *in extenso* in his inaugural lecture at Cambridge in 1885.[9] It must be emphasized that Marshall did not consider that he was in fundamental disagreement with his fellow economists, but only that he was presenting a more appropriate characterization of the commonly recognized scope of the subject. In the practical world Marshall is content to consider economics as examining

that part of individual and social action which is most closely connected with the attainment and with the use of the material requisites of well-being. Thus it is on the one side a study of wealth; and on the other, and more important side, a part of the study of man.[10]

But Marshall was well aware of the misleading character of such a definition, in so far as the *essence* of economic activity is concerned. In his inaugural lecture he said:

The outward form of economic theory has been shaped by its connection with material wealth. But it is becoming clear that the true philosophic *raison d'être* of the theory is that it supplies a machinery to aid us in reasoning about those motives of human action which are measurable. In the world in which we live, money as representing general purchasing power, is so much the best measure of motives that no other can compete with it. But this is, so to speak, an accident . . .[11]

Marshall is at pains to explain that it is in the *measurability* of motives that the homogeneity of economic activity is to be found. That it is money which in real life lends itself to such measurement is merely a convenient accident. In the course of developing this point, Marshall uses the arguments of Cliffe Leslie.

If with Cliffe Leslie we analyse all the infinite variety of motives that are commonly grouped together under the term "love of money," we see that they are of all kinds. They include many of the highest, the most refined, and the most unselfish elements of our nature. The common link that binds them together is that they can be more or less measured; and in this world they are measured by money.[12]

Marshall envisages the possibility of an economy in which incentives are in the form, not of money, but of a graduated system of decorations of honor. All this attributes "high and transcendent universality to the central scheme of economic reasoning." [13] Nevertheless, "for practical purposes . . ." it will be best to go on treating it as chiefly concerned with those motives to "which a money price can be . . . assigned." [14] In brief, economics deals with the play of measurable motives reinforcing and counteracting one another, "but it also sets out that most complex play of human motives that changes the purchasing power of money, and thus alters the measure of all motives." [15]

In his *Principles* Marshall expresses himself quite frequently in similar terms. "The *raison d'être* of economics as a separate science is that it deals chiefly with that part of man's action which is most under the control of measurable motives." This is a characteristic statement of Marshall's position.[16] It will be noticed that Marshall does not consider this definition to be a watertight one, since he is constantly employing qualifying phrases such as "chiefly," "more or less," and the like. This was, indeed, frankly acknowledged by Pigou. In 1912 Pigou had stated that economic welfare arises from that part of the community's income that enters "easily into relation with the measuring rod of money," [17] and had asserted that the "methodological principle at the basis of economic science, and that which separates it from the other social sciences, is the reference it makes to a measure, namely, money." [18] Later, in his *Economics of Welfare*, Pigou admits the haziness of such definitions:

It is not, indeed, possible to separate [the economic part of welfare] in any rigid way from other parts, for the part which *can* be brought into relation with a money measure will be different according as we mean by *can*, "can easily" or "can with mild straining" or "can with violent straining." The outline of our territory is, therefore, necessarily vague.[19]

Money as a Universal Measuring Rod

Before we discuss this fresh conception of economic affairs, it will be of interest to draw attention to a view that has the doubtful distinction of running precisely counter to that of Marshall while yet being built on the very same foundation. The French sociologist Gabriel Tarde, in the course of a campaign to prove that most of the "economic" categories are really common to all the social sciences, attempted to show that *money* too is not a strictly economic phenomenon. It is true, Tarde wrote, that money is a measure of wealth, but it is not a measure of wealth alone. Money, besides measuring wealth, measures desires and beliefs; it is a universal measure of all social "quantities," of which wealth is only one.[20] Tarde believed that he had thus broken the link that chained money exclusively to economics, whose subject matter, despite some fairly advanced statements in his writings, he still identified solely with *richesses*.

Both Marshall and Tarde, it will be observed, look upon money as significant primarily on account of its suitability to serve as a measuring rod of human motives. But in postulating the suitability of money as a measure of human motives, Marshall had by the same token held these motives to be *economically* relevant. Tarde, on the other hand, working unwaveringly on the assumption that only the phenomena of wealth are economic, and confronted with his own conception of money as measuring human desires, is forced to the triumphant conclusion that money itself pertains to noneconomic phenomena.

Clearly the conception of money as a measuring rod is something also of a two-edged sword, capable, perhaps, of replacing wealth as the criterion of the economic, but capable too of forcing itself outside the scope of economics altogether if the latter is defined as the science of wealth.

Measurement and Economics

Several points of criticism present themselves in the consideration of the Marshall-Pigou view of economics. The description of the subject in terms of the possibility of measuring human motives could conceivably be interpreted as stressing the *comparison* of motives with one another. Economic activities would be those in which the relative strength of human desires would be expressed, through the allocation of resources, in the visible phenomena of the market. But this is not the sense in which Marshall wrote that money measures human motives.

What Marshall had in mind is a means of escape from the dim, hazy realm of desires and feelings into a sharply defined world of quantities brought into clear focus, free of the fuzziness of merely qualitative differences. There is a groping towards the "quantification" and the endowment with "objective measurability" of the numberless subjectively felt urges and drives. Economic phenomena, we are to understand, are in the unique and apparently highly-prized position of being able to reflect in measurable (and hence presumably "scientific") terms, at least some part of the uncharted wilderness of the human mind. Now there is, no doubt, some satisfaction in feeling that not *all* human desires remain submerged within individual consciousness; that some of them at least register delicate, but measurable, changes on some external scale for all to see. But it is not clear that the inherence of such a fortunate property in certain motives and feelings offers a valid criterion for a common scientific treatment. As Croce asked Pareto on a slightly different point: "What intrinsic connection is there between this merely accidental attribute, measurability, of the objects which enter into an economic action, and the economic action itself?" [21] At least Marshall himself shows appreciation of the good fortune that the motives measured by money all admit of analysis by similar types of reasoning. "The problems which are grouped together as economics," he wrote, "because they relate specially to man's conduct under the influence of motives that are measurable by a money price, are found to make a fairly homogeneous group." [22] But surely this homogeneity, under Marshall's definition, is no more than a happy accident.

Moreover, the whole idea of the measurement of subjective desires by means of money is one that involves serious and controversial problems. It may be readily conceded that human motives, acting in the market place, exert definite effects on money prices. It is by no means clear that the resultant prices offer in any valid sense a means of *measuring* such motives. Discussions on the possible conception of a cardinal utility may invite ingenious suggestions purporting to measure such a utility. Money has never in any but the crudest of senses been able to serve as such a measure. Undoubtedly Marshall's idea of money as a measuring rod is related to his frequent use of the hypothesis that money is exempt from the "law" of diminishing marginal utility, but this was never more than a simplifying analytical technique. Prices are not *measured* in money; they are simply amounts of money given in exchange for goods. Prices are expressed in terms of money, not because money represents any sort of "measuring rod," but simply because it is money that is commonly used as the *quid pro quo* for goods.[23] One need not draw attention (as Marshall himself did) to the violent fluctuations in the purchasing power of money in order to feel the force of a characteristic sentence of Professor Knight: "If we accept the aphorism, 'science is measurement,' as a definition of science, which is its only intelligible meaning, then there is no such thing as 'economic' science . . ." [24]

Marshall's was not the only attempt to see economic science as essentially a consequence of measurability. An interesting point of view in this regard was presented in an essay in 1893 by an eminent American contemporary of Marshall, Simon Patten. In the classical economic system, Patten explained, economics was unfortunately divorced from utilitarianism.

Utilitarianism was abstract, and treated of pleasures and pains as purely subjective phenomena. Economics was concrete and treated of utilities as material wealth conditioned by the laws of the objective world . . .[25]

The achievement of subjective economics and the development of the theory of consumption makes possible their unification.

When the basis of economics is broadened by making the unit of measurement subjective, and the basis of utilitarianism narrowed by separating it from ethics, the unity of the two, both in the method they use, and in the field they occupy, becomes apparent . . . There is only one science for measuring the welfare of society and its progress through the gains or losses of those positive utilities which men create or destroy.[26]

The term "positive utility" is used by Patten in contradistinction to "absolute utility." By "absolute utilities" Patten understands those which cannot be measured and hence cannot enter into the utilitarian calculus. As instances of such absolute utilities, Patten cites "water in a desert," "honesty," and the like. "Positive utilities" are those which, by their susceptibility to measurement, enter into the utilitarian calculus.

Economics is the science of positive utilities—the realm where no other motives are recognized except those resulting from changes in the amount of our measurable pleasures and pains.[27]

It is true that Patten's stress on the measurability of economic motives refers to their comparison with one another. Honesty is not directly relevant to economics because it is immeasurable, in the sense that no finite utilities can reach up to it. It is an absolute good.[28] But Patten's position reflects also the felt need for a conception of "quantities" of utility. Of course, in a scheme in which a label bearing for each individual a definite number of "units"

of utility is mentally attached to every good, it is difficult to treat
in terms of such units those values to whose utility the individual
can imagine no limit to be assigned. This difficulty led to the
postulation of a difference *in kind* between "positive" and "absolute" utilities. Economics became neatly identified with the first
of these; and measurement, for Patten as for Marshall, constituted
the decisive criterion.

But in the absence of a demand to know the "quantity" of a
utility, the distinction between "positive" and "absolute" utilities
disappears of itself. The modern idea of the role of *preference*
in human action offers a completely adequate view of the matter.
When forced to choose between two alternatives, the individual
exercises his preference in a way that remains essentially the same
regardless whether the alternatives represent "positive" or "absolute" utilities. In the process of preferring, *all* possible values
are placed in an ordered array. "If honor cannot be eaten, eating
can be forgone for honor." [29] Measurability becomes a criterion of
doubtful worth simply because any results that it brings for comparing utilities with one another can be obtained even more easily
without it. A considerable number of writers who cite the Marshall-Pigou view of economics have drawn attention to these weak
points in the whole idea of measurement.[30]

Money and Price-Economics

In a chapter on the role of money in definitions of economics,
mention should be made of the part that it has played in the
emergence of so-called "price-economics." In the literature of the
second and third decades of this century there was a lively discussion of whether economics should deal with subjective utilities,
with welfare itself, or whether it should deal only with the external manifestation of those utilities, with objective prices. The
"price-economists" attempted to avoid reference to the underlying
motives, desires, and satisfactions that are reflected in market
prices. They rejected "explanations" of prices that invoked these
subjective concepts. They conceived of economics as concerned,
not with the causes of human behavior, but with its consequences

as seen in the patterns of prices. Pareto, Cassel, Davenport, and
Mitchell are representative of this line of thought. Writers such
as Fetter and Viner in the United States, on the other hand, were
among those who saw price-economics as an inadequate means of
understanding the operations of the market and insisted on the
need to dig below the surface phenomena of prices for their explanation.[31] It is not necessary for present purposes to go further
into the origin and causes of the emergence of a price-economics.
In so far as it represents a distinct outlook on the nature of economic phenomena, price-economics can be largely subsumed
under the catallactic view of the subject, especially under that
conception of the latter that stresses the purely functional relationship between different prices.[32]

What is of relevance to the present chapter is the degree to
which the presence of a general medium of exchange and the
identification of economic activities with those involving such a
medium may have contributed to the price-economics line of
thought. Prices are the corollaries of acts of exchange. Every act of
exchange, by definition, is associated with a definite ratio according to which the goods are exchanged against each other. The
phenomenon of price is one with a peculiar fascination of its own,
especially when the whole *structure* of prices—the interrelationships between different prices in the same market and between
prices at different times—is grasped. It is not difficult to understand the temptation to treat these ratios as "things" in themselves,
moving in accordance with their own "laws of motion," rather
than as the manifestations of acts of human choice. The part
played by money in the market has only heightened this temptation.

Money prices make possible a system of rational calculation in
which any economic decision is influenced by all the relevant factors. The producer and the consumer are alike guided by money
prices to adjust their actions in the most advantageous way to the
real conditions of the market. In the discussion over the possibility
of rational economic calculation of gain and cost in a socialist
economy, one fact has emerged with overwhelming unanimity. It
is almost universally conceded that in an economy without prices,

real or "quasi," there is no means of judging the economic wisdom or folly of any action. Every prospective buyer or seller, if he is to act in a rational way, must be able to compare his prospective situation at the completion of the transaction with his present situation. This involves the comparison of innumerable "economic quantities" with one another: those actually under his control initially, those to be brought under his control through the transaction, and those possibilities of control which his initial position enables him to command through alternative transactions. The expression of market prices in terms of money is an inestimable boon to the solution of this complex problem. As a common medium of exchange for *all* marketable goods, money fuses all the alternatives confronting the marketer into an immeasurably simpler chain of decisions. The money price paid for one good expresses succinctly, and more convincingly than is ever conceivable in a barter transaction, a preference for this good over a definite set of alternative goods.

The implications of these well-recognized considerations for the construction of a theoretical "price system" in which the relative movements of different prices are to be reduced to all-embracing "laws" are obvious enough. A conception of a price structure ultimately depends on the sensitivity of each part of the structure to changes in other parts. When changes in prices in one area do not generate related price movements throughout the economy because of undefined "frictional" forces clogging the system, then the concept of "laws" of price movements becomes less and less realistic. The introduction of a monetary *numeraire* to describe the relationships among the prices in such a system is more than a matter of convenience. The assumption of rational behavior, guided by prices, which the concept of a system of prices postulates would be almost wholly untrue in a barter economy. Besides the extraordinary difficulty that would be entailed in the exposition of a system of barter prices, there would be the more serious objection that the loosely knit relationships that would perforce exist between barter "prices" would make the recognition of any "system" of such prices of negligible significance.

To present the matter briefly: in a market without money prices exchange ratios are of a type almost completely analogous to the transformation functions under which a Crusoe economy operates. In a Crusoe economy no analysis is possible without explicit assumptions regarding subjective categories that price-economics is anxious to avoid. The attempt to see economics as a system of laws governing the movements of prices that are the consequences of human behavior must depend on a common monetary denominator.[33] The possibility, of course, exists that improved means of calculation could enable rational comparison of alternatives to take place without guidance by external market prices. But this possibility would destroy the entire field investigated by price-economics. From a point of view that sees economics as essentially concerned with prices, it has been asserted, for example, that if linear programming could set up a system of shadow prices to guide managers, the borderline of economics might need to be reviewed.[34] In so far as the signals of shadow prices are not available and guidance must be sought in money prices, it is the preoccupation of economic activity with money that made possible the idea of an economics that could be "positive," disregarding the realm of dim mysteries of feelings and dealing with definite, observable market prices.

Money as an Economic Institution

Closely associated with the considerations of the previous section is the stress that has been laid on the essentiality of money for economic activity because of its unique role as an *institution*. Economic affairs, on this view, are monetary affairs, not because money is a passive *sign* of the presence of economic activity, but because it plays an active role in shaping the character of such activity. According to Marshall, as has been seen, money characterized economic activity by serving as a measure of certain motives. The presence of money was not seen in any way as influencing these motives themselves, or at least it was not because of any such influence that money was taken to be the criterion of the economic. Money was seen as merely expressing the real motives operative in the phenomena of the market. The fact that it served at the same time as a measuring rod was the reason why economics came to be defined in monetary terms.

But it is clear that the use of money is a real factor that has profoundly affected the entire pattern of economic activity. And in the literature on this subject attempts have been made to treat money as the definitive criterion of the economic by virtue of the peculiar influence it exercises on human action. Economic activity becomes such through its reflection of this influence. Professor Mises has pointed out that rational economic activity became possible only with the widespread adoption of a medium of exchange.[35] As we have seen in the previous section, the recognition of this fact led to the emergence of the concept of price.

It was Wesley Mitchell who stressed the role of money as an active institution that has shaped human activity in a definite pattern. Of the writers on this subject Mitchell was perhaps the most insistent on the necessity of confining economics to monetary affairs. "Money may not be the root of *all* evil, but it is the root of economic science." [36] Most of all, Mitchell wanted to avoid discussions on subjective concepts. "When the definite and objective interrelations among money prices have been analyzed it is time enough to penetrate into the dim mysteries of our feelings about utilities . . ." [37] But Mitchell paid considerable attention to the positive influence that money has exerted.

Writing within the framework established by Veblen, Mitchell contrasts his "institutional" view of the economic significance of money with Marshall's concept. The latter sees money as "an indispensable tool for measuring the force of opposing motives; but it remains merely a tool . . ." To predict what men will do "one needs to know the motive force of the satisfactions and sacrifices promised by alternative lines of action. That force can best be expressed in terms of money; but the use of money does not alter the substantial character of economic behavior." But, Mitchell continues, on Veblen's view of the matter, the whole picture changes.

Money becomes a most significant thing in the economy of society, because it shapes the habits of thought into which our native propensities grow. Instead of being a machine for doing quickly and commodiously what would be done, though less quickly and commodiously, without it, the use of money "exerts a distinct and independent influence of its own" upon our wants as consumers, upon our skill as planners, and upon our ideals as citizens.[38]

Because of the manner in which the monetary calculus promotes rational behavior, the student of economics cannot picture economic logic without money and without prices.[39]

Now, while the positive influence on economic activity that money exerts has been rather widely recognized,[40] this does not of itself provide a valid criterion of economic activity. Professor Robbins, for example, has complained that the restriction of economics to monetary phenomena confines the subject to a particular institutional setting.[41] The influence that money and monetary calculation has exerted is not so much a matter of innovating as of accelerating and facilitating a pattern of activity that, at least in principle, could exist without it. Nevertheless, the role that money has played in the conception of economic phenomena has been broadened by the "institutional" concept. Money has, in fact, played a role in economic activity, not merely as a passive tool, but also as an active force. The superposition of the ideas on the money criterion presented in this section contributes to fuller appreciation of what has been meant by the statement that money is an essential element in economic affairs.

6

Economics and Economizing

Before Wicksteed wrote, it was still possible for intelligent men to give countenance to the belief that the whole strucure of Economics depends upon the assumption of a world of economic men, each actuated by egocentric or hedonistic motives. For anyone who has read the *Common Sense,* the expression of such a view is no longer consistent with intellectual honesty.

Lionel C. Robbins

Before Robbins explained the "nature" of economic science, it was still possible for the economist to hold to the so-called "materialist" definition of economics, or to similar ones . . .
. . . Similarly, before Robbins' definition, criticism of economics on the ground of its being "too wide" or "too narrow" was still understandable. Now, however, such discussions have become meaningless: economics is a given pie, which the economist is only allowed to dress a bit, to cut as deeply and into as many parts as he wishes, and to eat according to his need.

G. Tagliacozzo

Something of a turning point in discussions on the nature of economic science and of economic affairs came in 1930 with the appearance of Robbins' *Nature and Significance of Economic Science.* Professor Robbins brought to the problem a method of attack that clearly revealed the logical inadequacies of earlier conceptions of the economic sector of affairs. At the same time he set forth his own positive definition of economics with effective simplicity and persuasive literary charm. The problem of definition was treated by Robbins as an integral part of the exposition of his general views on the appropriate tasks and methodology of economics. As such, the book as a whole and Robbins' definition of economics attracted widespread attention. Although Robbins claimed no originality for his definition, he effectively presented to the English-speaking world a group of earlier views with a clarity and a vigor that made them the focus of a newly awakened interest and unmistakably left his own stamp on the formulation he espoused. Since the publication of his book, discussions of the problem of definition have invariably tended to revolve around Robbins' definition, or at least to take it as a starting point.

The Economics of Professor Robbins

"Economics," wrote Professor Robbins, "is the science which studies human behavior as a relationship between ends and scarce means which have alternative uses." [1]

From the point of view of the economist, the conditions of human existence exhibit four fundamental characteristics. The ends are various. The time and the means for achieving these ends are limited and capable of alternative application. At the same time the ends have different importance. Here we are, sentient creatures with bundles of desires and aspirations, with masses of instinctive tendencies all urging us in different ways to action. But the time in which these tendencies can be expresed is limited. The external world does not offer full opportunities for their complete achievement. Life is short. Nature is niggardly. Our fellows have other objectives. Yet we can use our lives for doing different things, our materials and the services of others for achieving different objectives.

Now *by itself* the multiplicity of ends has no necessary interest for the economist. If I want to do two things, and I have ample time and ample means with which to do them, and I do not want the time or the means for anything else, then my conduct assumes none of those forms which are the subject of economic science . . .

Nor is the mere limitation of means *by itself* sufficient to give rise to economic phenomena. If means of satisfaction have no alternative use, then they may be scarce, but they cannot be economised . . .

Nor again is the alternative applicability of scarce means a complete condition of the existence of the kind of phenomena we are analysing. If the economic subject has two ends and one means of satisfying them, and the two ends are of equal importance, his position will be like the position of the ass in the fable, paralysed halfway between the two equally attractive bundles of hay.

But when time and the means for achieving ends are limited *and* capable of alternative application, *and* the ends are capable of being distinguished in order of importance, then behavior necessarily assumes the form of choice. Every act which involves time and scarce means for the achievement of one end involves the relinquishment of their use for the achievement of another. It has an economic aspect.[2]

Several highlights stand out in Robbins' conception of the nature of economic affairs. Central to the whole idea is the concept of *scarcity*. The limitations that prevent the attainment of the desired ends fundamentally affect the character of all activity directed towards these ends. The importance of the role assigned to scarcity as a governing condition of realizing ends makes possible the rejection of the idea that economics is concerned with specific *kinds* of ends. Robbins' definition rejects the identification of economics with certain *kinds* of behavior; it attempts, on the other hand, to bring out the economic *aspect* of behavior of all kinds. *All* kinds of behavior that occurs under the shadow of inadequate means present such an economic aspect to the observer.

In fact, the recognition that there can be distinguished in human actions a pattern of behavior that depends for its uniqueness, not on any one type of end pursued, but on the economizing aspect of actions directed at ends in general, led Robbins several years later to take yet a further step. Having emancipated economics from the bonds that tied it to particular ends, Robbins was led to suggest that the "economic" motive refers precisely to actions that are *not* directed to any particular ends. By saying

that a man's motive in doing a certain thing is wholly economic, what we really mean is simply that *he regards it only as a way of securing means for satisfying his ends in general*. If he does it with only one end in mind, we do not regard his motive as economic;

we regard it as having the character of the end to which it is specific. But if he does it with the desire to increase his power to satisfy ends in general, then we regard it as economic . . .[3]

The core of Robbins' conception is thus the act of economizing scarce means with regard to numerous, differently valued ends. A considerable body of literature has grown up in the past few decades in which this central concept has been subjected to careful scrutiny by economists generally, and economic methodologists in particular. The implications of these ideas for the substantive content of economic science have been thoroughly investigated; and the minute dissection of Robbins' definition has provided several distinct topics for debate. In this chapter we shall proceed to survey the area covered by this literature, after briefly glancing at some earlier ideas to which Robbins' definition owes its source.

Scarcity and Economics

Economists had long recognized, at least to some extent, the role played in economic phenomena by the factor of scarcity. The physiocrats had excluded from their subject matter "free goods" (such as air) because, being abundant, they were not objects of exchange. Among classical writers, Lauderdale explicitly required a degree of scarcity for individual (but not public) wealth; [4] most of the classical economists succeeded, in one way or another, in excluding from the scope of the science of "wealth" those goods whose supply was unrestricted. In the classical use of the "law of supply and demand," what was relevant was the *scarcity* of the supply.[5]

With the movement away from the objectivism of the classical science of wealth and with the increasing interest, during the second half of the last century, in man and his behavior, the idea of scarcity as a factor conditioning human action assumed ever greater importance. Economists who recognized the uniqueness of the maximization-pattern of behavior and the paramount position of the so-called economic principle could hardly fail to be aware of the fact that the basic source of both is to be found in the

phenomenon of scarcity. A clear understanding of the fundamental character of scarcity as a condition of human action began with
the work of Carl Menger.[6] Menger still considered economics as
concerned essentially with goods, but his definition of "economic
goods" and of "economizing" placed the condition of scarcity in
the forefront. The four components of the activity of economizing,
Menger explained in 1872, are called into play only when "the
requirements of men for many goods are greater than the quantities available to them." [7]

It is of some importance that writers such as Menger used the
criterion of scarcity as a refinement of the definition of economics
couched in terms of goods. This circumstance throws light on the
relation of the idea of scarcity to the emergence of a clearly recognized "economic principle." Such a relationship was perceived
very soon. Dietzel, in attacking the notion that the economic principle provides a valid means of describing the scope of economic
science, remarked that the criterion of scarcity suffers from the
same inadequacies as the economic principle, to which it is, indeed, equivalent.[8] It is obvious that conformity to the economic
principle is called forth by scarcity. In fact, what the economic
principle is to economics, considered as the analysis of *behavior,*
scarcity is to economics, viewed as the analysis of goods.

Although several German writers, including Schäffle and Cohn,[9]
had laid stress on the phenomenon of scarcity and its importance
for economics, there is reason to believe that this did not imply
the recognition of the role of "economizing" in Menger's sense.
Scarcity can be associated with economic affairs, not necessarily as
a means of genuine demarcation, but merely as a simplifying
device for the theorist. Anything appertaining to the satisfaction
of material wants, let us say, may be considered as economic, but
in order to facilitate analysis it may be necessary to confine attention to scarce goods. Determinate solutions of economic problems,
it is found, are yielded only when scarce goods are involved. And
this property of scarce goods may be employed in marking out the
scope of economic science without seeing scarcity as affording any
real means of distinguishing the economic from other phenomena.
The accident that makes scarce goods particularly amenable to

theoretical manipulation may not lead to the discovery of any uniqueness in the act of economizing at all.

Something of this seems to underlie Neumann's treatment of the definition of economics in terms of scarcity. In his survey, made in the eighties of the last century, of attempts to define economics, Neumann rejected the criterion of scarcity on rather surprising grounds, which reveal his limited appreciation of the real nature of this criterion. Scarce goods, Neumann asserted, are sometimes used for noneconomic purposes, e.g., for artistic ends. Moreover, Neumann added, there are cases of economic activity that involve only nonscarce goods. Thus, when an entrepreneur acquires sea water, a nonscarce commodity, for the purpose of renting out sea-water baths, he is surely engaged in economic activity, even though he is dealing in what, according to Menger's definition, is a "noneconomic" good.[10] It is fairly obvious that an understanding of the nature of the act of economizing would have prevented Neumann from offering these objections. In so far as sea-water baths are scarce, their provision surely entails economizing and is hence an economic activity, no matter how plentifully one of the materials may be obtainable in some other situation. And in so far as the materials for the expression of artistic impulses are scarce, their provision is also governed quite as powerfully by the economic principle.

Outside Germany there were, before the turn of the century, far fewer references to scarcity as a possible criterion for defining the nature of economic activity. Walras was one of the few writers who stressed this criterion. He required that what he called *richesse sociale* be both useful and scarce. It is not an accident that Walras' term for marginal utility is *rareté*. One writer has remarked that "Walras' *rareté* appears to be a truer concept than the common notion of marginal utility, for . . . he gives clear recognition to the fact that supply limitations are included and expressed in it." [11] For the rest, the focusing of attention by mathematical economists generally on the role of maximization must be accompanied by a lively awareness, even if not explicitly expressed, of the restriction of such behavior to cases admitting of a finite *maximandum*.

During the present century scarcity definitions of economics have become decidedly popular. Precursors of Robbins' formulation in terms of the act of economizing scarce means for the attainment of competing ends include a number of prominent figures. Besides Menger (in the last century), Robbins himself cites such writers as Wicksteed, Mises, Fetter, Strigl, Schönfeld and Mayer in this regard. Moreover, Robbins' formulation has been described as in some degree akin to ideas expressed by Spann and Oppenheimer. Both Voigt and Max Weber paid explicit attention to this point of view.[12] Any number of writers could be mentioned who, without endorsing Robbins' definition of economics, yet ascribe the central economic role to scarcity. In fact, one or two writers have felt bound, in reaction to this trend, to moderate the general enthusiasm for the conception of scarcity by asserting the possibility of an economics of "abundance." [13] It must be admitted that these writers do not demonstrate any partiality to the notion of "economizing," from the standpoint of which abundance is meaningless in any other than a relative sense.

There was thus a long tradition in economic literature in which the importance of the limitation of resources was recognized, and there were, moreover, many indications pointing to the possibility of using the administration of scarce means as *the* distinguishing criterion of the economic.[14] In pressing the scarcity of means into service as the very core of everything economic, and by discovering in the effects of coping with such scarcity an economic aspect to activity in general, Robbins was crystallizing ideas that had already been in ferment for some time. Perhaps the most useful service afforded by the fresh formulation lay in the clarity with which the conception of economic activity as consisting in "economizing" was contrasted with the older definitions. Perhaps never before had the notion of the allocation of scarce means among competing ends been so consciously and vigorously presented as independent of the particular nature of the ends and means that may be involved.

Economizing and Maximization

Besides the sources for Robbins' formulation to be found in earlier references to scarcity and the approaches to the fundamental notion of economizing, yet another line of thought that was historically relevant to the emergence of the new definition must be recognized. This was the stress on the *maximization* principle, the getting of the most out of the least, as the distinctive mark of economic activity. The appearance and development of this line of thought has been outlined in an earlier chapter; at this point the relationship between the two concepts—maximization and economizing—must be briefly pointed out.

Maximization as a possible criterion for distinguishing economic phenomena had been clearly suggested towards the last quarter of the past century and even earlier. In its earlier expressions the so-called economic principle usually referred to the maximization of some tangible entity such as wealth and thus bore little resemblance to economizing. However, when maximization is understood to refer to something less objective, such as pleasure or satisfaction, then its similarity to the act of economizing becomes fairly close. After all, the economizing of scarce means in the face of competing arrays of ends is undertaken with the purpose of squeezing as much "satisfaction" out of available resources as their shrewd management will permit. Just as the bare concept of economizing abstracts from the concrete ends at which activity is aimed and the specific means utilized to attain them, so does the idea of getting the greatest return at the least cost. It was seen in an earlier chapter, in fact, that the shift in emphasis to the maximization principle was closely associated with the denial of any specifically economic impulse.

But while the allocation of scarce means among competing ends can be subsumed under the concept of maximization, the converse is not true. And the differences between the two classifications of action, maximization and economizing, are perhaps even more significant than their similarities. Robbins himself pointed out in a footnote that the "maximization of satisfaction" simply replaces the array of "ends" of action by an ultimate goal, viz., satisfaction, to the achievement of which our "ends" are to be regarded as proximate.[15] The scarcity of means then enforces the relinquishment of some of our "ends," at the same time that the task of maximizing satisfaction determines the way in which the available means are disposed among the various "ends" chosen. Maximization, with one ultimate end in view, is thus the source of economizing limited resources among alternative subordinate "ends." This description of the relationship between maximizing satisfaction and economizing reveals several features of the former category of action that restrict its usefulness as a characterization of the nature of economic activity and perhaps helps to explain the limited part played by the concept of maximization in the line of thought that led to the allocation view of economics.

In substituting an ultimate end such as satisfaction for the intermediate "ends" chosen as conducive to it, the conception of economic activity as maximizing behavior suffers from two weaknesses. On the one hand, it involves setting up such an ultimate end, with the presumption that it can be meaningfully "maximized"; on the other hand, it ignores the multiplicity of intermediary "ends" and the effects that their very number has on the allocation of resources. The first weakness, the postulation of an ultimate "satisfaction" that can be maximized, is brought into relief by the way in which the alternative notion of economizing scarce resources among competing ends avoids altogether this awkward idea of "quantities" of satisfaction. The concept of economizing dispenses with the necessity of assuming that men act as if they were constantly scanning a potential "store" of satisfaction and striving to accumulate the largest possible stock. Instead, this concept recognizes that men act to change their situation until no further action promises to lead to a condition preferred to the present one. The advance in economics from the stress on maximizing satisfaction to that on economizing thus parallels the advance from the older utility analysis (especially where it involved cardinal utility) to the more recent indifference techniques.

The second weakness of the concept of maximization, that it ignores the multiplicity of intermediate "ends," is a consequence of the fact that it abstracts too drastically from actual economic activity. It may be true to say that the economizing of resources is merely the maximization of a more ultimate satisfaction, but to speak in such terms is to miss one of the really significant features of economic activity, the *allocation* of these resources among the *different* uses clamoring for these limited means. The whole idea of the allocation of limited resources and their economic distribution among the competing demands for them is hidden under the facile phrase, "the maximization of satisfaction." The constraint to *administer* resources, to apportion them judiciously among alternative uses by the careful comparison and weighing of relative degrees of importance—a necessity imposed by the fact that the intermediate "ends" are numerous—is overlooked in the maximization formula. By its stress on allocation as the characteristic feature of economic activity, the concept of economizing, on the other hand, leads directly to the appreciation of the significance for economics of the idea of *price* and *exchange at the margin.* Hence, this formulation is eminently suitable for characterizing the subject matter of economics.

These considerations thus clearly set Robbins' definition apart from the earlier definitions of economic activity in terms of maximization, despite the undoubtedly important part that the latter conception, in conjunction with the literature on scarcity, played in the emergence of Robbins' view of economics. Robbins' formulation of this view, which sees the essence of the subject matter of economics in the peculiar quality of economizing behavior, attracted the critical attention of economists to an extent achieved by no previous attempt at definition. Several waves of debate were set in motion concerning various aspects of the freshly expounded view. These must now be examined more closely, and their investigation will provide an opportunity to glance at the most important of the opinions inspired by Robbins' work.

The Character of Robbins' Definition

Robbins was at some pains to point out that the conception of economics that he expounded had an entirely different character from that of the previously accepted conceptions of the subject. The earlier definitions had almost invariably been *classificatory,* marking off certain kinds of behavior, i.e., behavior directed to certain types of ends, as the subject matter of economics. Robbins' own formulation, on the other hand, is *analytical.* It "does not attempt to pick out certain *kinds* of behavior, but focuses attention on a particular *aspect* of behavior, the form imposed by the influence of scarcity." [16] Hitherto it had been believed possible to describe certain acts and activities as being "economic"; Robbins' definition, however, does not consider the adjective "economic" as at all appropriate for the description of any act as such, but sees it as singling out a point of view from which actions may be examined. Whereas the earlier definitions of economic affairs had searched for criteria sufficiently comprehensive, and yet sufficiently exclusive, to describe accurately a given *class* of acts, Robbins' definition sets forth the particular interests that actuate the singling out of the economic aspect of an act. An act pertains to economic science in so far as it reveals the consequences of a compulsion to allocate scarce resources among conflicting ends. Robbins' formulation thus differs from others perhaps less in its choice of a criterion for definition than in its radically different conception of the kind of idea that is to be defined.

The critics subjected this feature of Robbins' contribution to close attention and expressed a wide range of opinions concerning its validity and significance. Writers who hailed Robbins' book as an auspicious turning point in the conception of economic science and who viewed his definition as a final and definitive pronouncement on the particular problem with which it grappled saw one of its principal merits in this concern with an aspect of action rather than with a particular kind of action.[17] Writers assessing the difference between Robbins' definition and earlier attempts recognized this approach as one of the most significant features of his contribution.[18] Those who have described (and deplored) Robbins' definition as the "dominant academic doctrine" have had especially in mind its lack of concern with the particular ends involved and its concentration on viewing action from a given "aspect." [19]

As the essential component of Robbins' definition, this disregard for the kinds of ends pursued in action had certain further consequences that aroused lively discussion. Perhaps the foremost of these is the ethical neutrality of the economic point of view as set forth by Robbins. If the economist is, as such, exempted or interdicted from choosing particular ends of action as his special concern, then the results of his researches will be achieved with ethical indifference towards the data with which he deals. This consequence of the definition of economics in terms of a particular aspect of action is reserved for separate discussion later in this chapter.

Two implications of this ethical neutrality have led to sharp criticism of the definition as a whole. On the one hand, the abandonment of the search for particular ends of action meant that the range of economic interest is widened to cover the "economic aspect" of actions that had not been able to qualify for inclusion in the class of "economic" acts on the basis of any of the previous definitions. On the other hand, the lack of concern for the nature of ends facilitated an academic detachment from the full reality of actions and the cultivation of a "purely formal" view of the economist's interest in the relationship between ends and means.

A. THE "BREADTH" OF ROBBINS' DEFINITION

The former of these two implications led to immediate attacks on Robbins' definition condemning it as being far too wide, i.e., as bringing within the scope of economics phenomena in regard to which the economist has no professional competence and to which economists have historically paid no attention whatsoever. Some writers have tended to see in this alleged shortcoming an opportunity to indulge their wit in describing the problems—whether literary controversies, games of chess, or even affairs of the heart—with which Professor Robbins, on the basis of his own definition of economics, should, as an economist, be equipped to deal.[20]

Ultimately these attacks and the consequent pronouncements

rejecting the concept of economizing as a criterion for defining the nature of economic phenomena provide yet another instance of the similarities between the conception of economics as a science concerned with economizing and the conception of it as a science concerned with maximization. Writers in the eighties of the last century who had considered the essence of economic behavior to consist in the impulse toward maximization had found themselves vulnerable to the objection that this propensity characterizes *all* human activities. The fact that economizing, like maximization, is an operation capable of being performed in widely differing situations means that the use of such a concept as a criterion for defining the nature of the economic cuts across many traditional boundaries. But clearly if a definition is to be rejected as too wide, some area must be accepted as the standard of reference. The stress that economists in the past have laid on the phenomena of the market as the area to which their researches applied makes suspect a definition that sees an essential economic unity existing in activities ranging far beyond this area.

Nevertheless, there is an important sense in which the definition of the economic in terms of economizing is less suspect in this regard than that couched in terms of maximization had been. The latter had been used in the form of the so-called economic principle, which was seen as essentially a principle of *explanation*. Market phenomena were explained on the hypothesis of the existence of such an economic principle. The concept of a form of behavior characterized by maximization was found to yield the results required to understand the real economic world. From this point of view, the definition of economics as the science concerned with the maximization pattern of behavior drew the boundaries of the subject in such a way as to include all phenomena that admitted of explanation on the hypothesis of the existence of such a principle. Any activity that involved maximization was thus *prima facie* economically relevant. And here the objection was immediately raised that such a criterion embraced all human behavior, including areas in which maximization did not lead to "explanations" such as economists had successfully provided in what was then accepted as the domain of economics.

Robbins' definition of economics in terms of economizing was in a somewhat different case. The concept of economizing was not being used as an explanatory device at all, but only as a means of characterizing certain behavior. The fact that such behavior proved more amenable to economic analysis in regard to market phenomena than in other cases does not necessarily void the use of this definition, since the latter is not predicated on its suitability for this kind of economic analysis. At most, the criticisms aimed at Robbins' definition could cast doubt on its suitability for readily characterizing the day-to-day problems to which economic theory is most frequently applied. Professor Robbins himself has presented the case for his exemption from this type of criticism.[21]

B. THE "FORMALISM" OF ROBBINS' DEFINITION

The other implication of the ethical neutrality inherent in Robbins' definition has occasioned perhaps even warmer debate. If economic theory is seen as focusing interest, not on the actual ends of action, but merely on the bare relationship that scarce resources have to these ends, then the theory becomes very formal, very pure indeed. Robbins stressed this feature of his conception of economics as finally detaching the essentially *economic* structure of action from the clutter of concrete data necessarily enveloping it in the real world. But several critics saw this "formalism" as an arid scholastic exercise that succeeded only in leaving out the important features of an economic problem.

This view found its most forthright expression in Souter's bitter essay in 1933 fiercely defending the "Living Classical Faith," reverently associated with the name of Marshall, against the "Austrian" position as set forth by Robbins. Apparently Professor Robbins came to be identified as a "juggler with a static verbal logic" and a "profane sunderer of 'form' from 'substance.' " Perhaps the principal target for Souter's scathing denunciation was the attempt to define economics as distinct from other disciplines in terms of its *attitude* towards a subject matter that it shared in common with these other disciplines. Souter's attack on Robbins' "formalism" arises from his burning belief in the status of economics as a member in a "society" of sciences, each of which can be sealed in an airtight receptacle only on the penalty of death.[22] The issue raised by the "formalistic" approach to economics is whether the science "is to enter upon the fatal path of fastidious withdrawal from organic intercourse with its fellows; or whether it will have the courage and honesty to assume its rightful place in the *society* of sciences." [23] As a member of such a society, economics is "necessarily and inevitably dependent upon sociology, upon psychology, upon technology," [24] and progress in economics must derive from "organic" relationships with the other disciplines.

All this leads to the almost emotional rejection of Robbins' conception of ends that the economist treats from the outset merely as data. Economics may legitimately take over from ethics or psychology the finished results of their study of the determination of the concrete means and ends involved in human action. But any attempt to consider economic analysis or the conception of an economic aspect of a problem as possible without taking into account such factual information concerning the content of action is "mere hocus-pocus." [25] To treat the concrete ends of action as "given," in the "perverted" sense of not affecting economic analysis, is a display of instincts that are "corruptly sophisticated" [26] and involves the bartering of the Mecca of "economic biology" for the mess of pottage of an illusory "static precision." [27]

Professor Parsons, in a paper following shortly after that of Souter, provided a calmly reasoned appraisal of the issues involved in the Robbins-Souter controversy. Parsons pointed out that the "formalism" that Souter denounces is not quite the same formalism that Robbins is rather pleased to find in his conception of economics. According to Robbins, economics is formal in the sense that it is abstract, making use of "logic," which is not confined to specific historical situations. Souter, on the other hand, attacks Robbins' definition on the grounds that it makes economics a "purely formal science of implications" in the sense of "having no reference whatever to empirical facts." If exception is taken to Robbins' view of economics as necessarily abstract because it involves the use of logical reasoning, then the road is open to a complete "empiricism"and *Historismus*.[28] The only room left for debate on Robbins' formalism is the fruitfulness of the particular abstractions that Robbins requires for his conception of economics.

Such criticisms of Robbins' view of economics, objecting to the degree to which it makes abstraction from reality, have, of course, been made. One writer has recently deplored the fact that by "eliminating *economic* ends *per se,* the concept of 'economizing' has diverted attention from the really significant aspects of behavior in modern economy (for example, pecuniary thinking and acquisitive drives) . . ." [29] But there is some difference between this kind of criticism and that of Souter. In the type of complaint that is voiced here there is room for recognition of the validity of an independent category of economizing. There is even room for recognition of the fundamental and possibly universal character of the category in its significance for economic problems. It is only objected that too-exclusive concentration by the economic theorist on this aspect of action may hinder adequate recognition of the particular, empirical content of a concrete economic problem. When the economist comes to apply his professional skills to the understanding of actual economic phenomena, it is argued, his attempt may be handicapped by the attitude with which he approaches the task. His conception of the nature and role of economic theory may prevent recognition of the actual facts of the situation the understanding of which could explain matters, whereas treating it purely as a case of economizing does not lead to an immediate solution. In other words, this objection does not necessarily question the validity of the concept of economizing as a criterion, but merely condemns it as inadequate in its application to the problems of the real world because of the "misleading" or "unfruitful" abstraction that it may make from significant elements of these problems. Souter, on the other hand, is objecting to theory, not in this way, as unsuitable for practical application, but altogether. He is opposed to the conception of a theory that has no reference to the phenomena of the real world. Yet, as Parsons pointed out, the alternative to the "aspect" type of definition propounded by Robbins must consistently lead all the way in an empiricist direction to the ultimate repudiation of the legitimacy of analytical abstraction to any degree and for any purpose.

In the last analysis, the attempts to condemn Robbins' definition of economics on account of its "formal" character fall into the same class as attempts to discredit economic theory as such and to construct an "economics" altogether free of theoretical propositions. The search for the definition of economic science in a particular "aspect" of the phenomena with which it deals simply brings to the task of definition the analytical attitude with which economic theorists have always expounded the substantive content of the discipline.

The Nature of Ends and Means

Apart from the more general considerations surrounding the "formal" character of Robbins' definition, couched as it is in terms of abstract ends and means, there has been some discussion of a narrower and perhaps more technical character concerning the nature and validity of the concepts of ends and means.[30]

Several writers have seen the relationship of ends and means in terms of which Professor Robbins defines economic science as an artificial schema that does violence to the true nature of human action. In a book in which the concept of an end of action is used many, many times, Robbins devoted very little space to explaining the nature of an "end" and to elucidating the difficulties that the notion involves. Robbins had described human ends as associated with "tendencies to conduct which can be defined and understood." This description was seized upon as typical of a certain "positivism" that critics believed themselves to have detected in Robbins' position. Robbins is eager, it is contended, to invest a study of economizing—which is a subjective notion—with the objectivity of science. He has sought to achieve this by pressing human action into a mould involving ends and means that can be defined and understood. Ends are in this respect conceived of as quite analogous to the definite "external" resources of nature that constitute means. Ends, that is, are considered as "external" to the actor. The relationship between the definite means, on the one hand, and equally definite ends, on the other, defines the scope of economic science. This view of Robbins on the nature of ends has been severely criticized by several writers.

The critics, among whom may be named Souter, Parsons, and Macfie, pointed to a number of inadequacies in Robbins' schema.[31] The concept of *purpose* as fundamental to human action seems to be wholly excluded. Ends are simply correlates of "tendencies to conduct"; this draws attention completely away from the conscious *aiming* that pervades economic activity. By squeezing the element of purpose out of action, Robbins' structure of ends and means is "timeless" in the sense that it ignores the fact that ends are never presented to the actor coincidentally with the means. If an economic act apportions resources among desired ends in much the same way as a pie is shared among a hungry family, then the economic act does not exist. Ends can be conceived as observable states of affairs only *after* their achievement. At the time of the contemplation of action, ends are to the actor only anticipations of future hoped-for states of affairs. *After* an action has been completed, it can be described as having achieved a certain allocation of resources among ends, but to characterize an action on these grounds as having involved the subjective notion of economizing is to consider the action from a merely behavioristic standpoint.[32] This indictment of Robbins on the charge of "behaviorism" and "positivism" gains in interest in the light of the contribution of the praxeological conception of economics, to be taken up in the following chapter.

In addition to the criticisms of Robbins' concretization of ends, some debate has developed on the very obvious relativity of the ends-means schema. It has been pointed out that ends may be considered as means to further ends, and that means may be equally well considered as the ends of earlier actions. Consciousness of this flimsiness in the ends-means dichotomy must necessarily raise doubts about the validity of a category such as economizing whose claim to a definite status is based exclusively on the relationship between ends and means.

It may be observed that the facile manner in which Robbins assumes the existence of definite ends, without careful discussion of the fact that ends are, as a rule, set up merely as intermediate to the achievement of further chains of ends, is to some extent to be expected from his unconcern with the *purposive* element in action.[33] We have noticed criticism of Robbins' formulation on this score, and there appears to be a direct link between this attitude and the postulation of absolute categories of ends and means. Felix Kaufmann has drawn attention to the fact that it is because of the element of purpose in human conduct that immediate ends are only the means to further ends.[34] Kaufmann sees the lack of agreement concerning the definition of the subject matter of economics as arising out of the three possible "levels" of ends that may be considered relevant: the end of acquisition of goods, the further end of consuming them, and the supposed ultimate end of increasing one's happiness. But what is of moment in appraising Robbins' definition is not so much the particular "levels" into which ends may more or less arbitrarily be classified; it is rather the fact that ends, in so far as economic activity is described as directed towards ends, are such only relatively to the particular and immediate context of the action.[35]

This consideration of itself would not, of course, seriously threaten Robbins' conceptualization of action in terms of means and ends. Parsons,[36] following up a classification of the chains of means-end relationships into "ultimate ends" of action, "ultimate means," and an intermediate sector (in which actions involve both the means to more nearly ultimate ends and the ends of previous preliminary actions), has shown how economic action finds its place in the intermediate sector.

But while the concept of economy and the operation of economizing does not depend on the "absolute" status of an "end" of action, at least one writer has shown the weakness of the ends-means dichotomy as a method of separating the science of economics from technology. It had been one of the principal merits of Robbins' formulation that it provided an elegant and conceptually neat device for distinguishing between problems of economics, on the one hand, and problems of technology, on the other. Where alternative definitions of economics, being classificatory in character, failed to provide a satisfactory means of excluding technology, the analytical definition advanced by Robbins enabled him to use Mayer's distinction: "The problem of technique arises when there is one end and a multiplicity of means, the problem of economy when both the ends and the means are multiple." [37]

There will be occasion later in this chapter to review some criticisms of the validity of this distinction; at this point the objection must be noticed that the very nature of the concepts, ends and means, makes the distinction inadequate. In a recent paper Rivett [38] has contended that while Mayer's distinction is valid in itself, "it cannot be used to separate the science of economics from the science of technology, pushing some relationships into the first field and others into the second." This is ultimately due to the fact that any course of action undertaken to achieve a desired end thereby becomes itself an end intermediate to the achievement of the originally conceived end. In Rivett's example, if a pencil is picked up in order to accomplish the end of writing, there has been introduced an additional, subordinate end of picking up the pencil. Pursuing this line of thinking, Rivett has no difficulty in demonstrating that the attempt to attain the single end—which, according to the Mayer-Robbins view is the problem of technology—may involve the intermediate pursuit of various subordinate ends that may well conflict with one another. The same problem of securing the single end, a problem of technology from the point of view in which the subordinate ends are seen merely as means, thus becomes a problem of economy from the point of view of a more minute scrutiny in which the harnessing of any of these means is recognized as itself possessing all the qualities of an end.

Once again Robbins' disregard of these considerations seems in consonance with his lack of concern for the element of purpose in human action. Once an end has been postulated as the goal of action, then all the actions undertaken with this end in view can, *ex post facto,* be grouped in a separate class from that of the end. All the chains of subordinate ends and means leading up to the final goal can be telescoped together to form a homogeneous pool of "resources" and "means" for the final goal. But from the point of view of the actor, such a dichotomy is in no sense unique or even especially significant. To him these resources, means, and subordinate courses of action are all arrays pointing purposefully to the final end, but at the same time and for the same reason containing subpatterns of purposefully ordered arrays, within each of which the *ex post facto* dichotomy betweens ends and means could be distinguished with equal validity.

These criticisms of Robbins' formulation in terms of ends and means may perhaps be most illuminatingly summed up by reference to the very interesting discussion by Tagliacozzo.[39] In the course of an exhaustive analysis of the nature of economic "error," i.e., of "uneconomic" behavior in failing to resist the temptation of the moment, Tagliacozzo points out that in full reality action necessarily involves the complete identity of ends and means. Tagliacozzo's work has especial relevance for the praxeological view of economics and will be discussed more thoroughly in the succeeding chapter. At this point we note Tagliacozzo's contention that when the economic agent succumbs to a fleeting temptation (e.g., the purchase of wine) at variance with a prearranged economic program, his "error" exists only as relative to the arbitrarily postulated goal of the program. To judge his action as "uneconomic," because it involves an inappropriate disposition of "means," is to impose *from the outside* an ends-means schema that does not conform to the real situation. Seen from the standpoint of full reality, the purchase of wine, as an autonomous act, involves the full identity of the end and the means. Without becoming involved at this point in the significance of these ideas for the concept of economic "rationality," this discussion focuses attention very clearly on the weakness of Robbins' ends-means formulation. Ends and means are clearly *imposed categories* artificially dissecting the elements of action; recognition of the relativity of these categories leads to the demand for their far more careful use in attempts to define the nature of economic activity and the scope of economic science.

"Given" Ends and Means

Implicit in the formulation of the nature of economic activity in terms of the allocation of scarce resources with regard to alternative ends is the assumption that the ends of action are merely "data" for the economist investigating economic activity. This property of Professor Robbins' definition, that is, its treatment of wants as given (and, for the purpose of a given economic problem, constant), has been accorded considerable attention. It has, of course, already been noticed in this chapter that an important and widely discussed characteristic of Robbins' definition was its identification of the economic by singling out an *aspect* of phenomena. This, too, is closely related to his treatment of ends and wants as data. Where earlier definitions had identified economic activity with action directed toward certain more or less well-defined ends, Robbins cultivated an unconcern for the nature of the ends involved in action. Necessarily this meant the removal of these ends from the range of phenomena to be studied and their relegation to the realm of given information upon which the problem to be investigated is based. All this, of course, gave rise to criticism on the part of those wishing to see the economists, in close collaboration with students of the neighboring disciplines, pay more attention to the realities of concrete action.[40]

But apart from the complaint that the treatment of ends as mere data is an unholy attempt to extrude from economics the contributions of the psychologist and the sociologist, this notion of ends implies a profoundly important outlook on the very nature of human action and the possibility of its scientific explanation. In the full reality of human action the values of men and the ends to which they direct their energies are continually changing, continually becoming modified under the impact of outside changes as well as through the effect of changes wrought by the very action aimed at the original ends and by the very effort of pursuing those ends. The attempt to introduce scientific explanatory analysis into the study of human action has involved the isolation, from the tangled intricacies of the web of action, of an element in it that we call its economic aspect. According to Robbins' conception of the precise nature of this element, its isolation involves the analysis of action in terms of its relation to the array of ends as they are esteemed at a given moment in time. Any proposition deduced from the fundamental concept of the economic act will thus have relevance only within the particular frame of reference relatively to which the economic aspect of action has meaning—i.e., the ends whose respective values were the data of the problem.

This view of the nature of the assumptions implicit in economic theory involves two important corollaries. First, economic theory can only analyze the implications of given wants; it cannot as such explain or determine changes in wants themselves (although, of course, its explanations can throw enormous light on these questions). Second, economic theory has validity only on the assumptions of the constancy of wants throughout the duration of the problem under consideration.

The danger in the conception of ends as data has already been commented on in this chapter. To construct a model of action in terms of ends so conceived may well lead one unwittingly to disregard the fact that to the actor himself ends are not data at all, but have been purposefully *chosen* and are constantly in danger of being supplanted by newly prized ends.[41] In viewing economics as concerned with preselected ends that are the ultimate frame of reference for a particular economic problem, one must exercise constant care not to transform these chosen ends into objective "pulls" similar to physiologically conditioned "needs," for this would turn economic activity into a series of reflexes responsive to quasi-biological tropisms.

Several writers have pointed out that from the economic point of view it is not only the ends that are data, but also the means. The economic element is the *coordination* of given ends and means whose substance economic analysis does not and cannot attempt to explore. Professor Knight especially has deplored the unfortunate habit of describing economics as concerned with means, but not with ends. In any sense in which ends are data for economics and are thus not the concern of the economist, means are no less "given" and beyond the range of the economic problem.[42]

In this respect it is interesting to examine the formula with which Max Weber attempted to distinguish between economics and technology. The problem of expressing such a distinction seems to have exerted some fascination, as attested by the recurrence of passages in Weber's writings discussing this question. Weber brought the distinction into clear relief by asserting that "economic action is primarily oriented to the problem of choosing the end to which a thing shall be applied; technology, to the problem, given the end, of choosing the appropriate means." A genuinely economic character is that which "takes account of alternative ends and not only of means for a given end."[43] This way of expressing the distinction may at first give the impression that in economic action the means are given, and the ends are still to be selected, whereas in technology the ends are given, and the means are to be selected.[44] It would be an error, however, to draw the conclusion that Weber in any way disagrees with the writers who stress that in economics the ends as well as the means are given. Weber too recognized that the economic view of action takes the actor's valuation of ends as a datum. After all, it is this idea that is the cornerstone of the concept of *Wertfreiheit* that Weber championed as the proper setting for the analysis of economic activity. Weber too is thinking of a given array of ends ordered by the (not-to-be-studied) valuations of the actor. What he has in mind, of course, in describing economic action as the choice of ends to which given means are to be applied is simply the fact that a given ordering of ends will necessitate the allocation of means among these ends in a manner peculiarly consistent with this given order of estimation. Ends are to be "chosen," not in the sense of being arranged in order of relative esteem, but in the sense of their receiving allocations of resources. With alternative ends competing for given means, these means must be allocated by "choosing" for each resource an end such that its allocation is in harmony with the (already) adopted ordering of ends.

The conception of the ends of economic action as data involves, we have noticed, two corollaries. It is implicit in this conception that the selection and ordering of ends do not constitute an economic problem; and it follows that for the duration of any economic problem its analysis must assume constancy in the relative urgency of the wants that economic action seeks to satisfy. Both these implications of Robbins' formulation are revealing. It requires no great insight into the affairs of the world with which economists largely deal to realize that if the economist is to work under the restraints imposed by these implications, he must, in his capacity as an economist, renounce interest in perhaps the most fascinating and important aspects of the data with which he works. The economist *qua* economist (and this phrase of Robbins has been used by critics with characteristic, but hardly deserved, sarcasm) must ignore the fact that tastes and values are swiftly changing variables and must avert his eyes from the intensely interesting and important processes whereby men arrive at their judgments of value.

These limitations on the scope of the economist's area of competence have, of course, been condemned again and again by historically-minded and institutionally-conscious critics of economic theory. The fact that the validity of these limitations follows rigorously from Robbins' definition of economics reveals the close faithfulness with which this definition of the subject mirrors the procedures that economic theorists have, in fact, been following all the time. What the explicit recognition of the fact that the phenomena with which the economist deals are data does achieve is the appreciation that self-restraint by economic theorists does not spring from blindness to the facts of economic life. The "abstractions" of the economists, against which realistically-minded critics have so vigorously rebelled, are inherent in the nature of the problems to which they address themselves. Their subject matter forms a distinct field precisely because there exists an element in action that is distinct from the nature of the ends of action and at least conceptually independent of the processes whereby ends are selected and ordered. It must surely be regarded as a merit of Robbins' definition that it isolates this element with clarity. A grasp of the character of this element in action makes it immediately evident that the severely circumscribed applicability of the propositions enunciated by the economic theorist, far from being the necessary result of a crudely unrealistic methodology, is but the properly incomplete contribution of the specialist whose skills have been developed by a judicious and fruitful division of labor. Specific policy recommendations on economic affairs may require long and careful study of the actual attitudes of human beings, their wants, valuations, and expectations. Crucially important though such information may well be, the research and scholarship involved in its compilation is *different* from the application of economic reasoning. Robbins' definition brings this distinction into sharp focus.

Single End and Multiple Ends

One of the basic components of Robbins' formulation of the nature of economic activity is its assumption of the presence of a *multiplicity* of ends to which the scarce resources can be applied and among which they must be judiciously allocated. It has been seen that Robbins himself pointed out that where a single ultimate end, such as "utility," is considered as the goal of action, then the process of economizing resources among competing ends reduces to the operation of maximizing this ultimate end. It has been shown earlier in this chapter that the superiority of the definition of economics in terms of economizing over the definitions couched in terms of the maximization principle has its source in the more penetrating analysis of action that is made possible by the recognition of numerous competing wants whose satisfaction is conducive to the ultimate end of utility.

It was the conception of economic activity as involving numerous ends that enabled Robbins to adopt Mayer's distinction between economics and technology. Technology involves selection among means for the attainment of only a single end, whereas economics necessitates comparing the urgency of several competing ends.[45] At this point attention must be turned to the question of the actual multiplicity of ends which, it is alleged, are to be found in economic action, and, on the other hand, of the extent to which the idea of an underlying single ultimate end is to be considered essential to the Mayer-Robbins conception of economizing. The problem arises partly from the very premise from which the Mayer-Robbins formulation starts—the existence of a given ordered array of variously prized ends.

It was seen in the previous section that given wants in Robbins' sense implied an ordering of ends separate from the economic act itself. It is on the assumption of previously ordered ends that the process of allocation of resources can proceed. Professor Knight, among others, has repeatedly stressed, however, that the comparison of ends as to their importance and the allocation of resources consistently with such a comparison imply "quantitative comparability in the final results of all uses of any 'resource' "; they imply, in other words, that "there is really only one end." [46] It would have to be admitted, if this argument be accepted, that economic action too is merely a matter of technique in so far as the ultimate (single) end of action is concerned.

It must be noted that the reservations that these considerations inspire concerning the validity of the notion of a multiplicity of ends are rather different from those expressed by Souter and Parsons on the same topic. The latter writers too laid stress on the unified character of systems of ends, whether of the individual or society; but their criticisms focused chiefly on Robbins' exposition of the ends of individual economizing in terms of psychological "pulls" that, when unified into a "system," seem to contradict the very concept of economy.[47] The points raised by Knight, on the other hand, do not at all lose their force even if the nature of the ends of action is set forth in less "positivist" terms. If ends can be compared and arranged in order, it is argued, there must be some common denominator relating them to one another. However revealing and significant it may be to break down this single ultimate end of maximization into the numerous intermediate ends of economizing, the elegant Mayer-Robbins distinction between economics and technology seems difficult to salvage.

It is interesting to draw attention at this point to a somewhat different characterization of economic activity as directed to a single end, which was developed by Robbins himself, and which has been used with great effect by Hayek. This is the view that recognizes the economic motive as "merely desire for general opportunity, the desire for power to achieve unspecified ends." [48] Money has come to be linked with the economic motive, according to this view, because it offers the means to enjoy the widest choice of goods and services that we may desire. (One is reminded of a century-old definition of wealth that saw it, not as particular goods and services, but as the "power" to command goods and services in general.) [49]

The relation between this understanding of an economic "end" and the economic aspect of activity in general is clear. We have, in the description of the economically motivated act as one directed at gaining the power to achieve *unspecified* ends, the view precisely opposite to the older notion of economic activity as directed to a single, sharply defined end (such as material goods and the like). The first step taken by Robbins away from the older type of definition was the recognition of an economic aspect to activity in general, regardless of the concrete nature of the particular ends involved. With the adjective "economic" freed of positive association with specific ends, Robbins is now able to press still further and identify the economic motive with activity distinguished precisely by the *lack* of any specifically selected ends.

It is unnecessary to examine the doubts that have been expressed whether Professor Robbins has in fact been able to salvage a scientifically acceptable notion of an "economic" objective distinct, let us say, from military and political objectives.[50] What is of interest in the present connection is the significance of the very conception of an activity distinguished by its orientation to ends-in-general rather than to particular ends. The view of economic activity as the effort to gain power to obtain ends that are to be selected only later represents an analysis of action that is intriguingly parallel to that which ignores altogether the multiplicity of ends in human action. We have seen that activity, as analyzed from the economic aspect, may be described in terms of one of two patterns. Either it may, with Robbins, be seen as the allocation of means with regard to numerous, ordered ends; or it may, with Knight, be seen as the technique of maximizing, with given resources, the single ultimate end, "satisfaction," in terms of which alone the numerous intermediate ends can conceivably be compared. The concept of an activity directed at ends-in-general involves the isolation of one kind of activity, which is, indeed, related to numerous, desired ends, but in which the latter have been superseded by a single end, not as their resultant, but as the *preliminary* to their attainment. Action was entirely deprived of its economic aspect, in the Robbins-Mayer view, when the ends of action were replaced by the end of "satisfaction," to which they are conceived as being subservient. Where many ends were supplanted by a single end, viz., the *resultant* of them all, activity became merely a question of technique with regard to this single, ultimate end. Now, on the other hand, we have isolated an activity in which numerous desired ends are superseded by the single *intermediate* goal of attaining power in general to command the as-yet-unspecified further ends.

The recognition that a large part of human activity, that directed at gaining general purchasing power in the form of money, does, in fact, conform to this pattern is highly revealing. The maximization of money income, of "wealth," as the essence of economic activity was one of a group of concepts underlying many older definitions of economics. The maximization of some less specific entity, such as satisfaction, utility, welfare, and the like, came to be identified with economics as a result of the introduction of subjective thinking into the discipline in the latter part of the previous century. Robbins' formulation of the economic aspect of activity in terms of the allocation of scarce means among numerous alternative ends is now seen to occupy a very special position in respect to these two types of maximization. It begins by pressing on to the multiplicity of ends of action that lie behind the quest for wealth. It sees the economic aspect of action to exist precisely in the circumstances brought about by this multiplicity of real goals and action. But it is, on the other hand, able to retain its grip on this economic aspect of action only by deliberately refraining from submerging the multiplicity of these ends into a single, more ultimate end. The economic aspect of affairs, as seen by Robbins, is predicated on an interpretation of action that, while reaching beyond the false homogenization of ends implicit in the definition of all economic activity as the maximization of the single end, "wealth," is able to resist the parallel homogenization of ends in terms of their resultant that is implicit in the characterization of action as the maximization of "satisfaction."

Economics and Ethics: the Positive and the Normative

Mention has already been made in this chapter of one important implication of Robbins' formulation of the nature of economic activity, viz., the necessary ethical neutrality of the economic point of view. The highly controversial consequences that have been drawn from this principle and the profound effect that adherence to it must have on the role of the economist and on the nature of his analysis demand a more detailed account of this aspect of Robbins' definition as well as the criticism with which it has been confronted.

The demand that the economist preserve a scientific neutrality with regard to the desirability of particular situations explored by his analysis has been maintained with a fair degree of consistency. Nineteenth-century economic methodologists had stressed the distinction between the *science* of political economy and a possible *art* of political economy. "Almost all leading economists, from N. Senior and J. S. Mill onwards" had made pronouncement "that the science of economics should be concerned only with what is and not what ought to be . . ." [51] By the turn of the century the relationship between economics and ethics had become a lively topic for discussion in the German literature. Heated controversy over the place of the *Werturteil* (value judgment) in economics culminated, at the famous Vienna meeting in 1909 of the Verein für Sozialpolitik, in what Schumpeter describes as almost amounting to a row.[52] It was at this time that Max Weber was vigorously campaigning for professional and academic *Wertfreiheit* in the social sciences. What Robbins injected into this time-honored issue was the claim to have demonstrated that such ethical neutrality on the part of the economist follows with rigorous necessity from the very definition of an economic problem.

Previously, the question of freedom from judgments of value

on the part of the economist had been debated chiefly from considerations of scientific propriety. Weber had devoted great pains to demonstrating that investigation into the "cultural sciences" is not incompatible with an attitude of detachment. Now Robbins had attempted to make it clear that ethical considerations can, by definition, in no way affect the economic aspect of affairs. The economic point of view is concerned with a concept of the act in which the ends of action have been previously determined and for the duration of which those ends are not permitted to change. The content of these ends is completely irrelevant to the economic aspect of the act and hence to economic analysis. Introduction of judgments of value into the consideration of the economic consequences of action thus constitutes deliberate transgression of the proper scope of economic inquiry.

In Robbins' exposition, this point of view found its expression in the emphasis on the distinction between "positive" studies, on the one hand, and "normative" studies, on the other.[53] Between these two fields of enquiry Robbins saw a "logical gulf," and it is this unbridgeable chasm that separates economics from ethics. The two fields of study are "not on the same plane of discourse." "Propositions involving the verb 'ought' are different in kind from propositions involving the verb 'is.'" "Economics deals with ascertainable facts; ethics with valuations and obligations." [54]

Several years before the publication of his *Nature and Significance of Economic Science,* Professor Robbins, in objecting to Hawtrey's postulation of the ethical character of economic propositions, had been able to declare that Hawtrey's position was contrary to the general agreement of economists.[55] However, Robbins' more extended discussion in his *Nature and Significance* and especially his postulation of the gulf between the positive and the normative met with far from general agreement. Two streams of sharp dissent may be distinguished in the subsequent literature. The one group of critics, with Souter, denied the validity of Robbins' positive-normative dichotomy on the ground that it is a part of a wholly unacceptable view of the nature of economic activity and economic science. Their condemnation of this distinction followed consistently from fundamental disagreement with Robbins' principal theses. On the other hand, several writers, with Macfie, have built solidly on the general framework constructed by Robbins, but have reached conclusions on the possibility of a normative economics that are sharply at variance with those developed by Robbins himself.[56]

Souter's' rejection of Robbins' characterization of economics as a "positive" science is closely connected with his previously cited condemnations of Robbins' entire position as "positivist." The treatment of the ends of action as abstract might indeed justify a distinction between two levels of inquiry: one concerned with the concrete ends of action taken as the "norms," and the other wtih the "positive" disposition of means with regard to these ends considered in the abstract. But the norms themselves may be studied quite as "positively." The rules of logic, for example, offer a field of study altogether as "positive" as does the "psychology of reasoning," even though the former deals with how we "ought" to reason (with truth as our norm), and the latter with how we do.[57] The distinction between positive and normative levels of discourse is thus seen to be only a relative one, not at all necessarily warranting the withholding of the name "science" from normative disciplines.[58] Moreover, as we have seen, Parsons forcefully pointed out that Robbins' conception of a positive end in the abstract, free of any normative tinge, contradicts the very nature of an end, which necessarily involves the notions of effort and purpose. While the circumstance that men do *try* to economize *can* be described and analyzed in "positive" terms by abstracting from the normative aspect of action, such an abstraction must necessarily pass over the essential quality of purposive action.[59]

The Souter-Parsons critique of Robbins' dichotomy and especially of its application to problems of economy thus has its source in a fundamental disagreement with the conceptual framework into which Robbins has fitted the economic act. Of quite a different character is the position taken up by Macfie with regard to the possibility of a "normative" economics. Macfie vigorously pursues his theme, which leads him to the conviction "that economics is fundamentally a normative science, not merely a positive science like chemistry." [60] But Macfie arrives at this conclusion, diametrically opposed to that of Robbins, by enthusiastically accepting Robbins' general framework and building solidly upon it as the foundation for his own position. In acknowledging his indebtedness to the work of Robbins, Macfie expresses the belief that Robbins' essay is final, "within its chosen scope." Macfie's own contribution he regards as a "superstructure" erected on it.[61]

But the superstructure that Macfie has erected would turn the concept of economy and the entire science of economics in a direction completely different from that envisaged by Robbins. Macfie accepts the analysis of economic action as the allocation of means with regard to given alternative ends. He endorses with fervor the rejection of the view linking the concept of economy with specific types of ends. He, too, relies heavily on the notion of economy as an aspect of *all* kinds of human endeavor. Although Macfie stresses the purposive character of human action far more than Robbins does, he too stresses the essential homogeneity of the economic element in action regardless of the particular type of motivation involved. Where he parts company with Robbins and attempts to embark on the construction of his own "superstructure" is in his elevation of the idea of "economy" into a "value" in its own right.[62]

With earlier writers the concept of economy was treated simply as the neutral expression of the concrete purposes of action. Where given ends were the motives of human endeavor, the desire to encompass these ends in the face of inadequate resources enforced the application of "economy," of careful comparison of ends and means, simply in order to fulfil the given goals of endeavor as completely as circumstances would permit. The practice of economy fulfilled only the originally selected goals of action; the content of these goals having been selected *before* the economic act, analysis of such an economic act could be "positive," i.e., unconcerned with the nature of the ends of action.

What Macfie introduced into this schema was the idea that, with given competing ends of action and with scarce resources, economy is enforced on the economic agent as an end and final value in itself. By acting rationally to achieve the optimum satisfaction of his previously selected desires, economic man is realizing a reasonable objective. "And the realisation of an objective which is reasonable is in some sense good in itself." [63] The principle "that scarce means should not be wasted, or should be used to the best advantage" is seen as a universal human value that fundamentally affects all kinds of endeavor, whether singing, writing, or activity in the market. If this view of the nature of economy is accepted, then the economic act becomes immediately more than merely the allocation of limited means in order to achieve specific competing ends. Economy, the fitting of scarce means to ends, is imposed not merely by force of the originally selected ends, but "under the persuasiveness of a value, to maximize total satisfactions." Economics does not "just accept human desires, and give them back unchanged. The principle of economy itself transmutes them through its criticism." The choice that emerges from subjecting competing desires to judgment in terms of the value, economy, is something quite different from the originally selected ends. Ends cannot remain "constant" throughout economic action because such action in itself injects a new "end" into the system of the agent's desired ends.[64]

Economics as Macfie conceives it thus emerges as an essentially normative discipline, analyzing the impact on numerous desired ends of a new end, viz., the value, economy, which is introduced through the presence of scarcity. This view has found favor with Professor Knight,[65] among recent writers, but the basic thesis is not new. Macfie's value, economy, is strikingly reminiscent of Veblen's "instinct for workmanship." In Veblen's view there is in the human character "a taste for effective work and a distaste for futile effort . . . a sense of the merit of serviceability or efficiency and of the demerit of futility, waste, or incapacity . . ." [66] Man is "possessed of a discriminating sense of purpose, by force of which all futility of life or of action is distasteful to him . . . It is not a proclivity to effort, but to achievement—to the encompassing of an end. . . . Within the purview of economic theory, the last analysis of any given phenomenon must run back to this ubiquitous human impulse to do the next thing." [67] In this discussion of what he calls the "pervading norm of action," Veblen, in what, coming from his pen, must be considered a remarkable passage, is clearly covering the same ground as Macfie.

The Nature of Economic Science and the Significance of Macroeconomics

In a chapter devoted to the discussion of Professor Robbins' definition of economic science, attention must be paid to the complaint that his formulation excludes from the subject the entire field of the "consideration of the general level of economic activity." [68] In an era in which investigation into the causes of general unemployment of resources has assumed the most prominent place in the work of economic theorists and policy-makers, such a complaint, if well founded, would be a serious limitation on the practical usefulness of Robbins' definition.

The point at issue has been raised by several writers. Robbins' definition is predicated on the necessity, imposed by the scarcity of resources, to economize in order to satisfy most fully alternative human wants. The concept of economy depends on the necessity of comparing alternative ends. This is so because the allocation of resources for any one selected end involves the necessary withdrawal of these resources from possible allocation to another, alternative end. Where, for example in the case of a resource that is a free good, the devotion of the resource to a particular use does *not* require its withdrawal from an alternative use, no economy is called for and no concept of economic "efficiency" can be applied. What critics of Professor Robbins have pointed out is that the same absence of "economy" that characterizes the use of a free good may quite as certainly characterize the use of a "scarce" resource if there is, for any reason, a demand insufficient to bring the resource into employment. "Efficiency in the use of underemployed scarce resources is as irrelevant as it is in the administration of free resources . . ." [69] "The problem of utilizing these [i.e., idle] resources fully is not a matter of deciding whether they should be devoted to use A or use B, but of how they can be used at all." [70]

Parallel to the use of this criticism to deny altogether the adequacy of Robbins' definition of economics is the view that the prevalence of idle resources renders inapplicable the conventional economic analysis of which Professor Robbins' formulation is the (correct) definition. It cannot be too strongly emphasized, Barbara Wootton has declared, that the absence of scarcity (through underemployment) of resources "renders inoperative, irrelevant and unreal the *whole* corpus of economic studies as defined by Professor Robbins and as embodied in the classical analysis and its contemporary elaborations and refinements." [71]

The question that is here being raised relates, of course, to the impact that the demand for the reconstruction of economics implicit in Keynes' *General Theory* must have on the conception of the very nature of economic analysis. On the basis of the "classical" concept of the economy, according to which the idleness of resources could be only a temporary phenomenon of disequilibrium, economic science as defined by Professor Robbins could adequately analyze the economic problems of the real world. In the real world the use of a resource for any one purpose does, in fact, mean its withdrawal from some alternative purpose. But the economics that Barbara Wootton has in mind takes serious account of the Keynesian proposition that resources may be unemployed for reasons other than the fact that too much is asked for their use. This would certainly undermine the whole assumption of scarcity [72] and cast a definite shadow on Professor Robbins' definition of economics. It would be inconvenient indeed if the validity of a definition of economics were to be made dependent on the particular view taken of a proposition advanced by an economic theorist, no matter how controversial that proposition might be.

The identification of Robbins' conception of the nature of economic science with "classical" economics and its assumption of full employment must be considered, moreover, from yet another angle. As expounded by Robbins, the analysis of economic affairs proceeds exclusively from the consideration of economizing by individuals. A problem is economic because it involves the necessity for an individual to reconcile his numerous desires with the limited resources available to him. A social problem has an economic aspect only in so far as it affects the conditions in the light of which individuals are constrained to economize. The consideration of the general level of economic activity and the degree of employment of a nation's resources would thus be excluded by definition from an individualistic ends-means economics. Economics, as Professor Robbins conceives it, must, it would seem, remain exclusively a microeconomics.

Despite these misgivings concerning the problems falling within the scope of Robbins' conception of economics, it has been shown by Rivett that it is quite sufficiently elastic to embrace the problems of idle resources. In the relevant sense, it is pointed out, unemployed resources *are* scarce. While they may be abundant in relation to effective demand, they are most certainly scarce relatively to desire. The doctrine that a deficiency in the effective demand for services is a result of a lack of purchasing power associated with *low* prices for that factor of production does not necessarily deny that idleness would be removed by sufficiently low prices. "If labor were not scarce relative to demand and were expected never to be scarce again, wages would be nil and . . . all labor would soon be employed." [73]

The point is, of course, that it is precisely from the perspective of microeconomics that problems of unemployed resources are most obviously seen to be economic problems in Robbins' sense. If it is an economic problem whether to devote resources to use A or to use B, this is not because the uses A and B are valued, but because they are *differently* valued. Where the problem is how idle resources can be utilized, not for one or another use, but *at all*, then society is facing the tragedy of total waste of the means that could be applied to secure desired ends. What seems a resource robbed of its scarcity is clearly a valuable means, which, instead of being allocated to the most prized purpose, has been allocated by a breakdown in the economic system to no end at all. From the point of view of the ends of the members of society, a resource involuntarily idle represents, not a quasi-free good, but scarce means unprofitably withdrawn from a potentially fully-employed economy.

The determination of the circumstances tending to bring about the tragic misallocation (or rather nonallocation) of precious resources must, of course, be one of the principal tasks of a discipline dealing with the way in which the members of society, through the division of labor, concertedly economize the resources at their disposal, with respect to their desired ends.

7

Economics as a Science of Human Action

We must regard industrial and commercial life, not as a separate and detached region of activity, but as an organic part of our whole personal and social life; and we shall find the clue to the conduct of men in their commercial relations, not in the first instance amongst those characteristics wherein our pursuit of industrial objects differs from our pursuit of pleasure or of learning, or our efforts for some political and social ideal, but rather amongst those underlying principles of conduct and selection wherein they all resemble each other . . .

Philip H. Wicksteed

The whole subject matter of conduct . . . constitutes a different realm of reality from the external world . . .

The first fact to be recorded is that this realm of reality exists or "is there." This fact cannot be proved or argued or "tested." If anyone denies that men have interests or that "we" have a considerable amount of valid knowledge about them, economics and all its works will simply be to such a person what the world of color is to the blind man. But there would still be one difference: a man who is physically, ocularly blind may still be rated of normal intelligence and in his right mind.

Frank H. Knight

Thus far we have given an account of a number of different conceptions of economic science, each of which reflects a fundamentally distinct understanding of what is to be meant by the economic point of view. In the present chapter we bring our survey to a close with an exposition of yet another conception of the point of view taken by the economist. In its completest form this definition of economics, by virtue of which the discipline emerges as one of the group of *sciences of human action,* embraces an entire and unique epistemology of the branches of knowledge commonly subsumed under the cultural and social sciences. As such, the view of economics as a science of human action deserves a close and full discussion in its own right, together with a clear exposition of its points of contact, both of agreement and of conflict, with the views treated in previous chapters.

Such a discussion is all the more in order since it has been long overdue in the methodological literature on economics. The concept of a science of human action, or, to use the term applied by Professor Mises, the *praxeological* view of economics,[1] has been singularly unsuccessful in gaining the degree of attention that, in its significance for economic methodology, it unquestionably deserves. Although isolated aspects of the praxeological point of view have been perfunctorily treated in the literature, little attempt has been made to understand them as integral parts of a complete epistemological system of the social sciences. The result has been a tendency to replace the system as a whole, in the public view, with specific controversial propositions concerning such concepts as apriorism, rationality, and the like. Taken out of context and discussed against the background of radically different epistemological ideas, these propositions could rarely command the serious consideration to which they were entitled. Especially unfortunate has been the consequence that the praxeological view has come to be even more profoundly neglected.

It is therefore the task of the present chapter to outline in some detail the conception of the nature of economic science as viewed from the perspective of praxeology. In addition, an attempt will be made to relate this view to several of the alternative definitions treated in earlier chapters. In particular, its points of contact with that discussed in the previous chapter will require careful examination. It will be shown that, side by side with the emergence of the view of economics as the science concerned with the allocation of scarce means, which culminated in the work of Professor Robbins, there has, for over sixty years, existed a stream of thought that has recognized the praxeological aspect of economics. The view of economics as concerned with scarce means will be seen to take its place naturally as an example of a limited application of praxeological ideas; many of its apparent inadequacies are seen to disappear when it is related explicitly to the broader concepts of a general theory of human action.

Coming at the end of a book setting forth a series of widely diverging views on the nature of the economic in human affairs, the subject of the present chapter throws a revealing light on the sources of this remarkable range of disagreement. The exposition of the praxeological element in social phenomena will help to explain why it so long succeeded in eluding the attention of so many brilliant thinkers. The recurrent and unfortunate identification of this economic aspect with so many of the actual facets of social history with which the praxeological element is intimately connected will gain in intelligibility, it is believed, by an understanding of the nature of social phenomena as viewed from the vantage point of praxeology itself.

I

The Sciences of Human Action

The description of economics as a praxeological science must necessarily be preceded by a rather detailed exposition of the praxeological point of view in general. This will readily be seen to embrace a far wider range of phenomena than is considered in conventional economics. At this point it is sufficient that the praxeological view sees economic affairs as distinguished solely by the fact that they belong to the larger body of phenomena that have their source in *human actions*. The core of the concept of human action is to be found in the unique property possessed by human beings of engaging in operations designed to attain a state of affairs that is preferred to that which has hitherto prevailed. A person perceives the possibility of an improvement in his position, perhaps through possession of an additional commodity, perhaps by the abandonment of an unwanted piece of property, by a change in physical location, or through some other alteration in the configuration of matters that might affect his sense of well-being. The recognition of any such opportunity for improving his well-being sets in motion the actions that the person will take to secure the improvement. The pattern of action taken will be broadly defined by the circumstances surrounding the desired alteration of affairs. Sound logic will, in a given situation, point to one or several courses of action that give promise of most successfully securing the desired change. In so far as human behavior is guided by logic, then, conduct will follow a path that has been selected by *reason*. This path of conduct is what is known praxeologically as *human action*.

The concrete forms that human action may take are as innumerable as are the ways in which men can achieve relief from states of relative dissatisfaction. The particular form that an individual human action takes is determined by factors that include those making up the specific environmental conditions as well as those that have shaped the character and values of the actor. The conception of sciences of human action recognizes that the form of action as it unfolds in its historical reality is the result of influences that range from the physiological to the religious, the social to the geographical. An explanation of human action can be adequately undertaken only with full awareness of these varied influences. The historian seeking to understand what men have done in particular instances must draw on the disciplines whose task it is to explain the sequences of cause and effect in the physical, physiological, or psychological influences upon action.

The contribution that the praxeological point of view has made to the scientific explication of action in history is the isolation of an element in action the explanation of which is not exhausted by even the most complete application of the sciences concerned with the concrete manifestations of human action. This residual element is that of the operation of human action itself, which neither is explained by physical, physiological, or psychological theories nor requires the assistance of these doctrines for its own exposition. A praxeological science, using the rationality of human action as its foundation, is able to derive theorems describing the path of action under given circumstances. The reasoning that constructs these theorems mirrors the reasoning that is implied in action itself. New links in the chain of knowledge, in the form of praxeological theorems, are forged from the constraint that human purposefulness imposes on action, namely, that it be taken only with the sanction of reason.

Given all the physical, physiological, and psychological influences on the setting of an action, action of a specific form might be predicted with assurance. But such prediction is conceivable, not because these influences *in themselves* determine action, but because action is subject to the mandate of reason, which guides the act into the path that is to be preferred among those indicated by these external influences. A complete knowledge on the part of an observer of these external influences might allow prediction of the form to be taken by action only because the logic of the observer enables him to know with certainty the path that the actor's own logic will select. When a man is about to perform a mathematical computation upon given data, an observer of the data may attempt to predict the results that the computer will arrive at. But for such a prediction to be successful, it is not sufficient to rely on the fact that these results are "determined" by the data; it is necessary that the observer with his own logic be able to reproduce mentally the logical operations performed by the computer in arriving at his results. There is, of course, a definite meaning to the statement that the results of a mathematical computation are determined by the relevant data. An attempt at the computation by a human mathematician, however, yields these "determined" results only in so far as his logic constrains him to conform to the objectively correct computational operations. The case with human action in general is rather closely analogous to this example.

At the root of the notion of human action is the simple assumption that human reason plays a role in every action. Although, of course, by no means universally acceptable, this assumption remains a simple, and at least superficially, plausible one. No matter how compelling the physiological or physical factors that crave action may seem, it is within the power of reason to resist them. No matter how strong the psychological pressures on man may be, his actions have necessarily passed the scrutiny and gained at least the tacit assent of his reason. These pressures may well be overwhelmingly powerful, and, of course, in sanctioning or prohibiting action, men's reason is operating with the consciousness of these imperious, often contradictory forces. The concept of human action depends, however, on the introspectively valid fact that there is a form of conduct that is specifically human, i.e., conduct that is accompanied by the consciousness of volition, of something more than a bundle of reflexes responding to specific stimuli. The nature of these various stimuli and the directions towards which they variously tend to guide action are completely independent of the desires and will of the actor. As such they are part of the subject matters of the physical, physiological, and psychological sciences. Were action taken simply in instinctive obedience to these stimuli, it could be conceived as objectively determined by the data constituting its setting, in the same way as the results of a mathematical computation are determined by the data of the problem. But because man possesses the power to reject one course of action for another, to arrange the satisfaction to be derived from obeying specific impulses within a wider ordering of values, the physical, physiological, and psychological sciences do not exhaust the facts of action that are capable of scientific explanation. The element in conduct that is the reflection of man's power to weigh, arrange, and choose among courses of behavior is the specifically human element in action. The investigation of this element of human action and of its manifestation in various particular situations forms a field of study unique by virtue of the nature of human action itself. Sciences of human action will be distinct from other sciences in that the former begin where the latter end, viz., in the implications of the rationality that governs purposeful behavior.

The Emergence of the Praxeological View of Economics

Postponing for subsequent discussion the further details of the praxeological view and the consideration of the controversial points involved in it, we shall proceed to outline the development, during the past three quarters of a century, of the stream of thought to be regarded as the praxeological view of economic science. Since its emergence, the praxeological point of view has been most fruitful, not in the extensive exploration of new sciences of human action, but in the consequences of its recognizing the theorems of economics as being the propositions of a science of human action. The possibility of theoretical statements concerning economic activity was seen as not at all due to any supposed uniqueness in the phenomena of wealth or material welfare or money or any of the other numerous criteria that had been used in defining economics. It was perceived that economic theory derives from precisely that element in human behavior which we have described as human action. The particular forms of action that have been traditionally investigated by economists are, indeed, distinguished by close association with various institutions such as money or with specific patterns of action such as interpersonal exchange. But if there is any meaningful underlying unity in the theorems of economics, it is to be found only in the concept of human action. Seen from this vantage point, economic theory acquires immediately a position unique within the range of human knowledge. It is the discipline that has alone successfully sought to harness the element of human action to the scientific explanation of social phenomena.

The earliest formulations of the praxeological view of economics in anything approaching a complete statement appeared about the turn of the century. Before this there had been several penetrating attempts to elucidate the nature of economic science. Several of these, especially those seeking to distinguish a specifically "economic principle" in action, have been cited in earlier chapters. But the uniqueness of human action as seen by praxeology, that is, as making possible a characteristically distinct contribution to the understanding of social phenomena, had not been expounded. Aside from isolated statements by several writers, who seem to have caught a glimpse of such a possibility,[2] it was not until the nineties that economics was clearly identified with the logic of conscious choice.

Perhaps the first discussion of the role of economics as a science of human action in this praxeological sense is that of an American, Sidney Sherwood. Writing in 1897 on the "philosophical basis of economics," [3] Sherwood declared that a general science dealing with "consciousness in action," a "science of practical life," was the intellectual necessity of the time. Hitherto special disciplines such as history, law, politics, and sociology had groped forward in this direction. But a "master science" was required to give a common starting point and method to these special inquiries. Such a science "must explain all the conscious activities of men by reducing them to terms of the motives and choices of the individual consciousness." To Sherwood it seemed that economics is the science outstandingly fitted to play this role. "Economics deals with wants consciously felt, resources consciously perceived, and consciously directed to the end of gaining conscious satisfaction . . ." Any restriction of economic reasoning to the sphere of material goods is completely artificial. It seemed "inevitable" to Sherwood that economics must ultimately include all human values. "All pleasures, all values, all choices, all teleological activities, are, in fact, chosen and followed upon principles which economics alone has explained in a scientific manner."

All human self-directed conduct, Sherwood pointed out, proceeds from choices that are simply the valuations of certain courses of action. The motive power in the practical activities of man is to be found in his consciously felt desires. Sherwood sharply criticized the temptation, to which several sociologists of the period had succumbed, of applying physical and biological concepts to psychical phenomena. The fitness that survives, according to the biological notion of evolution, is an unforeseen fitness, an adjustment wrought out in consequence of the struggle. But psychical activities are essentially purposeful; the fitness that survives in social adjustments is prearranged. Sociologists are guilty of unscientific procedure when they group the phenomena of economic adjustments together with those of unexplained and fortuitous biological change.[4]

Sherwood's perception of the nature of human action and of the praxeological character of economics is unmistakably clear. The adjective "conscious," which he constantly uses to describe the types of conduct dealt with by economics, and his explicit relation of such conduct to human *motives* identify the "master science" for which Sherwood is searching as an all-embracing praxeology. That Sherwood's definition of economics represents, in this respect, an advance over that of his contemporaries becomes apparent from the originality of his attitude towards the use of the "economic principle" as the defining criterion. It was seen in an earlier chapter that several writers, such as Dietzel and Neumann in Germany and Hawley in the United States, had been deterred from using the economic principle as a criterion for defining economics on the very grounds that make the principal significant, namely, that it characterizes *all* kinds of human activity. These writers recognized the importance to economics of the rational element in economic activity; indeed, this element played so obvious and dominant a role in economic analysis that, as the "economic principle," it suggested itself to them as the natural mark identifying the phenomena with which the discipline dealt. This suggestion they found themselves forced to reject on the ground that *all* human activity displays the very same hallmark of rationality, that the economic principle governs *all* the conscious activities of man. And this left them no choice but to seek for some other quality in economic phenomena that they, among all other social phenomena, might uniquely possess in common.

Sherwood, starting from a position substantially similar to that of these writers, was able to reach a quite different conclusion. Once it had been suggested that economic phenomena are susceptible of analysis by virtue of their rational quality, Sherwood found it impossible to discard this idea. Instead of being dismayed at finding a similar purposefulness, a similar rationality and adherence to the economic principle, throughout the range of human activities, Sherwood was awakened thereby to a new appreciation of the role of economics. Instead of impelling him to look for other characteristics by which to delineate the scope of economic science, the realization of the all-pervasive influence of the economic principle convinced Sherwood of the futility and artificiality of erecting rigid boundaries purporting to separate economic activity from human action generally. The conscious direction of resources to the end of gaining conscious satisfaction was so fundamental to the very conception of economics and was at the same time so obviously a factor decisive in all action, that Sherwood could see economics transformed into a spearhead of a new "master science" that might investigate the consequences in activity generally of the consciously motivated element in action. Hitherto economics had been confined, to be sure, to specific kinds of phenomena, but this restriction was an artificial one and in no way corresponded to a unique field of knowledge.

This statement of the nature of economics seems to have passed unnoticed in the literature. Happily, similar ideas were being formulated at about the very same time by the celebrated Italian philosopher, Benedetto Croce. His views were set down with rather greater painstaking precision and expounded against the background of a fully articulated general philosophical and epistemological system. As such, Croce's position has attracted the attention of a number of subsequent writers. It has not always been appreciated, however, how closely Croce's view of economics mirrors the praxeological outlook. This feature of Croce's ideas on the nature of economy and economics is brought clearly into focus by their juxtaposition with the radically different views of Pareto, with whom Croce conducted an elaborate exchange of opinions on the subject. A brief review of Croce's opinions as expressed in this published correspondence will at the same time provide a remarkably clear, if not complete, statement of the view of economics as a science of human action.

The root of the difference between the outlook of Croce and that of Pareto, and the source of their celebrated debate on the nature of economics, is to be found in their attitudes towards *teleology*. According to Pareto, the act is a subject for science only in so far as it yields "facts and concrete cases." According to Croce, on the other hand, the act is aimed at a purpose, and economics obtains its distinctiveness and its homogeneity from this characteristic of the act itself. Croce's crusade against the behaviorism of Pareto [5] took the form of a vigorous rebellion against the latter's injunction to economists to confine their attention to the "result of action" and to leave the "nature" of action for the metaphysicians.[6]

Pareto's position, Croce complains, itself involves an implicit metaphysical postulate. It is implied that the facts of man's activity are of the same nature as physical facts; that in both cases regularities can be observed and consequences can be thereby deduced, but that the "inner nature of the facts" can never be exposed.[7] Upon the testimony of experience, however, Croce insists on the fundamental distinction between the physical and the mental, between mechanics and teleology, between passivity and activity. From this point of view, it is of the utmost relevance (Pareto's statements to the contrary notwithstanding) to recognize that the choice with which economics is concerned is not simply "the fact of choice," but the fact of *conscious* choice. And because the economic fact is a fact of conscious choice, a fact of will, its "inner nature" is not at all obscure. The nature of economic activity is grasped as immediately as is the nature of the operation of willing. An act is economic in so far as it is the consistent expression of a man's will, of his conscious aiming at a perceived goal.[8]

From Croce's position on the nature of economic activity flows immediately his praxeological conception of economic science. The purposefulness of human action—a category to which nothing in physical science corresponds—is the unique element that invests economic science with its individuality. The propositions of economics relate to the effective execution of the purposes willed by the actor. They are not descriptions, but *theorems* in the sense that they follow rigorously and necessarily from the postulated systems of ends and means. "Economic Science . . . is a mathematic applied to the concept of human action . . . It does not inquire what human action is; but having posited certain concepts of action, it creates formulae for the prompt recognition of the necessary connections." [9]

Croce's ideas will have been perhaps more fully set forth when we shall have considered his contributions to several points of detail in the praxeological conception of economics. Although his stature as a thinker drew more academic attention to these ideas than had been given to those of Sherwood, Croce's impact on the development of economic methodology has to this day not reached its full potential. Writings during the last half century on the proper conception of economic science could in many instances have greatly benefited from familiarity with Croce's work in this field. One author whose writings do deserve a place in any discussion of the evolution of praxeological ideas, although his contribution in this respect scarcely approaches that of Croce, is Max Weber.

Max Weber and Human Action

The great sociologist's views on the nature of economics and, in particular, the significance of his ideas for the development of praxeology are closely related to his views on the social sciences in general. These in turn revolve around the concept of *Verstehen,* which is the epistemological tool that Weber used to distinguish the *Geisteswissenschaften* from the natural sciences. It is of some interest to compare Weber's way of achieving this distinction with the method used by Croce.

Like Croce, Weber sees *purpose* as the most conspicuous feature in action, and, because it is the foundation for the notion of *Verstehen,* as the source of the possibility of separating the social from the physical sciences. A motive is "a meaningful complex . . . which appears to the actor himself or the observer to be an adequate . . . ground for his attitudes or acts." The significance of purpose in the scientific analysis of action is its introduction of a new notion of causality. It permits the grasping of the cause of an action through the understanding (*Verstehen*) of its motive. A correct causal interpretation of concrete action implies that "the outward course and the motive are each correctly grasped and that their relationship to each other is 'understandable.' " [10] And it is the possibility of making this kind of statement regarding the causation of a phenomenon of interest to the *Geisteswissenschaften* that marks these disciplines as distinct from the physical sciences. In the latter, events can be only "externally" observed, while the teleological orientation of social phenomena permits their being grasped completely.

Economics, like *verstehende Soziologie* in general, becomes in this way, for Weber as for Croce, a science of human action. That which is understood is purposeful human *action*.[11] But it is here that Weber and Croce part company and that Weber's progress in praxeological thought becomes diverted. Croce had not understood the economic aspect of human action to consist merely in the simple fact that action is aimed at a purpose. In perceiving the economic aspect, Croce recognized the constraint that purposefulness imposes on action, i.e., that action actually tend to achieve the purposes that serve as its inspiration. Economics, for Croce, is the science that investigates the extensive implications and consequences of precisely this tendency. But this aspect of purpose in action plays no role in Weber's conception of economic activity or of the nature of economic science. Weber's science takes notice of the teleological character of human action merely because this purposive feature opens a window on the "internal" nature of the act, not at all because it implies that the action is constrained to follow a specific path. The fact that human actions are motivated is in itself sufficient only to invest them with the property of being "understood"; it is not sufficient to set up a category of "economy," still less to establish an economic science.

Weber, indeed, is able to extend the concept of *Verstehen* to grasp the behavior of the most unreasonable or emotional human beings. To approach the construction of an economic science, it is necessary first for Weber to introduce the notion of the "ideal type," i.e., the formulation of abstract, arbitrary models of acting man. Only one of Weber's four ideal types finds a place in his concept of economics. This is the ideal type of rational action, the model of a coldly calculating human being conscious of ends and means. Within the range of actions that can be intuitively grasped because of their motivations there exist patterns of action that are distinguished in that they are in fact suited to the attainment of the chosen goals. Among these patterns are to be found the materials to be studied by the economist as Weber conceives him.

The necessity that Weber felt of introducing rationality into economic activity as a specific assumption limiting the general concept of human action reveals the limited extent to which he appreciated the praxeological content of action. For Weber, the common denominator of all human actions that are "understandable" is not their conformity to a rational pattern of utilizing given means towards a desired end, but simply their conscious "direction" towards an end as such. We can understand an action, not necessarily because we ourselves would, under similar circumstances, act likewise, but because we can sense and appreciate the possibility that such an action could be induced by the agent's mental posture of desire towards the end. For Weber, there is no presumption that the action so induced will at all hasten the attainment of the end concerned. A man seeking a desired object may, in his anger at being thwarted, or in the excitement of pursuit, act in a manner that, in the judgment of both the cool observer and subsequent history, is supremely capable of frustrating the attainment of the sought-for end. Such a conception of action is, of course, incapable in itself of serving as a foundation for economic science. Only by imposing an artificial abstraction of the ideal type is Weber able to reach economics. And it is apparent that when conformity to an ideal type must be assumed for the deduction of the propositions of economics, these propositions cease to be the logical implications of human action, and economics ceases to be a branch of praxeology.[12]

Acting Man and Economizing Man: Mises and Robbins

In the decades following the age of Weber, praxeological ideas developed in two directions, yielding two related, but significantly distinct, conceptions of economic science. On the one hand, there developed, partly under the influence of Max Weber, the conception of economics that has been treated in the previous chapter. Here the ends-means dichotomy came to serve as the framework for the construction of an economic science that took as its foundation the idea of *economizing*. The previous chapter has described the culmination of this stream of thought in the work of Professor Robbins. This must now be clearly related to another direction of praxeological thought, to the influence of which, indeed, the development of the first must in some degree be ascribed.

This second line of praxeological thought has been led by the work of Professor Mises. It is in this direction that we find the most complete and consistent development of the praxeological concept, and it is this development that the present chapter set out to describe. Mises' explicit enunciation of the character of economics as a science of human action, the most highly developed of the potential praxeological disciplines, represents one of his most seminal and original ideas. It may be reasonably asserted that most, perhaps all, of Mises' characteristic contributions to the various branches of economic theory are, in his eyes, simply the consistently worked out corollaries of this fundamental thesis concerning the nature of economics.[13] If economic theory, as the science of human action, has become a *system* at the hands of Mises, it is so because his grasp of its praxeological character imposes on its propositions an epistemological rationale that in itself creates this systematic unity. It is unfortunate, but not difficult to understand, that disagreement with some of Professor Mises' economic theories on the part of his critics has induced in them a tendency to ignore, if not to disparage, the epistemological basis from which Mises' conclusions seem to follow so rigorously. The truth is that the comprehension of economics as a science of human action provides a basis broad enough to support widely diverging conclusions. The validity of the praxeological approach must be tested on its own merits and by its internal epistemological adequacy.

Although praxeological ideas already appear in germinal form in Mises' first book, *The Theory of Money and Credit* (1912), it was not until the twenties that they became explicitly formulated. By the early thirties Mises' ideas on the nature and scope of economics had reached their full development,[14] and some of these ideas attracted the attention of writers on the methodology of economics in ,a number of countries.[15] The works in which Professor Mises has most fully presented the case for praxeology are his *Grundprobleme der Nationalökonomie* (1933), *National-ökonomie* (1940), and its English counterpart *Human Action* (1949). A vigorous restatement of the position of the sciences of human action and a spirited defense of their epistemological assumptions are to be found in Mises' recently published *Theory and History* (1957).

In comparing the two views of economics represented by the works of Mises and Robbins, it is necessary to notice carefully their points of similarity and to observe even more carefully the degree to which they differ from one another. Writers have tended to group Mises and Robbins together as continuators of Weber in their stress on the ends-means dichotomy and its importance for economic activity.[16] But the two views place economic science in two quite distinct positions.

Economizing consists in the allocation of scarce resources among competing ends. Acting, in the praxeological sense, consists in selecting a pattern of behavior designed to further the actor's purposes. Of course, the particular allocation that, in any given situation, will be made of scarce means in respect of different ends will constitute a course of action, a pattern of conduct designed to further the achievement of as many of those goals (in their preferred order) as possible. But the concept of action is wider and at the same time more fundamental than that of economizing. Although action may be described in terms of ends and means, such a description is quite different from that of an operation of economizing. In the concept of economy, ends and means constitute a scheme more or less artificially imposed on action so that the relative valuations of ends can be reflected in the specific pattern in which resources are allocated. The essential idea becomes, not the intent pursuit of a set purpose, but the almost mechanical translation of the scale of "ultimate" ends into appropriately apportioned shares at the level of means. "Means" are *required* for the notion of economy because they are the entities that must be "allocated"; it is in the *comparison* of different ways of utilizing resources that economizing finds its place.

With the broader notion of action, on the other hand, we are not primarily interested in the particular pattern in which resources will be apportioned among ends. Such an allocation, if carried out, will be of interest as one of the possible *implications* of action and will, of course, as such, find a place somewhere in the science of human action. But on the basis of Robbins' conception of the nature of economic science, economics can achieve homogeneity and individuality *only* by virtue of its concern with the existence of such operations of comparison and allocation of means. The praxeological approach, on the other hand, finds a basis for the homogeneity and individuality of economics at a deeper level, which does not necessarily require a clearly recognizable pattern of allocation. This basis is found in the fundamental characteristic of action, viz., that it is conduct directed at the achievement of a purpose.

In this characteristic, praxeology finds a sufficient source of explanation for the specific patterns of action, among which the judicious disposal of scarce means appears as a frequent example. But a really unique criterion for the definition of economics is not to be found in the idea of allocating scarce resources, nor can this concept serve as an adequate foundation on which that science can be constructed. The key point is not that acting man ponders the comparative efficacy in different uses of certain given "means," but that he behaves under a constraint that he himself has imposed, i.e., the necessity of acting in order to achieve what he wants to achieve, so that his behavior tends to conform to the pattern implied by his scale of ends. "Means" exist as such for acting man only *after* he has turned them to his purpose; acting is not apportioning, but *doing*—doing what seems likely to further one's purposes.

The remainder of this chapter, which attempts to set forth several details of the praxeological view and to consider various criticisms levelled against it, will serve at the same time as a commentary on the similarities and distinctions between an economics built around *homo agens* and one centered around economizing man.

II

Praxeology and Purpose

We shall begin the more detailed dissection of the category of human action and the discussion of its suitability to serve as the focus of the economic point of view with a survey of the role of *purpose* in action. It has already been noticed in this chapter that it is purpose that endows the behavior of men with the unique properties that praxeology finds in human action. The views of Croce and Weber have been cited in this connection as expressions of the discovery, in the act, of a phenomenon unlike anything coming within the range of observation of the physical sciences. Stones dislodged from a hillside by the elements and hurtling down on the unsuspecting traveller in the valley are part of a different "event" than stones hurled with intent by men waiting in ambush. The latter are hurled with purpose; they are—in this case literally—*aimed* by human beings. Stone-throwing by human beings is something that the scientist can in part "explain" by reference to an element not present in natural phenomena, viz., the conscious aim of the thrower. Praxeology takes this very element as its point of departure; it finds human actions amenable to analysis in that they bear the imprint of a constraint imposed by chosen goals.

Now, the recognition of purposefulness in economic activity did not begin with the emergence of praxeological ideas. It is, of course, true that the older conceptions of economic science, which saw it as concerned with an objective entity such as wealth or goods, did not require reference to the purposefulness of human action. The scope of their discipline was described completely by the character of the objects whose "laws" it investigated. But even here it was difficult to avoid the implication of purposefulness in men's attitude towards these objects. This implication was given tacit recognition in the substantive analysis that the classical economists employed, and it tended to be brought into the open in the more sophisticated of the classical attempts to define "wealth."

With the tendency, during the nineteenth century, to place man at the center of economics, the recognition of the role of purpose became almost a matter of course. Political economy was, in fact, the extended exposition of the consequences of one of man's many purposes, the acquisition of wealth. Discussions of the character that was thrust upon *homo oeconomicus* could hardly avoid the central fact of his purposefulness. Towards the close of the century economics came to be identified explicitly as a "teleological" discipline.[17] Wealth came to be endowed with a "teleological nature." Discussions of the assumption of rationality made by economists necessarily involved the notion of purposive behavior, of "ends" and "means," and consequently pointed to the distinction that this characteristic conferred on any human, as against physical, phenomena. The emergence, during the early decades of the present century, of the concept of *Verstehen* brought the teleological character of human action still further into the forefront.

However, it is of some importance to appreciate the quite different role that praxeology assigns to human purposefulness in economic activity from that assigned by other points of view. Wesley Mitchell could point out that economists cannot understand what men do if they treat them as molecules, leaving their purposes out of account. He and other economists could draw attention to the new element of causality introduced by teleology in human affairs. They could recognize a chain of cause and effect in which the usual temporal relation is reversed, the present being "caused" by the goals set up for the future.[18] But all this does not necessarily lead to a praxeological position. The economic point of view could be held to imply any arbitrary criterion that might be imagined, without in any way ruling out recognition of the causal element introduced by the teleological character of economic activity. Mitchell, for example, saw economic activity as essentially connected with phenomena of money. This

was perfectly consistent with his stress on the usefulness of referring to purpose in providing the economists with "explanations."
The phenomena of the real world are the products of a number
of diverse chains of causes and effects. The investigation of any
group of phenomena in the real world must take into account as
many such causal relations as possible. In the class of phenomena
constituted by "economic affairs," there exists a causal relation,
the consequence of human purposefulness, that is absent among
phenomena of the physical world. But no attempt need necessarily
be made to state explicitly the distinctive qualities of "economic
affairs" in terms of this purposefulness or of the causality to
which it is admitted to give rise.

The part played by purposefulness in the praxeological conception of economic activity is a far more important one. Purpose is not something to be merely "taken into account": it provides the sole foundation of the concept of human action. When
Engliš defined economics as a teleological discipline, he was
attempting to place his finger on the very nerve center of the
subject.[19] There is place for a distinct science of economics *only*
because the teleological quality of action makes possible a unique
kind of "explanation." The theorems of economics are derived
for praxeology exclusively on the basis of the purposefulness of
human behavior. Other determinants of behavior—heredity, environment, and the like—are on a completely different level of
"explanation"; as such, they belong to other disciplines; they have
no place in a "pure" economic science.

The crucial position that purpose fills in the praxeological system is intimately connected, of course, with the conception of
human action as rational. Rationality in human behavior consists, after all, in the consistent pursuit of one's own purposes; in
selecting the means that appear best adapted to the achievement
of one's goals; in refraining from courses of action that might frus-
trate their achievement or promise only the attainment of less
valued, at the expense of more highly prized, objectives. The
place of the rationality of action is sufficiently important for the
praxeological point of view to deserve separate discussion in a
subsequent section of this chapter. It is sufficient at this point, for

the appreciation of the praxeological importance of human purposefulness, to emphasize as much as possible that a concept of rationality exists for praxeology only as the expression of human purposes.[20]

Emphasis of this kind is called for, perhaps, in order to disassociate the praxeological approach from what may be called the "positivist" conception of rationality in human action. It was seen in the previous chapter that Professor Robbins has been charged with employing the ends-means dichotomy in too positivistic a fashion. An "end" in Robbins' scheme, it has been alleged, is set up by an external observer as something positive, as a "correlate of a tendency to conduct"; it is used by Robbins in a way that abstracts from the conscious aiming and striving that characterizes human actions *before* they have been completed. "Rationality" in the disposition of means with regard to such denatured ends becomes simply the mechanical ordering and sharing of resources according to a given pattern.

Without our entering here into a discussion concerning the justice of this objection to Robbins' system, it is worthwhile to make explicit the quite different kind of rationality that is central to the praxeological view. Action is not described as rational because it involves the automatic manipulation of resources into a pattern faithfully reflecting a given hierarchy of ends. Rationality consists rather in the transference, to conduct involving means, of those features in behavior that accompany the direct pursuit of ends. Rationality involves the conscious effort to make one's conduct conform to a given path; it calls for the same aiming and striving by the economic agent towards necessary intermediate goals as he displays towards the "final" goals themselves. It is only from the "outside" that such rationality can be described merely in terms of a particular pattern of resource allocation. The full praxeological grasp of human action perceives its rationality as completely pervaded by the "aiming" quality bestowed on action by its teleological character. This aspect of purpose leads, in fact, directly into the more detailed exposition of the praxeological view of rationality, which is the subject of the succeeding section.

Praxeology and Rationality

Few features of the praxeological position seem to have been more seriously misunderstood than the very special significance that it attaches to the rationality of human action. In the praxeological view, action is rational by definition; and this has been attacked from two directions. On the one hand, it has been branded as palpably false and contrary to the facts of experience.[21] On the other hand, it has been interpreted as a vicious misuse of language, in which the word "rational" has been emptied of all meaning, so that its use to describe action, while not false, conveys no information whatsoever. The insistent description of action as rational is thus a misleading attempt to appear to be saying something, without, in fact, doing anything of the sort.[22] To say that a man acts rationally, it is complained, tells us nothing more about what it is that he does than that he does it. Both these types of criticism rest on a quite incomplete appreciation of how the rationality of action is used in the praxeological system.

The concept of rationality in human behavior has long been a topic for discussion in the literature on the methodology of economics. Attacks on the undue reliance which economic theory has been accused of placing upon human reason are as old as attacks on the very notion of an economic theory. Historically-minded critics of theory long ago discovered that man is possessed of "instincts," that he is a creature of "habit," that he is capable of being carried away by mass hysteria and other psychological aberrations. Economic theory, it was found, had blindly ignored the realities of life. Where it had not explicitly endowed economic man with an exclusive thirst for "wealth" or with an utterly selfish character, economics had apparently proceeded on the quite gratuitous assumption that men behave sensibly from the point of view of their own interests. It was easy to demonstrate how far from the truth economics must be; it was easy to point out the true character of men with their full array of impulses, instincts, and stupidities. On the other hand, it was not difficult for economists to defend their theorems as hypothetical constructions with a definite, if limited, applicability to the real world, or, alternatively, as providing *norms* for the appraisal of actual performance. And debates on these lines abound in the economic journals of the decades around the turn of the century and later.

In all these discussions the assumption of rationality made by traditional economic theory was treated in a special sense; and what is chiefly responsible for the misunderstandings mentioned above is the confusion of this traditional conception of rationality with the conception of it employed in praxeological discussions. The point at issue in the earlier discussions concerning the empirical validity of economic theorems that treat men as reasoning beings free of irrational impulses and instincts was the fruitfulness of a particular simplifying abstraction. The social phenomena of the real world are the consequences of human actions in which all types of influences have played a part. One of these influences stems from man's reasoning powers, which urge him to pursue a selected goal with a steadfastness and tenacity unperturbed by human weaknesses and passions. Economic theory, it was believed, investigates social phenomena on the assumption that this influence of cool reason is, in fact, sufficiently powerful to make man pursue unwaveringly a goal once chosen. And this assumption, introduced in order to make analysis possible, was criticized or defended in respect to its justifiability, in the light of the realities of human nature.

It was quite natural for the conception of rationality that was made central to praxeological ideas to be discussed in a similar fashion. When these ideas are made to hinge on a conception of rationality as a pervasive quality of all human action, they of course invited criticism as being in contradiction to the facts. And when it is pointed out that in the sense in which the praxeological view sees human actions as rational, no such contradiction exists, then the praxeological postulate of rationality is criticized as a misleading and empty use of words. It is explained, for example, that a man who is swayed from the pursuit of his own best interests by falling prey to a fleeting temptation is yet acting "rationally" in the praxeological sense. In the praxeological view, the man has simply substituted a new set of ends, represented by the fleeting temptation, for the previously chosen ends. The fact that in the eyes of an outside observer, or even in the eyes of the man himself at a cooler moment, it is the original set of ends that constitutes the man's "best interests," is not sufficient to justify our labeling the man's pursuit of his newly selected goal as "irrational." The selection of an end can never, as such, be judged in regard to its rationality; and there is no reason to question the rationality with which the man pursues his newly chosen end.

It is this kind of explanation that provokes the annoyance of the critics and incurs the charge of using the word "rational" in a viciously misleading manner. These strictures are, in fact, quite undeserved; and it is worthwhile to devote attention to clearing up the confusion on this point. We can perhaps best succeed in this by considering in some detail the contribution of Tagliacozzo, mentioned in the previous chapter, to the clarification of the notion of "economic error" or "uneconomic behavior." Tagliacozzo deals with the "Rhine-wine" situation which had been involved in the Pareto-Croce correspondence cited earlier in this chapter at the turn of the century.

The "Rhine-wine" case concerned the man who does not wish to indulge in gluttony, who has in fact budgeted all his money for other, more highly valued purposes, but who, yielding to the temptation of the moment, buys and drinks Rhenish wine. Croce had written that by so acting the man has placed himself in contradiction with himself [23] and that his sensual pleasure will be followed by a judgment of reprobation, an *economic* (to be carefully distinguished from a moral) *remorse*.[24] The man is guilty of what Croce has elsewhere called "economic error": the "failure to aim directly at one's own object: to wish this and that, i.e., not really to wish either this or that." [25] By contrasting this concept of economic error, as an error of will, with a technical error, which is an error of knowledge, Croce was enabled to criticize Pareto's distinction between logical (i.e., rational) actions, which are economic, and illogical actions, which are not. Action, Croce explains, is a fact of will, not of knowledge. The will presupposes reasoning, it is true, but action, which is the expression of will, cannot itself be qualified by adjectives such as "logical" or "illogical," which pertain only to the application of reason.[26]

It was with this example of an economic error, the consumption of wine in defiance of a previously chosen program, that Tagliacozzo dealt at length. Tagliacozzo pointed out that the purchase of wine can be appraised from various vantage points. From the standpoint of full reality, no distinction between means and ends need be made at all. Wine has been purchased because such a purchase was desired, and that is all. There is no recognition of any "program" against which the man's action is to be compared and in terms of which it can incur disapproval or excite remorse. There is, consequently, no notion of an "end" separate from the means that might "bring about" the realization of the end.

From the point of view of the man's own budget plan, however, the case is very different. Here a yardstick has been set up by the man himself against which the "economic" correctness of his actions can be measured and found wanting. The artificial creation of a "plan" in the form of a prior selection of ends necessarily carries with it a "point of view" from which it is possible *to appraise* the wine purchase and to convict it of economic error.

Finally, the man's action can be contemplated with the realization that any one yardstick in the form of a program will necessarily be quite arbitrary; that the span of time over which such a "program" is to have validity may be as long or as short as we please. From this point of view it is clear that what is a "temptation" from the standpoint of a long-range program becomes itself an independent "program" in its own right in relation to a suitably brief span of time taken as a frame of reference. The consumption of wine has now become the desired end; the man's actions can still be appraised, but only for their consistency with *this* newly adopted "program."

The distinguishing of these possible attitudes towards the wine purchase and the recognition of the relativity of the notion of an economic error enable Tagliacozzo to pursue Croce's theme to its ultimate praxeological conclusion. In a real action, taken as an independent event, there is no room for any discrepancy between the conception of a program and its realization; the two concepts coincide completely. But this understanding of the situation does not at all exhaust its significance. Actions *can* be "judged" with regard to the faithfulness with which they conform to "programs." And there can exist a complete range of such "programs" against which any action may be appraised, depending on the particular frame of reference selected. The important fact is that the very conception of an economic "judgment" implies a particular *tendency* on the part of human beings such that deviation from it incurs (economic) "disapproval." This tendency is one that makes for an identity of means and end, comparable to the intrinsic coincidence of means and end that is present in any real action considered as an independent event with no frame of reference other than itself. It is this "tendency" that demands "that given programs be respected; that wine not be bought, if the program does not provide for such purchase; that given means go as far as they can in the fulfilment of the ends." [27]

Together with the consciousness of a chosen set of ends that comprise a program there is an inevitable consciousness of an inclination to reduce all the means and resources required for the attainment of the program to the same rank as the chosen purposes themselves. Failure to achieve such a complete coordination of ends and means, which spells susceptibility to the distractions of "temptations of the moment," can be sustained only at the expense of fighting free of this conscious inclination—a struggle that makes up the sense of economic error. Now in so far as all human action is teleological and is the expression of purposes consciously chosen, it is clear that *all* action must necessarily be part of the operation of the tendency toward the identification of means and end. The man who has cast aside a budget plan of long standing in order to indulge in the fleeting pleasure of wine still acts under a constraint to adapt the means to the new program. Should a fit of anger impel him to forgo this program as well and to hurl the glass of wine at the bartender's head, there will nonetheless be operative *some* constraint—let us say the control required to ensure an accurate aim—which prevents his action from being altogether rudderless. It is here that praxeology has grasped the possibility of a new scientific range of explanation of social phenomena. Precisely because man's actions are not haphazard, but are expressions of a necessity for bringing means into harmony with ends, there is room for explanation of the content of particular actions in terms of the relevant array of ends.[28]

During the course of this discussion of the nature of economic error, the sense in which praxeology sees human action as "rational" will have become abundantly clear. It will also have become clear how the praxeological use of the concept of rationality is quite unaffected by both types of criticisms that we noticed to have been levelled against it. Its description of all human action as rational constitutes a proposition that is, in fact, incapable of being falsified by any experience, yet does, nevertheless, convey highly valuable information. Action is necessarily rational because, as we have seen, the notion of purpose carries with it invariably the implication of requiring the selection of the most reasonable means for its successful fulfilment.[29] Such a proposition cannot be proved empirically false because, as we have seen, programs *can* be changed, so that evidence that a man no longer "follows his best interests" proves only that he has chosen a new "program" the necessary requirements of which no longer permit him to follow—what used to be identified as—his best interests. Despite the impossibility of its empirical contradiction, this proposition yet conveys highly useful information because the insight it provides makes possible the derivation, *in regard to whatever program is relevant in given circumstances,* of highly developed chains of theorems. The kind of knowledge that such theorems can convey, their dependence on the praxeological postulate of rationality, and the implications of the italicized qualification in the previous sentence will become more easily comprehensible in the subsequent sections of this chapter.

The Assumption of Constant Wants—the Praxeological Context

Closely related to the preceding definition of the sense in which praxeology depends on the rationality of human action is the further clarification of the relevance of such rationality for a praxeological science, and especially of the character of the assumption of a constancy of wants. A praxeological theorem becomes possible because of the quality of purpose in action. This quality enables the praxeological theorist, by resorting to his own reason, to predict the path that a given person will follow under the requirement of using *his* reason in order to fulfil his purposes.

The appreciation of the character of a praxeological theorem so derived throws immediate light on the notion of "given ends" and the assumption of a constancy of wants, both of which are inevitably involved in such a theorem. The previous chapter dealt in some detail with Robbins' conception of ends as data for economics. It will be noticed that the praxeological view places equal emphasis, and for substantially similar reasons, on the notion of given wants and purposes. The point at issue hinges on the very possibility of knowledge acquired through praxeological excogitation.

A great city is served by alternative means of transportation; one of these means of transportation has been crippled by an accident. It will be obvious to the observer of the effects of the accident that the alternative means of transportation will tend to be employed in larger than normal volume. In making this prediction the observer has made a simple application of his reasoning powers to a problem of human action; he has applied a theorem of praxeology. The knowledge that he has so acquired is a piece of information different from the data from which he began, but which was, nevertheless, implied in the assumptions concerning human purposes that the observer felt entitled to make. Because he was able to assume that many people desired transportation with sufficient urgency, the observer was able, from his own knowledge of the alternatives open to them, to predict the course of action that they would take. It is clear that this newly acquired knowledge was gained only because of the existence of given purposes, and *it is only in relation to these given purposes* that this praxeological knowledge has significance.

Analysis of human action can proceed only by the treatment of given purposes as data; the effects of a change in surrounding circumstances can be deduced only on the assumption that these purposes are adhered to with constancy, that no new "program" has been substituted for the old. These restrictions on the derivation of praxeological knowledge follow from what has been said in the previous section concerning the rationality implicit in the concept of human action. It was seen that the rationality of action can be appraised relatively to various mutually inconsistent programs that a person may, under different sets of conditions, have chosen. Because this is the case, it is essential, for the derivation of a praxeological theorem, that it be formulated in reference to one such program, whose dominance and relevance must, along with other information, be supplied by the data. Once the data have been supplied, theorems may be derived that will possess necessary truth, but their validity remains strictly dependent on the data; their truth is limited to the "programs" to which they are relevant.

It is a curious fact that critics of economic theory have time and again seized on this feature as a central and damning weakness. The application of economic theorems to the explanation of concrete historical situations requires careful scrutiny of the data on which such theorems are to be grounded. The data will vary, of course, from one concrete case to another. The correct use of economic propositions in particular real situations presupposes, as a matter of course, adequate factual information regarding changes in the data. The writers who have from time to time disparaged the work of economic theorists altogether and urged economists to devote themselves more or less exclusively to the description and classification of those changing facts themselves have pointed to the "relativity" of theories. They considered the necessary limitations on theoretical constructions, which are imposed by virtue of the fact that they are valid only in relation to given programs, as grounds for believing that economic knowledge can be derived more efficiently by simple reference to the changing programs themselves. An economic theory might be an elegant source of intellectual satisfaction, but the severe circumscription of its applicability made it of only academic interest.

It seems worthwhile to point out that, as our discussion of the foundations of praxeological knowledge makes clear, the acknowledged relativity of a praxeological theorem to a given program as its frame of reference is, in fact, not a weakness at all, but is, on the contrary, a reflection of remarkable scientific achievement. Contemplation of the raw data alone presents a range of social phenomena that seem to defy orderly explanation altogether. It seems impossible to develop chains of cause and effect that can bring any semblance of determinacy into the data. Certainly mere analysis of the masses of empirical figures cannot yield any stable "laws" and relationships. The very fact of changing programs, changing tastes and prejudices, makes for an area in which no logical necessity is visible at all and in which everything seems to be in a condition of haphazard flux.

It is into this bewildering mass of empirical data that the economic point of view throws a ray of light. It enables us to grasp an element that does introduce a measure of explanation into social phenomena. This element is laid bare by subjecting the empirical data to a systematic abstraction, made possible by recognition of the character of human action. By taking a cross section of social phenomena at a particular instant in time, by considering the programs that members of society have chosen at that instant and by mentally arresting program changes, one can apply praxeological theorems to these various programs and deduce the consequences. The conclusions so derived are valid in relation to the assumed programs, and provide an explanation of the concrete phenomena of the real world in so far as there *is* a tendency for men to adhere to programs once they have been initiated. Moreover, once the possibility of this type of explanation is grasped, it is clear that *all* historical phenomena admit, at least in principle, of being treated in such terms. It becomes merely a matter of feeding the suitable assumptions and data into the theoretical system and extracting the appropriately complicated chains of reasoning.

The crucial point is that the perception of any kind of explanatory framework has been made possible only by prescinding from any conceivable change in a given set of programs. The introduction of any kind of order into the jungle of empirical data has been accomplished by abstracting from full reality and accepting a hypothetical state of affairs as a frame of reference. It is the outstanding achievement of economic theorists to have been able to recognize determinate causal chains within the tangles of statistics; they were able to succeed in this only by treating social phenomena as the systematic working out of the praxeological consequences of *given programs* that were adhered to. A *particular* program may not necessarily be adhered to, but the emergence of human action at all presupposes the existence of some program that was adhered to, and it is in reference to this that praxeological reasoning provides the explanatory key.

An economic proposition referring to a given set of circumstances, a particular configuration of demand, a specific technological context will provide information concerning this definite situation. Changes in the data, a revolution in tastes, the acquisition of new habits, the discovery of more efficient techniques will all make up a situation to which a new praxeological solution will be relevant. To deny the applicability of economic reasoning because of the change in conditions is to deny that the old set of conditions did set up specific "forces" constraining action; it is to deny that these "forces" provide an interpretation of action that goes beyond a mere cataloguing of observed events. "But," as Professor Knight has commented, "this fact certainly cannot be denied." [30]

The position that the praxeological element occupies within the whole class of social phenomena has been set forth by various writers. Professors Mises and Knight have devoted considerable attention in their writings to the elucidation of this point. [31] Within narrow limits man can be observed and his behavior explained purely mechanically. At this level of interpretation human behavior is considered only in the positive terms of stimulus and response; it is completely "caused" in the sense that the problem-solving elements in human conduct are ignored. On higher levels of interpretation, however, the conduct of men involves recognition of their putting forth effort, of their attempt to solve problems—in short, of their human actions.

Here again various levels of discussion are possible. Unquestionably the most "interesting" and, for the business of living, the most important is the consideration of the ways in which men have acquired their particular interests; the development of particular programs that men believe worthy of undertaking; the forces that determine people's value judgments and the emergence of their sense of absolute moral appraisement. The level of interpretation on which praxeology has a contribution to make is, however, a more modest one. It is willing to accept the interests and programs of men as data and seeks to understand, in terms of these interests and programs, the chains of consequences that can be deduced. The principles of human action make it possible to ascribe and refer back historical events to such interests and programs as "final causes" that can be accepted without further explanation.

Praxeology, Apriorism, and Operationalism

The considerations set forth in the previous section are sufficient to make clear what writers have had in mind when they have characterized economics as an a priori science. This description of economic knowledge has been repeatedly misunderstood; it has been repeatedly taken out of context and held up for ridicule.[32] But the matter is essentially logical and clear.

Professor Mises in particular has stressed the a priori nature of praxeological knowledge. A theorem of a praxeological science provides information that has been derived by sheer reasoning; it is the product of pure logic without the assistance of any empirical observation. As such, a praxeological theorem is congeneric with a theorem of geometry; being the rigorously derived consequences of given assumptions, it partakes of the "apodictic certainty" that is necessarily possessed by such an exercise in logic.

Disagreement with this approach has been vigorously expressed by a number of writers. Dissatisfaction has arisen from several points of view. On the one hand, it is pointed out that an a priori theorem, being derived by sheer logic from given axioms, is necessarily circular, in that it merely tells us in a different way what we already know by our knowledge of the axioms themselves. All the information provided by economic reasoning is thus merely extended circumlocution. So long as economics was not acknowledged as a praxeological science, it is argued, this objection could not be raised. So long as it had been necessary to introduce specific postulates about the way in which people actually behave, an economic theorem did tell something new. If, for example, it was postulated that men behave "rationally" and rationality was defined so as to possess definite empirical content, such as a pattern of behavior that maximized money profits, and the like, then the consequences of this assumption do provide new information. Deduction from the specific assumption made has yielded a theory, against which the assumption could, in fact, be tested for its faithfulness to the facts. But with the emergence of the view of economic knowledge that saw it as completely independent of particular empirical assumptions, the situation became completely altered. A theorem describing the consequences of human behavior that does not take into account the concrete content of that behavior must remain, it has been repeatedly asserted, simply a different way of saying that people behave as they behave.[33]

Closely connected with this criticism of economics a priori are the objections raised against its supposed misuse of a method of doubtful respectability, viz., introspection. Implicit in much of the unfavorable discussion of apriorism in economics is the current belief that only "operationally meaningful" propositions ought to find a place in science.[34] A theorem which makes no direct reference to observable facts, and which therefore cannot be "tested" against observable facts, is one the interpersonal validity of which must remain in doubt and to which "scientific" status is to be denied.

Now, these are issues that concern basic epistemological problems far wider than the range of this book. Closely though they relate to the praxeological view of the nature of the economic aspect of affairs, they themselves are concerned with inquiries into the nature of science and knowledge that would carry us far away from our own subject. Professor Robbins has gone so far as to relegate completely to philosophy all such discussions concerning the a priori character of economics.[35] Mises, Knight, and Hayek have most vigorously justified the kind of introspection that is necessary for the conception of economic knowledge as "scientific" without being empirically "testable." [36] We are not so much concerned here with the scientific validity that may be attributed to a priori economics as with the clarification of the precise sense in which the praxeological conception of the economic point of view does, in fact, imply a strictly a priori position.

The concept of human action is sufficient, in the praxeological view, for the deduction of complex chains of reasoning concerning the choices men will make, the alternatives from which they will be forced to choose, and the like. Human action relates to real entities, goods, or services; it develops against the background of objectively measurable price relationships. Economic science seeks to provide an explanation of these real phenomena; it seeks to explain the consequences of given changes in data, to relate market phenomena to the underlying human motives. Praxeology envisages the successful attainment of these goals through the scrutiny of human affairs from a specific point of view that recognizes the teleological and rational nature of human action. This point of view makes possible the construction of chains of reasoning that are purely formal, in the sense that they refer to goods, services or factors of production only abstractly; they depend for their validity not on the specific objects with which human action may be concretely concerned, but only on postulated attitudes of men towards them. The propositions that can be deduced in this manner may thus, of course, include the analysis of situations that may be quite unreal. And in order to be of service in the understanding of reality, praxeology must direct its attention exclusively to the analysis of situations that correspond to the actualities of the external world. It would be possible, for example,

to examine the consequences of a world in which labor was preferred over leisure. Economics could certainly deduce theorems
concerning prices, incomes, and production in such a world. But
this would be intellectual gymnastics of a fruitless kind.[37]

To maintain contact with situations that do in fact require
explanation, economics must thus resort to experience for guidance. It must take the facts as they are and apply to them the a
priori logic of human action. "It adopts for the organized presen-
tation of its results a form in which aprioristic theory and the
interpretation of historical phenomena are intertwined." [38] It is
clear that the exposition of economics as an a priori science has
never implied that it can dispense with references to factual observation in the final statement of its results. Particular economic
propositions will concern human attitudes and conventions that
do conform to those of the real world. The sense in which it is
maintained that economics is an a priori branch of knowledge
is a much narrower one. It concerns the contribution that the
recognition of the concept of human action makes to the explanation of social phenomena.

The observation of facts provides useful knowledge. This is the
procedure of history. But observation does not exhaust the knowledge and understanding that we can attain concerning these affairs. The economic point of view injects an immediate sense of
order into these affairs, an order that brings with it a large measure
of *explanation*. This explanation is achieved by subjecting the
observed data to a specific scientific procedure, praxeological reasoning. This procedure is in itself quite independent of the facts
to which it is applied. It could be applied to conditions that are
nonexistent. It is itself the contribution of human logic and
reasoning alone. In this sense the theorems of economics, closely
though they refer to concrete reality, are to be described as a
priori. They are derived purely from the knowledge that the
human mind possesses of the category of action.[39]

The separation that is thus emphasized, between the facts and
their logical analysis through economic reasoning, is a fruitful
one. It stresses the quite distinct operations that are being performed in the observation of economic history and in the devel-

opment of economic theorems. It focuses attention on the new source of knowledge that is provided by our understanding the nature of action. It illuminates the striking fact that pure reason can convey knowledge concerning brute facts of the real world. Because men act as reasoning beings, it is possible to explain their concrete patterns of behavior by applying to their attitude the theorems that our own reason has supplied.

All this does not prevent the praxeologist from maintaining a becoming modesty with regard to his own contribution. He does not in any way believe that his theorems can exhaust all that can be known about social phenomena; he does insist on the unique assistance he can provide. He does not deplore close attention to market data, to masses of statistics, and the like; but he does deprecate the view that this kind of scrutiny can be a substitute for economic reasoning or that it needs to be resorted to as a "test" for the correctness of such reasoning. His recognition of the category of human action does impress upon him most forcefully the utter helplessness with which the masses of facts must be faced without the illumination provided by a procedure of analysis that itself owes nothing to these facts—the application of economic reasoning.

The Economic Point of View and Praxeology

Our discussion thus far in this chapter has made no attempt to distinguish a specifically economic point of view from the general praxeological outlook. We set out, in this book, to examine the various points of view held to characterize economic science and through which an "economic" aspect of social phenomena has been distinguished. Our search has led us in this chapter to consider the filiation of ideas that have found the specifically economic point of view to be merely part of a broader perspective, the praxeological view. The economic aspect of affairs is simply the praxeological; a theorem of economics is simply a praxeological proposition.

To be sure, the praxeological perspective embraces a range of human action far wider than that usually treated in economic theory. All human actions, motivated though they may be by the entire range of the purposes that have inspired and fired men to act, come within the sway of the ideal praxeological discipline. The constraint that men feel to fulfil their purposes in spite of obstacles pervades all aspects of life. It is the position of praxeology that the common category that embraces the entire range of human efforts is the key to economic science. We have seen at various points in this book that economists have again and again searched for something in economics that should *differentiate* it from the rest of human action. These thinkers were deterred from expounding the praxeological character of economics for the very reason that this character is common to other aspects of social life.

The praxeological view sees economic science as the branch of praxeology that has been most highly developed.[40] Perhaps other branches will one day attain a similar stage of development. The important point is that distinctions between various "branches" of praxeology must be arbitrary. Economics *is* a "given pie"; it is not a pie that every economist can make at will or for which he can prescribe his own recipe. Economic theory *has* a "nature of its own" that must be respected; certainly it must be recognized if its distinctive contribution is to be made at all. But the pie that is the economic aspect of affairs is bigger than that traditionally treated by economists; it embraces all human action. The slice that makes up economic theory may—so long as it is cut from the correct pie—be cut in any arbitrary way. "It is impossible to draw a clear-cut boundary around the sphere or domain of human action to be included in economic science." [41] "The scope of praxeology, the general theory of human action, can be precisely defined and circumscribed. The specifically economic problems . . . can only by and large be disengaged from the comprehensive body of praxeological theory." [42]

Economic theory has traditionally dealt with the phenomena of the market, prices, production, and monetary calculation. In these spheres of human activity, theorists have developed constructions that help to explain the regularities these phenomena evince and to bring into clear focus the tendencies for change in these phenomena consequent upon given autonomous changes in the data. Writers on economics have striven to present precise definitions of the scope of this discipline. From the point of view of praxeology, the earlier attempts suffered from their tendency to seek for the defining criteria in the nature of the specific affairs with which market phenomena are concerned. The consequence of these searches was the series of formulations examined in the earlier chapters of this book. The subject matter of economics came to be connected with the material things that are the objects of traffic in the market; it came to be linked peculiarly with the use of money in market transactions or with the specific social relationships that characterize the market system. Where writers came closest to the recognition that these criteria were only accidental characteristics of the affairs upon which economic analysis could be brought to bear, where they were able to glimpse the congenerousness of the specifically economic type of analysis with the underlying *actions* of men, they were unable to follow this clue to the conclusion to which it pointed. Precisely because those features in action that made it susceptible of economic analysis seemed common to *all* human activities, these writers were driven back to look for some other defining characteristic. And this meant again the search for some arbitrary quality to justify selecting the particular slice of pie that made up economic theory; but it meant in addition the relegation yet further into the background of the true recipe of that larger pie from which their conception of economics was being arbitrarily hacked.

From this point of view the formulation of the nature of the economic in terms of the allocation of scarce means among competing ends occupies a rather special position. This definition, discussed at length in the previous chapter, differs from the rest in its approach to the problem. It defines an *aspect* of human activities in general; it does *not* look for the key to economic phenomena in the specific *kinds* of activity with which they are mostly concerned. In finding the economic aspect of activities in general to consist in concern with the ends-means relationship, this conception too includes within its scope kinds of actions with which economics has had traditionally little to do. From the praxeological standpoint, in fact, the idea of economizing scarce means in allocating them among alternative ends, when used as a criterion for defining the domain of the economic, is nothing but a convenient, though artificial, framework in which human actions can be analyzed. The allocation among competing goals is a technical concomitant of a good deal of purposeful behavior. Human action *does* frequently call for carefully apportioning scarce means among competing projects. In a formal sense it is even possible to consider *all* human action as consisting in such allocation; but this involves the kind of artificiality in the conception of ends and means with which Professor Robbins' definition was charged. The principal merit of the latter is thus its implicit dependence on the concept of human action; its apparent inadequacies stem from its attempt to consider action as conforming to a particular technical pattern. Much of the criticism Robbins' definition received will be seen to dissolve when his conception of economics is related more clearly to the idea of human action. The allocation of scarce means among alternative ends simply signifies the consistent pursuit of ends, the consistent pursuit of the more highly valued ends taking precedence over the fulfilment of the less highly esteemed ends. It means, in fact, the exercise of the human faculty for purposeful action.

It is not to be denied that the ends-means formulation seems to fit with remarkable neatness the phenomena treated by economic theory. But this neatness has been achieved at the cost of a failure to press on to the very crux of the economic point of view. We are not thereby apprised, as the expression of this economic point of view *is* able to apprise us, how an analysis of human affairs by economic science is made possible by the very perspective from which the economic theorist views them. The ends-means dichotomy does not show how the recognition of the principle that governs the allocation of means conduces at the same time to a recognition of the possibility of scientific analysis and explanation of economic phenomena. Only when the economic point of view is conceived as focusing attention on the nature of human action is it able to provide the key to economic science. And in this sense it can indeed be contended that the definition of economics in terms of the economizing of scarce means (like others before it) "fails to convey an adequate concept of its nature," [43] until this definition is superseded by the fully developed conception of economics to which it logically leads, viz., the praxeological point of view.

"Economists would agree," Cannan wrote, "that 'Did Bacon write Shakespeare?' was not an economic controversy. . . . On the other hand, they would agree that the controversy would have an economic side if copyright were perpetual and the descendants of Bacon and Shakespeare were disputing the ownership of the plays." [44] This is so, Professor Robbins explains,[45] because the supposed copyright laws would make the use of the plays scarce and would in turn yield their owners scarce means of gratification that would otherwise be differently distributed. Of course, Professor Robbins is correct, but the same explanation can be given in terms that make it immediately clear how the economic side of such a controversy is able to yield material for the economic theorist.

It can be explained, that is, that the controversy has an economic aspect because the assumed copyright laws affect the conditions of human action in either or both of two ways. In the first place, as they render the use of the plays scarce, the laws will have altered the pattern of action on the part of prospective producers. An additional obstacle has been placed in the way of persons desiring to produce the plays; and it will be obvious that a prospective producer will be constrained to forgo some less highly prized gratification in order to fulfil his dramatic purposes. On the other hand, it will be clear that this state of affairs opens up a new avenue by which the legal owner of the plays may possibly be enabled to fulfil his own purposes more completely, through taking advantage of the producers' attitudes. Either of these two influences of the controversy on human actions is sufficient to invest it with interest for the economic point of view. This way of expressing the nature of this point of view, however, reveals at the same time the very nature of the analysis that it makes possible.

Notes

NOTES TO CHAPTER I

1. *Memorials of Alfred Marshall,* ed. A. C. Pigou (London: Macmillan & Co., 1925), p. 499.
2. R. Robinson, *Definition* (Oxford, 1950), p. 15.
3. B. Croce, *Historical Materialism and the Economics of Karl Marx* (English ed.; London: Macmillan & Co., 1915), p. 29.
4. These considerations will account for the absence of references in this essay to the achievements in recent years in mathematical programming, input-output analysis, and game theory. Rivett has suggested, in "The Definition of Economics," *Economic Record,* November, 1955, pp. 229-230, that progress in linear programming might one day require review of the borderlines of economics. Apart from its special relevance to Rivett's own definition of economics, this suggestion can refer only to the scope of the subject, not at all to the delineation of the economic point of view. On this point see especially W. J. Baumol, "Activity Analysis in One Lesson," *American Economic Review,* December, 1958, p. 837.
5. E. Cannan, *Wealth* (3rd ed.; London, 1945), p. 4.
6. For examples of the specific restriction of definitions of economics to "economic theory," or even more narrowly to "price theory," see J. A. Schumpeter, *History of Economic Analysis* (New York, 1954), pp. 535-536; F. H. Knight, "The Nature of Economic Science in Some Recent Discussion," *American Economic Review,* Vol. XXIV, No. 2 (June, 1934), p. 226.
7. On the distinction between real and nominal definitions, see, e.g., J. S. Mill, *A System of Logic* (10th ed.; London, 1879), I, 162 f.; L. S. Stebbing, *A Modern Introduction to Logic* (6th ed.; London, 1948), p. 426; C. K. Ogden and I. A. Richards, *The Meaning of Meaning* (3rd ed. revised; London, 1930), p. 109 n.
8. For examples of writers who saw in the multiplicity of definitions a proof of their fundamental weakness, see L. Walras, *Eléments d'économie politique pure, ou Théorie de la richesse sociale* (Lausanne, 1874), p. 3; A. P. Usher, "The Content of the Value Concept," *Quarterly Journal of Economics,* August, 1917, p. 712; F. Kaufmann, "On the Subject Matter and Method of Economic Science," *Economica,* November, 1933, pp. 381-382.

9. For Pareto's views on the usefulness of defining economic affairs, see the translation of his paper "On the Economic Phenomenon" (first published in *Giornale degli economisti*, 1900, II, 139-162) in *International Economic Papers*, No. 3, p. 194. See also V. Pareto, "L'économie et la sociologie au point de vue scientifique," *Rivista di scienza*, 1907, p. 294. Myrdal's views are expressed in his *The Political Element in the Development of Economic Theory* (Harvard, 1954), pp. 154-155; for those of Hutchison see his *The Significance and Basic Postulates of Economic Theory* (London: Macmillan & Co., 1938), p. 53.

10. G. Tagliacozzo, "Croce and the Nature of Economic Science," *Quarterly Journal of Economics*, Vol. LIX, No. 3 (May, 1945), p. 308.

11. For examples of earlier views recognizing the importance of an adequate definition of economic affairs, see E. de Laveleye, "Les lois naturelles et l'objet de l'économie politique," *Journal des économistes*, April, 1883, p. 92; S. Patten, "The Scope of Political Economy," *The Yale Review*, November, 1893, reprinted in S. Patten, *Essays in Economic Theory* (New York, 1924), p. 178.

12. L. Robbins, *An Essay on the Nature and Significance of Economic Science* (2nd ed.; London: Macmillan & Co., 1935), p. 3. Robbins put forward the same view, as well as the suggestion for a history of the stream of thought leading up to modern definitions, in his Introduction to Wicksteed's *The Common Sense of Political Economy* (London, 1933), I, xxii. See also L. Robbins, "Live and Dead Issues in the Methodology of Economics," *Economica*, August, 1938, p. 344, for an acknowledgment of the minor importance of the precise wording in the expression of the (correct) definition.

13. F. H. Knight, review of L. Mises, *Nationalökonomie*, in *Economica*, 1941, p. 410 n.

14. A. L. Macfie, *An Essay on Economy and Value* (London, 1936), pp. 2-3.

15. For examples of economists convinced of the insuperable difficulty of achieving a determinate definition of economic affairs, see P. T. Homan, "Issues in Economic Theory, an Attempt to Clarify," *Quarterly Journal of Economics*, May, 1928, pp. 349, 364; F. St. Leger Daly, "The Scope and Method of Economics," *The Canadian Journal of Economics and Political Science*, May, 1945, p. 169.

16. G. Tagliacozzo, "Croce and the Nature of Economic Science," *Quarterly Journal of Economics*, May, 1945, p. 307.

17. See, e.g., R. Robinson, *Definition*, pp. 162-172.

18. B. Croce, "On the Economic Principle II," translated in *International Economic Papers*, No. 3, 1953, pp. 197-198, from *Giornale degli economisti*, I (1901). See also *International Economic Papers*, No. 3, p. 203, for an interpretation by Pareto of the differences between Croce and himself in terms of the philosophical clash between the medieval nominalists and realists.

19. F. A. Hayek, "The Trend of Economic Thinking," *Economica*, May, 1933, p. 131.

20. On these points see, e.g., L. Robbins, *The Theory of Economic Policy in English Classical Political Economy* (London, 1952), p. 3; M. Bowley,

Nassau Senior and Classical Political Economy (London, 1937), pp. 27 f.

21. See, e.g., A. Amonn, *Objekt und Grundbegriffe der theoretische Nationalökonomie* (2nd ed.), pp. 23 f.

22. J. S. Mill, "On the Definition of Political Economy: and on the Method of Investigation Proper to It," (in *Essays on Some Unsettled Questions of Political Economy*) London reprint, pp. 120 f.

23. See the *Centenary Volume* of the Political Economy Club, London, 1921, p. 44.

24. It was in this period too that one of the earliest denials of a specifically economic side of affairs was put forward by Comte. Any such separation was "irrational" and evidenced the "metaphysical" character of economics. For an account of Comte's criticism of economics and of J. S. Mill's reaction to it, see Ashley's Introduction to his 1909 edition of Mill's *Principles*, pp. xi f. See also R. Mauduit, *A. Comte et la science économique* (Paris, 1929); F. A. Hayek, *The Counter-Revolution of Science* (Glencoe, 1952), pp. 181-182. An early discussion of Comte's views on economics is J. E. Cairnes' "M. Comte and Political Economy," in *Essays in Political Economy* (London, 1873).

25. Knies required of a definition of economics that it comprise a) "das Gebiet der Untersuchungen," b) its "Aufgabe," and c) its "Methode." (K. Knies, *Die politische Oekonomie vom geschichtliche Standpuncte* [Braunschweig, 1883], p. 157.) Menger required a similar scope for a definition. (C. Menger, *Untersuchungen über die Methode der Sozialwissenschaften und der politischen Oekonomie insbesondere* [Leipzig, 1883], p. 238.)

26. The distinction between the "individual" (or concrete) and the "general" (or abstract) in economic phenomena was made famous by Menger in his *Untersuchungen*, pp. 3 f.

27. Prominent United States writers who applied themselves to the careful definition of the economic point of view during this period include in their ranks Ely, Patten, Davenport, Taussig, Hawley, Giddings, Hadley, and Ward.

28. Among French writers of the period who concentrated most directly on definition may be mentioned: R. Worms (*La science et l'art en économie politique*, Paris, 1896); E. Levasseur (*De la methode dans les sciences économiques*, Paris, 1898); A. Jourdan (*Des rapports entre le droit et l'économie politique*, Paris, 1884); G. Schmidt ("Rapports de l'économie politique avec la morale et le droit," *Revue d'économie politique*, 1900); G. Tarde (*Psychologie économique*, Paris, 1902).

29. Cammillo Supino, *La definizione dell'economia politica* (Milan, 1883).

30. L. M. Fraser, *Economic Thought and Language* (2nd printing, 1947), ch. 2.

31. The following references support the conclusion that writers who have sought to define the scope of economics have done so with regard to the discipline as it has actually developed, not to any projected subject: A. Marshall, *The Present Position of Economics* (London, 1885); L. Robbins, *Nature and Significance of Economic Science* (2nd ed.; London, 1935), p. 22; R. T. Bye, "The Scope and Definition of Eco-

nomics," *Journal of Political Economy*, October, 1939; A. Amonn, *Objekt und Grundbegriffe der theoretischen Nationalökonomie* (1911), p. 12.

NOTES TO CHAPTER II

1. L. M. Fraser, *Economic Thought and Language* (London, 1947), pp. 21 ff.
2. Contrast, however, Cunningham's appraisal of Adam Smith's achievement as consisting "in isolating the conception of national wealth, while previous writers had treated it in conscious subordination to national power" (quoted in A. Marshall, *Principles of Economics*, [8th ed.; Macmillan & Co.], p. 758 n.).
3. Adam Smith, *An Inquiry into the Nature and Causes of the Wealth of Nations*, ed. Cannan (Modern Library, 1937), p. 643.
4. See, e.g., *op. cit.*, p. 403.
5. *Op. cit.*, p. 397. John Neville Keynes has remarked (*The Scope and Method of Political Economy* [4th ed.; London, 1930], p. 39 n.) that although Smith's work has the form of a science, he himself conceived his subject primarily as an art. In this connection, however, a note of Jeremy Bentham is of considerable interest. He wrote (*Economic Writings*, ed. Stark, Vol. III [George Allen and Unwin, 1954], p. 318 n.): "To Adam Smith, the science alone has been the direct and constant object in view: the art the collateral and occasional one."
6. L. Robbins, *The Theory of Economic Policy in English Classical Political Economy* (London, 1952), pp. 170-171.
7. James Steuart, *An Inquiry into the Principles of Political Economy* (1767), cited in L. Haney, *History of Economic Thought* (4th ed.), p. 138.
8. On the attitudes of some of the earliest economic writers towards the right of private property, see, e.g., E. Halévy, *The Growth of Philosophic Radicalism* (Boston, 1955), p. 45; L. Robbins, *The Theory of Economic Policy*, pp. 50 f.; J. Bonar, *Philosophy and Political Economy* (3rd ed.; London, 1922), pp. 142 f. Perhaps the most clear example of an economist who was stimulated by concern with private property rights was Samuel Read. Read, one of the economists "rediscovered" by Seligman ("Some Neglected British Economists," *Economic Journal*, 1903), called his book *Political Economy. An Inquiry into the Natural Grounds of Right to Vendible Property or Wealth* (Edinburgh, 1829). He treated economics, not as concerning wealth, but as concerning the "right to wealth." It is of interest to note that the alternative name which Read suggested (p. xvii) for political economy, "Political Justice," is the title of Godwin's book of 1793 fiercely attacking the institution of private property.
9. Gunnar Myrdal, *The Political Element in the Development of Economic Theory* (English ed.; Harvard, 1954), pp. 69 f. Contrast Schumpeter's remark in this regard (*History of Economic Analysis*, New York, 1954), p. 120.

10. The intellectual ancestry of classical political economy has been traced variously to the *moral* tradition represented by the Mandeville-Shaftesbury-Hutcheson realm of thought and to the *political* tradition of the Grotius-Pufendorf-Hobbes-Locke filiation. See, e.g., J. T. Merz, *History of European Thought in the Nineteenth Century* (Edinburgh, 1914), IV, 127-128; J. Bonar, *Philosophy and Political Economy*, pp. 6, 85, 151; W. Hasbach, *Untersuchungen über Adam Smith* (Leipzig, 1891), pp. 23 f., 140 f. See also F. A. Hayek, "Individualism: True and False" (reprinted in *Individualism and Economic Order*, Chicago, 1948).

11. B. Mandeville, *Fable of the Bees* (ed. of 1723), pp. 427-428.

12. W. Röpke, *The Social Crisis of Our Time* (English edition; Chicago, 1950), p. 68.

13. F. A. Hayek, *The Counter-Revolution of Science* (Glencoe, 1952), p. 107.

14. See, e.g., W. H. Hutt, *Economists and the Public* (Jonathan Cape: London, 1936), pp. 301-302.

15. See E. Halévy, *The Growth of Philosophic Radicalism* (Beacon Press: Boston, 1955), pp. 13, 19, 57.

16. R. T. Malthus, *Principles of Political Economy* (1820), p. 27. Ricardo in his *Notes on Malthus (ibid.)* seems to agree with Malthus.

17. For a discussion of the significance of this distinction in Smith's work and of the later controversies over it, see, e.g., E. Cannan, *A History of the Theories of Production and Distribution in English Political Economy from 1776 to 1848* (3rd ed.), pp. 14 f.

18. Earl of Lauderdale, *Inquiry into the Nature and Origin of Public Wealth* (Edinburgh, 1804), p. 57.

19. It is not quite clear whether Lauderdale really intended his definition to be interpreted as broadly as it was. It is noteworthy that in his reply to the scathing review of his book in the *Edinburgh Review,* Lauderdale speaks of himself as having defined wealth as consisting "of the objects of man's desire." Lauderdale, *Observations on the Review of his Inquiry into the Nature and Origin of Public Wealth, published in the VIIIth number of the Edinburgh Review* (Edinburgh, 1804).

20. R. T. Malthus, *Principles of Political Economy* (1820), p. 27.

21. J. R. McCulloch in the *Supplement to the Encyclopaedia Britannica,* quoted in Malthus, *Definitions in Political Economy* (London, 1827), pp. 70 f.

22. See n. 16 above; Read, *Political Economy* (Edinburgh, 1829,), p. 1.

23. D. Ricardo, *Principles of Political Economy and Taxation* (1817). Original Preface . (Everyman's ed., p. 1); P. Sraffa, ed., *The Works and Correspondence of David Ricardo,* Vol. VIII, Letter No. 392, Ricardo to Malthus, 9th October, 1820. Ricardo's stress on distribution was noticed by, among others, G. Ramsay, *Essay on the Distribution of Wealth* (Edinburgh, 1836), p. v. There is perhaps room for conjecture concerning Ricardo's position in 1817. Early in 1817 Malthus had written to Ricardo referring to "the causes of the wealth and poverty of nations" as the "grand object" of economic enquiries (Sraffa ed., Vol-

ume VII, Letter 200), and we have no record of any adverse reaction from Ricardo. Although in his *Principles* (1817) Ricardo had referred to distribution as the "principal problem" in political economy, this is not quite the same as his declaration to Malthus in 1820 that the laws of distribution are "the only true objects" of the subject. To Malthus in 1820 Ricardo was writing that he was "every day . . . more satisfied" of the correctness of his view. This might support the conjecture that Ricardo's 1817 statement was meant to be less emphatic than his later views. There is some support for the view that the scope of Ricardo's *Principles* (which treated distribution as the "principal problem") was not meant to cover the whole science. On this see Ricardo's letter to Mill (Sraffa ed., Vol. VII, Letter No. 196); see also T. De Quincy's remarks to this effect in *Dialogues of Three Templars on Political Economy*, in Vol. X of De Quincy's *Works*, 1877, p. 205. For a contrary view see Trower's letter to Ricardo (Sraffa ed., Vol. VII, Letter No. 214).

24. M. Bowley, *Nassau Senior and Classical Political Economy* (London, 1937), p. 303 n., and see above n. 8.

25. Read, *Political Economy*, Preface, p. ix.

26. On Hume's views in this regard, see J. Bonar, *Philosophy and Political Economy*, p. 107.

27. See above n. 7.

28. Ganilh in his *Inquiry into the Various Systems of Political Economy* (English ed.; New York, 1812), pp. 2-4, cites Palmieri's *Pubblica felicità* (1787) and Canard's *Principes d'économie politique* (1801) for the view that wealth is *superfluous*. Boileau (*An Introduction to Political Economy* [London, 1811], Ganilh himself (*op. cit.* p. 22) and the American economist Raymond (*The Elements of Political Economy*, [2nd ed.; Baltimore, 1823], p. 40) all defined wealth as surplus over current expenditure for "wants." This position seems to have considerable bearing on the classical attitude towards the consumption of wealth. (On this see J. N. Keynes, *Scope and Method of Political Economy*, [4th ed.; London, 1930], pp. 105 f; L. Robbins, *The Theory of Economic Policy*, p. 7.) The conception of wealth as surplus after expenditure implies a finite area of human "needs" which are objectively fixed. This conception led to the view that the consumption of wealth is the *destruction* of wealth rather than the *consummation* of the process of production. One recalls J. S. Mill's unhappy description of the desire for present enjoyment of goods as being antagonistic to the desire for wealth (*Essays on Some Unsettled Questions of Political Economy*, London reprint, p. 138).

29. Bentham recommended the use of the term "matter of wealth" in place of "wealth" to 'make it absolutely clear that political economy was not confined to the treatment of great riches. Malthus in a letter to Ricardo in 1817 explicitly included the *poverty* of nations in the scope of economics (Sraffa ed., Vol. VII, Letter No. 200). Samuel Bailey, celebrated critic of Ricardian value theory, ascribed the popular view of political

economy as a "degrading" inquiry to the mistaken belief that it treats only of excessive wealth. S. Bailey, *Discourses on Various Subjects Read Before Literary and Philosophical Societies* (London, 1852), p. 125. For examples of later writers clinging to the "surplus" view of wealth, see Sargent, *Science of Social Opulence* (London, 1856); M. Liberatore, *Principles of Political Economy* (English ed.; London, 1891).
30. F. H. Knight, *The Ethics of Competition* (Harper & Bros.), p. 24. See also on this point K. Mannheim, *Essays on the Sociology of Culture* (New York, 1956), p. 35. For bibliography on the materialist interpretation of history, see W. J. Blake, *Elements of Marxian Economic Theory and Its Criticism* (New York, 1939), pp. 686-691. See also T. Parsons, "Some Reflections on 'The Nature and Significance of Economics,'" *Quarterly Journal of Economics,* May, 1934, p. 534, n. 4.
31. K. Marx, *Capital* (English ed.; Ch. Kerr & Co., Chicago, 1915), I, 406, n. 2. See, however, the significantly different translation of this note by E. and C. Paul (Everyman's ed.; 1930), p. 393 n.
32. K. Marx, *A Contribution to the Critique of Political Economy* (translated by N. Stone, Chicago, 1904), pp. 10-11.
33. See E. R. A. Seligman, *The Economic Interpretation of History* (New York: Columbia University Press, 1902), p. 43.
34. See Eastman's edition of selections from Marx (Modern Library), p. 10.
35. F. Engels, *The Origin of the Family, Private Property, and the State* (English translation, Moscow, 1940), p. 5. For another statement by Engels in virtually the same words, see Knight, *Ethics and Competition,* p. 24 n.
36. From a letter by Engels to *Der sozialistische Akademiker* (1895), quoted in Seligman, *The Economic Interpretation of History,* pp. 58-59.
37. Karl Kautsky, *Die materialistische Geschichtsauffassung* (Berlin, 1927), I, 3-6.
38. The following references are to later writers who seem to have formulated their definitions with stress on "subsistence": B. Hildebrand, *Die Nationalökonomie der Gegenwart und Zukunft,* ed. by Gehrig (Jena, 1922), p. 305: E. Sax, *Das Wesen und die Aufgaben der National-ökonomie* (Vienna, 1884), p. 12; P. Leroy-Beaulieu, *Précis d'économie politique* (Paris, 1888), p. 1; C. Perin, *Premiers principes d'économie politique* (Paris, 1896), p. 2.
39. Thorstein Veblen, *The Theory of the Leisure Class* (Modern Library, 1934), p. 24.
40. T. Veblen, *The Place of Science in Modern Civilization and Other Essays,* (New York: Viking Press, 1919), p. 91.
41. T. Veblen, "The Limitations of Marginal Utility," *Journal of Political Economy,* 1909; reprinted in *The Place of Science in Modern Civilization,* p. 241. A list of passages in Veblen's writings in which the material-means-of-life criterion is used would include: T. Veblen, "Why Is Economics Not an Evolutionary Science?" *Quarterly Journal of Economics,* 1895, reprinted in *The Place of Science in Modern Civilization,* pp. 71, 76; T. Veblen, "Mr. Cummings' Strictures on 'The Theory of the Leisure

Class.' " *Journal of Political Economy*, 1899, and "The Instinct for Workmanship and the Irksomeness of Labor," *American Journal of Sociology*, 1898, both reprinted in *Essays in Our Changing Order* (New York, 1943), pp. 27, 78, 80. It is of special interest to note that Veblen uses the phrase "material means of life" as synonymous with the object of Marx's materialism. (See his "The Socialist Economics of Karl Marx and His Followers," *Quarterly Journal of Economics*, 1906, reprinted in *The Place of Science in Modern Civilization*, p. 415.)

42. Franklin Giddings, "The Economic Ages," *Political Science Quarterly*, June, 1901, p. 195. For a similar distinction between human economy and its biological analogues, see Lester F. Ward, "Psychological Basis of Social Economics," *Annals of the American Academy of Political and Social Science*, 1893, pp. 464-465.

43. S. Sherwood, "The Philosophical Basis of Economics," *Publications of the American Academy of Political and Social Science* (October 5, 1897), p. 71.

44. J. E. Cairnes, *The Character and Logical Method of Political Economy* (London, 1875), p. 31. (The lectures published in the book were delivered during the 1850's.)

45. Cairnes, *op. cit.*, p. 18.

46. Bonamy Price, *Chapters on Practical Political Economy* (London, 1878), p. 19. For further references in which the wealth-focus of economics was retained, see the quotation from a speech by Robert Lowe in Cliffe Leslie, *Essays in Political Economy* (2nd ed.; 1888), p. 21; H. Sidgwick, *The Principles of Political Economy* (2d ed.; 1887), p. 12; W. F. Marriott, *A Grammar of Political Economy* (London, 1874), p. 1; J. N. Keynes, *The Scope and Method of Political Economy* (4th ed.; 1917), p. 100. Jevons and Marshall made free use of such terms as "the laws of wealth" and the "study of wealth." W. S. Jevons, "The Future of Political Economy," *Fortnightly Review*, November, 1876, reprinted in his *Principles of Economics and Other Papers* (London, 1905), p. 193; A. Marshall, *Principles of Economics* (8th ed.; London, 1920), p. 1. When Mr. Norman, a veteran member of the Political Economy Club, rose at the club dinner in 1876 to express his sentiments, he was not fighting an uphill battle when he asserted that the "real essence of Political Economy" is the explanation of wealth phenomena; *Revised Report of the Proceedings at the Dinner of 31st May, 1876, held in Celebration of the Hundredth Year of the Publication of the "Wealth of Nations"* (Political Economy Club: London, 1876), p. 26.

47. References to writers in German who defined economics with special attention to *Güter* or *Sachgüter* include: G. v. Schönberg, "Die Volkswirtschaft," *Handbuch der politischen Oekonomie* (4th ed.; Tübingen, 1896), p. 15; K. Knies, *Die politische Oekonomie vom geschichtliche Standpuncte*, (Braunschweig, 1883), p. 158; C. Menger, *Untersuchungen* (1883), p. 232 n.; E. v. Philippovich, *Über Aufgabe und Methode der politischen Ökonomie* (Freiburg, 1886), pp. 20-21; E. Sax, *Das Wesen und die Aufgaben der Nationalökonomie* (Vienna, 1884), H. Dietzel, *Ueber das Verhältnis der Volkswirthschaftslehre zur Sozialwirthschafts-*

lehre (Berlin, 1881), p. 9; see also Dietzel "Beitrage zur Methodik der Wirtschaftswissenschaft," *Conrads Jahrbucher,* 1884, p. 18.

48. See J. K. Ingram's Preface to Ely's *Introduction to the Study of Political Economy* (quoted by Ely in his Introduction to the enlarged edition of Ingram's *A History of Political Economy* [London, 1915], p. xvii); and Cliffe Leslie, "On the Philosophical Method of Political Economy," *Hermathena,* 1876 (reprinted in his *Essays in Political Economy,* p. 189).

49. Cliffe Leslie, *op. cit.,* p. 212.

50. Besides the references to Dietzel's works in note 47 above, see also his "Der Ausgangspunkt der Sozialwirtschaftslehre und ihr Grundbegriff," *Tübinger Zeitschrift,* 1883; and his article "Selbstinteresse" in the *Handwörterbuch der Staatswissenschaften* (3rd ed.; Jena, 1911), VII, 435 ff.

51. H. Dietzel, *Theoretische Sozialökonomik* (Leipzig, 1895), p. 182.

52. R. T. Ely, *The Past and the Present of Political Economy* (Baltimore, 1884), p. 20.

53. E. de Laveleye, "Les lois naturelles et l'objet de l'économie politique," *Journal des économistes* (April, 1883), p. 92. French writers of this period stressing *richesses* include: Arendt, Limousin, Landry, Beauregard, Herve-Bazin, Courtois, Worms, and Levasseur.

54. For an interpretation of classical economics generally as seeing the central economic problem in the struggle of man against nature, see M. Dobb, *Political Economy and Capitalism,* pp. 19 f.; H. Myint, *Theories of Welfare Economics,* pp. 2 f.

55. H. Storch, *Cours d'économie politique* (St. Petersburg, 1815), I, ii.

56. See W. E. H. Lecky, *History of the Rise and Influence of the Spirit of Rationalism in Europe* (1865; American ed., 1955), pp. 335 f. On the possible influence on Lecky exerted by Comte, see Hayek, *Counter-Revolution of Science,* p. 187.

57. For passages in his writings in which the *Aussenwelt* is stressed, see A. Schäffle, *Die Nationalökonomie oder allgemeine Wirtschaftslehre* (Leipzig, 1861), pp. 2, 24; *Das gesellschaftliche System der menschlichen Wirtschaft* (3rd ed.; Tübingen, 1873), p. 2; "Die ethische Seite der Nationalökonomischen Lehre vom Werthe," *Gesammelte Aufsätze* (Tübingen, 1885).

58. On Mangoldt's and Sax's position, see E. Sax, *Das Wesen und die Aufgaben der Nationalökonomie* (Vienna, 1884), pp. 14-15. On Cohn's position, see Menger, *Untersuchungen,* p. 243. Julius Lehr in his *Grundbegriffe und Grundlagen der Volkswirtschaft* (Leipzig, 1893), p. 67, instead of referring to *Güter,* speaks of "die Dinge der Aussenwelt."

59. C. A. Tuttle, "The Fundamental Economic Principle," *Quarterly Journal of Economics,* 1901, p. 218.

60. On the existence of a line of subjective development in economics after the death of Ricardo, see M. Bowley, *Nassau Senior and Classical Political Economy,* ch. II.

61. See A. Schäffle, "Mensch und Gut in der Volkswirtschaft" (1861) in his *Gesammelte Aufsätze,* pp. 158 ff.; Droz's very strongly held position is cited by an American economist, Stephen Colwell, in a preliminary

essay to an edition of F. List's *National System of Political Economy* (Philadelphia, 1856), p. xxxvii; see also P. Cauwès, *Précis du cours d'économie politique* (Paris, 1881), p. 6.

62. R. T. Ely, *An Introduction to Political Economy* (New York, 1889), p. 105.

63. This continuity between the classical conception of economics as a science of wealth and the later emphasis on welfare gains in significance if classical economics is interpreted as "welfare analysis at the physical level" on the grounds that the classical economists implicitly assumed "that quantities of satisfaction of given wants are roughly proportional to quantities of physical products." H. Myint, *Theories of Welfare Economics,* p. xii.

64. E. Cannan, *A History of the Theories of Production and Distribution in English Political Economy from 1776 to 1848* (3rd ed.; London, 1917), p. 312. The quoted passage first appeared in the second edition (1903).

65. On the distinction between "classificatory" and "analytical" definitions of economics, see L. Robbins, *Nature and Significance of Economic Science* (2nd ed.), pp. 16 f.; A. L. Macfie, *An Essay on Economy and Value,* p. 2; L. Fraser, *Economic Thought and Language,* pp. 26 f.

66. "Welfare was like a fluid or a gas which, although perhaps difficult to measure, was in principle measurable . . ." I. Little, *A Critique of Welfare Economics* (Oxford, 1950), p. 9.

67. Dugald Stewart, *Political Economy,* ed. Hamilton (1855), I, 9. The passage was written about 1810. Cf. Bonar, *Philosophy and Political Economy* (London, 1922), p. 152.

68. J. C. L. Simonde de Sismondi, *Nouveaux principes d'économie politique* (3rd ed.; Geneva, 1951), p. 66.

69. See W. S. Jevons, *The Principles of Economics* (London: Macmillan & Co., 1905), p. 49; H. H. Powers, "Wealth and Welfare," *Publications of the American Academy of Political and Social Science* (April 4, 1899), p. 16.

70. Among French writers of the period who expressly condemned the objectivism of the definitions formulated in terms of *richesses* were: H. Dameth, *Introduction à l'étude de l'économie politique* (Paris, 1878), p. 89; A. Girault, "Les grandes divisions de la science économique," *Revue d'économie politique,* 1900, p. 796; E. Villey, *Principes d'économie politique* (Paris, 1894), p. 5; C. Gide, *Principles of Political Economy* (2nd American ed.; Boston, 1905), p. 3 n.; G. Tarde, *Psychologie économique* (Paris, 1902), I, 127.

71. See L. Robbins, *Nature and Significance,* p. 4 and footnotes.

72. For a more detailed discussion of Marshall's conception of the economic point of view, see below, chap. V. See also T. Parsons, "Wants and Activities in Marshall," *Quarterly Journal of Economics,* November, 1931, pp. 106 ff. For a discussion of the limitations circumscribing Marshall's adoption of the welfare formulation, see also F. Fetter, "Price Economics Versus Welfare Economics," *American Economic Review,* 1920, p. 721.

73. E. Cannan, review of L. Robbins' *Nature and Significance in Economic Journal*, September, 1932, pp. 424-427.
74. F. Fetter, "Price Economics Versus Welfare Economics," *American Economic Review*, 1920; W. C. Mitchell, *The Backward Art of Spending Money and Other Essays*, p. 381.
75. For an informative survey of these problems, see Streeten's Appendix to his translation of Myrdal's *The Political Element in the Development of Economic Theory* (1954).
76. D. H. Robertson, "Utility and All What?" *Economic Journal*, December, 1954, reprinted in his *Economic Commentaries* (London: Staples Press), pp. 57-58. Robertson has coined the term "ecfare" to denote the specific area of human welfare which is of concern to the economist.
77. S. Bailey, "On the Science of Political Economy," in his *Discourses on Various Subjects Read Before Literary and Philosophical Societies* (London, 1852), p. 125. This essay was written about 1835.
78. On the disrepute in which the "economic virtues" had been held, see, e.g., R. H. Tawney, *Religion and the Rise of Capitalism* (London, 1926), ch. IV.
79. In his *Inquiry into the Various Systems of Political Economy* (translated by D. Boileau, New York, 1812), Ganilh devoted some thirty pages to a survey of classical and modern civilizations, attempting to show that in the latter the desire for wealth bears no similarity to its objectionable counterpart in the former.
80. See R. Whately, *Introductory Lectures on Political Economy* (4th ed.; London, 1855), p. 25; M. Longfield, *Lectures on Political Economy* (Dublin, 1834), p. 3.
81. R. Jennings, *Natural Elements of Political Economy* (London, 1855), p. 41.
82. W. Bagehot, *Works* (Hartford, 1889), V, 224.
83. See W. S. Jevons, *The Theory of Political Economy* (1871); (4th ed.; London: Macmillan & Co., 1911), p. 26; F. Y. Edgeworth, *Mathematical Psychics* (London, 1881), pp. 52-53.
84. See W. S. Jevons, "Future of Political Economy," reprinted in *Principles of Economics and Other Papers*, pp. 197-199.
85. See F. A. Hayek, *The Road to Serfdom* (Chicago, 1956), pp. 88-89, for an interesting commentary on the possible sinister consequences of the belief that economic affairs pertain to the more sordid sides of life.

NOTES TO CHAPTER III

1. J. Ruskin, *Unto This Last*, Preface, sec. 5, note.
2. H. T. Buckle, *History of Civilization* (New York, 1871), II, 343. See also W. H. Hutt, *Economists and the Public* (London, 1936), p. 301, n. 2.
3. Mill's essay was published originally in the October, 1836, number of the *London and Westminster Review*. The essay had been written several years previously. On this point see J. Bonar, *Philosophy and Po-*

litical Economy (3rd ed.; London, 1922), p. 239; see also Ashley, Introduction to his 1909 edition of J. S. Mill's *Principles of Political Economy,* p. xvi.

4. J. S. Mill, "On the Definition of Political Economy," reprinted in *Essays on Some Unsettled Questions of Political Economy* (1844), p. 127. (All references are to the 1948 reprint by the London School of Economics and Political Science.)

5. *Ibid.,* pp. 129-132.

6. *Ibid.,* p. 137.

7. *Ibid.,* p. 140.

8. The earlier classical economists had used the concept of "economic man" but had not felt the need to define his nature, to state explicitly the degree of abstraction of which he is the product, or even to say whether he exists at all. This is easily understandable. In a science of wealth it is an obvious simplification to take into account only those aspects of human nature that seem to bear most directly on the phenomena of wealth. It is only for a Mill, for whom political economy deals exclusively with the "laws of mind," that it becomes imperative to demarcate those areas in human nature that pertain specifically to the investigations of political economy. For an analysis of the role of economic man in classical political economy, see A. Fey, *Der Homo Oeconomicus in der klassischen Nationalökonomie, und seiner Kritik durch den Historismus* (Limberg, 1936).

9. J. S. Mill, *System of Logic,* Book VI, ch. 9, sec. 3. A position remarkably similar to that of Mill seems to have been taken independently by Samuel Bailey, the author of *A Critical Dissertation on the Nature, Measures, and Causes of Value; Chiefly in Reference to the Writings of Mr. Ricardo and His Followers* (1825). It is unfortunate that Bailey's other writings, especially his essay *On the Science of Political Economy,* have received less attention. This essay was published as Discourse IV in S. Bailey, *Discourses on Various Subjects Read Before Literary and Philosophical Societies* (London, 1852); a footnote on p. 112 declares the essay on political economy to have been written in 1835 (that is, about a year before the publication of Mill's essay). Bailey objects forcefully to the usual definition of the subject in terms of wealth (pp. 107 f.). Like Mill, Bailey is concerned with distinguishing between the *technical* laws of production (which involve the physical sciences) and the *economic* laws relevant to political economy. Bailey unequivocally shifted the conception of economics from that of a science of wealth to that of a science of man and, in so doing, seems to have been tempted to create something suspiciously resembling Mill's economic man.

10. R. Whately, *Introductory Lectures on Political Economy* (4th ed.; London, 1855), p. 16; N. Senior, *An Outline of the Science of Political Economy* (London, 1938), p. 27; for Senior's view of Mill's economic man, see M. Bowley, *Nassau Senior and Classical Political Economy,* pp. 61 f.

11. See F. Y. Edgeworth, *Papers Relating to Political Economy* (London, 1925), I, 173. Edgeworth was aware of Marshall's denial of the necessity

of self-interest for economics. See Edgeworth's review of the third edition of Marshall's *Principles* in *Economic Journal*, V, 586. On Cunningham, see his "The Perversion of Economic History," *Economic Journal*, II, 498. For a fuller discussion of the place of self-interest in neoclassical economics, see W. H. Hutt, *Economists and the Public* (London, 1936), ch. XIX. See also F. H. Knight, "Professor Parsons on Economic Motivation," *Canadian Journal of Economics and Political Science*, 1940, pp. 461 f.

12. See especially M. Bowley, *Nassau Senior and Classical Political Economy*, ch. II.

13. N. Senior, *An Outline of the Science of Political Economy* (George Allen & Unwin), p. 26.

14. Henry George, *The Science of Political Economy* (New York, 1898), p. 88.

15. F. Hermann, *Staatswirtschaftliche Untersuchungen* (2nd ed.; Munich, 1870), pp. 67-68. See especially p. 68 n., where Hermann cites from a review that he wrote in 1836 ideas closely similar to those written at the same time by Mill and Bailey.

16. W. S. Jevons, *The Theory of Political Economy* (Macmillan & Co.), p. 23. See also the quotation from Jevons in Cliffe Leslie, *Essays in Political Economy*, p. 101.

17. See A. Schäffle, *Das gesellschaftliche System der menschlichen Wirthschaft* (3rd ed.; Tübingen, 1873), I, 46, cited in C. Menger's *Untersuchungen*, p. 242.

18. See A. Wagner, *Grundlegung der politischen Oekonomie*, Vol. I, *Grundlagen der Volkswirtschaft* (2d ed.; 1879), p. 9; and (3rd ed.; 1892), p. 81.

19. See H. Dietzel, "Der Ausgangspunkt der Sozialwirtschaftslehre, und ihr Grundbegriff," *Tübinger Zeitschrift für gesamte Staatswissenschaften*, 1883; H. Dietzel, *Theoretische Sozialökonomik* (Leipzig, 1895), p. 81; F. J. Neumann, *Grundlagen der Volkswirtschaftslehre* (Tübingen, 1889), pp. 4 f; see also E. V. Philippovich, *Grundriss der politischen Oekonomie*, Vol. I (1913), p. 2, and W. Sombart, "Die Elemente des Wirtschaftslebens," *Archiv für Sozialwissenschaft und Sozialpolitik*, 1913, XXXVII, for similar expressions. For Sax's views on the usefulness of the economic principle for definition, see his *Das Wesen und die Aufgaben der Nationalökonomie* (Vienna, 1884), p. 12.

20. It is of interest to note that Robbins has in fact used an argument almost identical with that of Dietzel to reject the material-welfare criterion towards which Dietzel was drawn. To the material-welfare economists Robbins points out the peculiar accident that generalizations valid for material-welfare activities prove to have equal applicability to other activities as well. L. Robbins, "Robertson on Utility and Scope," *Economica*, May, 1953, p. 105.

21. A. T. Hadley, "Economic Laws and Methods," in *Science Economic Discussion* (New York, 1886), p. 93; for other United States writers of the period who discussed the economic principle, see J. B. Clark, *Philosophy of Wealth* (Boston, 1892), p. 57; R. T. Ely, *Introduction*

to Political Economy (New York, 1889), pp. 58-59; E. R. A. Seligman, *Principles of Economics* (10th ed.; 1923), p. 4.

22. F. B. Hawley, *Enterprise and the Productive Process* (New York, 1907), p. 73.

23. H. J. Davenport, *Outlines of Economic Theory* (New York, 1896), p. 32.

24. See, however, K. Kautsky, *Die materialistische Geschichtsauffassung* (Berlin, 1927), I, 3-6, for the denial of this.

25. Of course, where maximization is itself expressed in terms of wealth, it leads back to the old notion of a specifically economic impulse (see, e.g., B. M. Anderson, *Social Value* [Cambridge, 1911], pp. 144-145).

26. James S. Early, "The Growth and Breadth of Theoretical Economics," in *Economic Theory in Review*, ed. C. L. Christenson (Indiana University, 1949) p. 13.

27. W. Roscher, *Geschichte der National-Oekonomik in Deutschland* (Munich, 1874), p. 1033.

28. P. Wicksteed, *Common Sense of Political Economy*, ed. Robbins, I, 163-165. For some later views on the subject see Z. Clark Dickinson, "The Relations of Recent Psychological Developments to Economic Theory," *Quarterly Journal of Economics*, May, 1919, p. 388; see also his book *Economic Motives* (Harvard, 1922); T. Parsons, "The Motivation of Economic Activities," *Canadian Journal of Economics and Political Science* (1940).

29. Among the writers who rejected the economic principle as a means of definition of the economic point of view, see especially the discussion by Oswalt of a paper by Voigt in *Verhandlungen des ersten Deutschen Soziologentages*, published in *Schriften der Deutschen Gesellschaft für Soziologie*, 1911, p. 270; H. Halberstaedter, *Die Problematik des wirtschaftlichen Prinzips* (1925), p. 76; F. Zweig, *Economics and Technology* (London, 1936), p. 19. Compare also P. Wicksteed, *The Common Sense of Political Economy*, ed. Robbins, I, 159 f.

30. J. Viner, "Some Problems of Logical Method in Political Economy," *Journal of Political Economy*, March, 1917, (Copyright 1917 by the University of Chicago), p. 248.

31. K. E. Boulding, *The Skills of the Economist* (Cleveland: Howard Allen, 1958), p. 179.

32. A. L. Macfie, *An Essay on Economy and Value* (London, 1936). For further discussion of Macfie's position, see chapter VI of this essay.

33. See Professor Robbins' Introduction to his edition of Wicksteed's *Common Sense*, p. xxi.

34. Wicksteed's "non-tuism" was noted by Roche-Agussol in his *Etude bibliographique des sources de la psychologie économique* (1919), p. 61, n. 1. Roche-Agussol also points out the similarity of Wicksteed's "non-tuism" to the ideas of Hawley (see especially "A Positive Theory of Economics," *Quarterly Journal of Economics*, 1902, pp. 233 f; and his *Enterprise and the Productive Process* [New York, 1907]).

35. P. Wicksteed, *Common Sense of Political Economy*, ed. Robbins, p. 175.

36. P. Wicksteed, "Scope and Method of Political Economy" (reprinted in *op. cit.*, II, 782).

37. P. Wicksteed, *Common Sense*, p. 182.
38. To be compared with Wicksteed's position is that of Viner, "Some Problems of Logical Method in Political Economy," *Journal of Political Economy*, March, 1917, (Copyright 1917 by the University of Chicago), p. 249: ". . . the economic transaction becomes non-moral in the sense that each party excludes the other from his moral situation."
39. N. Senior, *An Outline of the Science of Political Economy* (London: George Allen & Unwin, 1938), p. 28. One recalls, in connection with this analogy, Gossen's claim to qualify as the Copernicus of economics.
40. M. Pantaleoni, *Pure Economics* (1889; English translation, London, 1898), p. 5. (The term "mathematical economics" thus had for Pantaleoni an unusual meaning, for he gave it the task of solving "the problem of inscribing in a given triangle a rectangle of maximum dimensions, or that of circumscribing a given sphere with a minimum cone.") See also I. Little, *Welfare Economics* (1950), p. 21.
41. See Pantaleoni, *op. cit.*, pp. 7, 19. See also M. Pantaleoni, "An Attempt to Analyse the Concepts of 'Strong and Weak' in their Economic Connection," *Economic Journal*, 1898.
42. See B. Croce, "On the Economic Principle I," in *International Economic Papers*, No. 3, p. 177.
43. See J. Schumpeter, *Das Wesen und der Hauptinhalt der theoretischen Nationalökonomie* (Leipzig, 1908), p. 86, for the explicit view that the economist must consider the changes in "economic quantities" as if they were caused automatically, without paying attention to the human beings who may have been involved in the appearance of such changes.
44. Schumpeter's outlook on economics may be related to the influence which Mach in Vienna was exerting at the time on scientific thought. For a characterization of mechanics parallel to Schumpeter's view of economics, see Ernst Mach, *The Science of Mechanics* (Chicago, 1919), pp. 256 f. It is to be remarked that Schumpeter was surprisingly reticent about precisely what he understood under his *güter*. (See *op. cit.*, p. 80 n.) At least one of his critics seems to have understood Schumpeter to include all that is meant by "utility." (See A. Amonn, *Objekt und Grundbegriffe der theoretische Nationalökonomie*, 1911, p. 129.)
45. J. Schumpeter, *Wesen und Hauptinhalt*, pp. xvi, xvii, 47, 64.
46. See, e.g., Schumpeter's paper "Über die mathematische Methode der theoretischen Ökonomie," *Zeitschrift für Volkswirtschaft, Sozialpolitik, und Verwaltung*, XV (1908), 30-49.
47. For the similarity of Pareto's position to that of Schumpeter, see his "On the Economic Phenomenon," in *International Economic Papers*, No. 3, p. 184, and his "Anwendungen der Mathematik auf Nationalökonomie," in *Encyclopädie der mathematischen Wissenschaften*, 1902, pp. 1107-1108. For a recent example of the hardiness of the Schumpeter view, see Boulding, *The Skills of the Economist*, pp. 28-29.
48. B. Croce, "On the Economic Principle II," in *International Economic Papers*, No. 3, p. 197.

NOTES TO CHAPTER IV

1. T. Malthus, *Definitions in Political Economy*, pp. 70 f. Mill's position is in his *Commerce Defended* (1808), p. 22; McCulloch's, in his *Principles of Political Economy* (1825), part I, p. 5. Parallel to the exchangeability condition required for wealth by these writers is the requirement that items of wealth be capable of appropriation and alienation. (See, e.g., S. Read, *Political Economy* [Edinburgh, 1929], p. 1.) Sismondi explicitly denied that exchangeability is a prerequisite for wealth (*Nouveaux principes d'économie politique* [Geneva, 1951], p. 71).

2. Count DeStutt de Tracy, *A Treatise on Political Economy* (English ed., Georgetown, 1817), "Of Action," pp. 6, 15.

3. R. Whately, *Introductory Lectures on Political Economy* (4th ed.; London, 1855), p. 4.

4. *Ibid.*, p. 5. See N. Senior, *Outline of the Science of Political Economy*, p. 25. Torrens, apparently, was in disagreement (*ibid.*). See also E. Cannan, *Theories of Production and Distribution, 1776-1848*, p. 7.

5. On the existence of a Dublin "school" in economics during this period, see R. D. Black, "Trinity College, Dublin, and the Theory of Value, 1832-1863," *Economica*, New Series, XII (1945), 140-148.

6. The Whately professors who endorsed the catallactic view were J. A. Lawson, *Five Lectures on Political Economy, delivered before the University of Dublin, 1843* (London and Dublin, 1844), pp. 12 f.; and W. N. Hancock, *An Introductory Lecture on Political Economy* (Dublin, 1849), p. 7. The writer who wrote under the pseudonym Patrick Plough (and was noticed by Seligman in his "On Some Neglected British Economists," *Economic Journal*, 1903), bestowed on his book (London, 1842) the following title: *Letters on the Rudiments of a Science, called formerly, improperly, Political Economy, recently more pertinently, Catallactics*.

7. Among writers who condemned the narrowness of the catallactic view were F. W. Newman, *Lectures on Political Economy* (London, 1851), p. 19; J. Cazenove, *Thoughts on a Few Subjects of Political Economy* (London, 1859), p. 70. See also W. E. Hearn, *Plutology* (London and Melbourne, 1864), p. 6. For later criticism of the narrowness of Whately's position, see W. Roscher, *Geschichte der National-Oekonomik in Deutschland* (Munich, 1874), pp. 844, 1072; P. Cauwès, *Précis du cours d'économie politique* (Paris, 1881), p. 7; P. Leroy-Beaulieu, *Traité théorique et pratique d'économie politique* (Paris, 1896), I, 16.

8. H. D. Macleod, *The Elements of Political Economy* (London, 1858), p. 5. Macleod stresses his independent arrival at the catallactic position. In his notion of exchange Macleod is narrower than some of his precursors. Thus he dismisses taxation from political economy on the grounds that it is not the subject of exchange. Whately expressly considered taxation as exchange (*Introductory Lectures*, p. 7 n.). Senior too (*Outline of the Science of Political Economy*, p. 87) viewed "all

that is received by the officers of Government as given in Exchange for Services. . . ." In his *History of Economics,* published some forty years later, Macleod carefully collected favorable references to his own work by later writers and cites the American Perry, about whom more below.

9. J. A. Lawson, *Five Lectures on Political Economy,* pp. 12-13.
10. A. Smith, *Wealth of Nations,* ed. Cannan (Modern Library edition), p. 13.
11. See J. A. Lawson, *op. cit.,* p. 26. (A similar ambivalence seems visible also in Plough's work cited above, n. 6.)
12. A. L. Perry, *Elements of Political Economy* (14th ed.; New York, 1877), pp. 1, 54.
13. F. A. Walker, *Political Economy* (New York, 1883), p. 3. Henry George's criticism is in his *The Science of Political Economy* (New York, 1898), p. 130.
14. Albert S. Bolles, *Political Economy* (New York, 1878), p. 3.
15. Franklin H. Giddings, "The Sociological Character of Political Economy," read at the second annual meeting of the association; published in the association's *Publications,* III (1889), 43. It is of some interest that Giddings, who here castigates the "absurdity" of the Perry position, has elsewhere (*Essays in Honor of J. B. Clark,* 1927) gratefully cited Perry's book as having been his own first textbook in economics.
16. See, e.g., A. Amonn, *Objekt und Grundbegriffe der theoretische Nationalökonomie* (2nd ed.), pp. 160 f., for Max Weber's position; Felix Kaufmann, "On the Subject Matter and Method of Economic Science," *Economica,* November, 1933, pp. 384 f; H. Halberstaedter, *Die Problematik des wirtschaftlichen Prinzips* (1925), p. 76. Schumpeter's position is discussed later in this chapter.
17. A. L. Perry, *An Introduction to Political Economy* (New York, 1877), p. 12.
18. P. Wicksteed, "The Scope and Method of Political Economy," *Economic Journal,* March, 1914, reprinted in *Common Sense of Political Economy,* II, 781.
19. See S. Newcomb, *Principles of Political Economy* (New York, 1886), p. 6; F. B. Hawley, "A Positive Theory of Economics," *Quarterly Journal of Economics,* 1902, pp. 233 f.
20. A. Marshall, *The Present Position of Political Economy* (London, 1885), pp. 22-25.
21. See especially G. Tarde, *Psychologie économique* (Paris, 1902), pp. 151 f., for the use of this aspect of exchange to distinguish between economics and politics. On Weber's position, see above, n. 16; see also Shils and Finch, eds., *Max Weber on the Methodology of the Social Sciences* (Glencoe, 1949), p. 63; M. Weber, *Gesammelte Aufsätze zur Wissenschaftslehre* (Tübingen, 1922), pp. 365-366.
22. Schumpeter's definition of economics in terms of exchange was set forth in his *Das Wesen und der Hauptinhalt der theoretische Nationalökonomie* (Leipzig, 1908); see especially pp. 55, 582. For Schumpeter's maturer view of exchange, see his *History of Economic Analysis* (1954), p. 911. For what seems to be a change in Schumpeter's appraisal of

Whately's stress on catallactics, see *Wesen und Hauptinhalt,* p. 50 n., and *History of Economic Analysis,* p. 536 n.

23. See A. Amonn, *Objekt und Grundbegriffe der theoretischen National-ökonomie* (1st ed., 1911), p. 128; L. Robbins, *Nature and Significance of Economic Science* (2nd ed.), p. 21 n.

24. E. R. A. Seligman, "Social Elements in the Theory of Value," *Quarterly Journal of Economics,* May, 1901, p. 327. See also L. Mises, *Socialism* (English ed., London: Jonathan Cape, 1936), pp. 114, 117.

25. J. A. Schumpeter, *Wesen und Hauptinhalt,* p. 53.

26. *Op. cit.,* p. 49.

27. Carl E. Parry, "A Revaluation of Traditional Economic Theory," *American Economic Review* (Supplement, 1921), p. 125.

28. "If economic theory is interpreted as a critique of the competitive system of organization, its first and most general problem is that of determining whether the fundamental tendencies of free contractual relations under competitive control lead to the maximum production of value as measured in price terms." (F. H. Knight, "Fallacies in the Interpretation of Social Cost," *Quarterly Journal of Economics,* 1924, reprinted in *The Ethics of Competition,* p. 218.)

29. J. E. Cairnes, "Bastiat," reprinted in his *Essays in Political Economy* (London, 1873), pp. 312 f.

30. F. Bastiat, *Harmonies économiques* (8th ed.; Paris, 1881), pp. 25-28.

31. R. G. Hawtrey, *The Economic Problem* (London: Longmans, Green & Co., 1925), p. 3.

32. F. A. v. Hayek, "The Trend of Economic Thinking," *Economica,* May, 1933, pp. 130-131. For similar passages stressing the economic *organization* for the purposes of definition, see R. T. Bye, "The Scope and Definition of Economics," *Journal of Political Economy,* October, 1939, p. 626; K. E. Boulding, *The Skills of the Economist* (Cleveland, 1958), p. 8. See also F. Oppenheimer, "Alfred Amonn's 'Objekt und Grund-begriffe,'" *Weltwirtschaftliches Archiv.* Bd. 27 (1928), I, *Literatur,* p. 170.

33. For samples of the literature on this point, see C. Menger's *Unter-suchungen* (Appendix I, "Ueber das Wesen der Volkswirthschaft"); G. Schmoller, "Die Volkswirtschaft, die Volkswirtschaftslehre, und ihre Methode" (1893), reprinted in his *Über einige Grundfragen der Sozial-politik und der Volkswirtschaftslehre* (Leipzig, 1898).

34. For one example of German influence in this regard, see Ely's approving reference to the definition of economics as the "science of national housekeeping," an idea which he relates to that of a "Volkswirthschaft" (*Introduction to Political Economy* [New York, 1889], p. 95).

35. See G. Schmoller, *Über einige Grundfragen,* p. 217.

36. See G. Schmoller, *Grundriss der allgemeinen Volkswirtschaftslehre* (11th and 12th ed.; 1919), I, 1.

37. W. Roscher, *System der Volkswirtschaft,* I (Berlin, 1906), 42.

38. F. Kleinwachter, "Wesen, Aufgabe und System der Nationalökonomie," *Conrads Jahrbucher* (1889), p. 639.

39. See especially A. Amonn, *Objekt und Grundbegriffe* (2nd ed.), pp. 153 f.

40. See especially the article by Oppenheimer cited above, n. 32.
41. See, e.g., D. Raymond, *The Elements of Political Economy* (2nd ed.; Baltimore, 1823), p. 35; Patrick Plough (pseud.), *Letters on the Rudiments of . . . Catallactics*, p. 4; R. Whately, *Introductory Lectures*, pp. 16, 33 f.
42. On this see T. Suranyi-Unger, *Economics in the Twentieth Century* (English ed., New York, 1931), p. 78. See also the next section in this chapter.
43. For J. S. Mill's emphasis on the social character of economic affairs, see his·*Essays on Some Unsettled Questions of Political Economy*, pp. 133, 135, 137, 140. Amonn, in his sharply critical review of Mill's position (*Objekt und Grundbegriffe*, 1st ed., pp. 35-36), does not seem to take notice of these passages. Gehrig (in an essay introducing his 1922 edition of Hildebrand's *Die Nationalökonomie der Gegenwart und Zukunft*, p. lx), ascribes it to the credit of the "new" economists to have first recognized the social character of their discipline.
44. See Comte's *Cours de philosophie positive* (2nd ed., 1864), IV, 194 f.; see also the works cited above, ch. I, n. 24.
45. On this see above, ch. II, n. 48. Compare Parsons' view that Marshall's conception of economics turned it into an "encyclopedic sociology," so that any separate identity of economic theory as a discipline is destroyed. (See, e.g., T. Parsons, *The Structure of Social Action* [Glencoe, 1949], p. 173.)
46. See, e.g., A. Amonn, *Objekt und Grundbegriffe* (1st ed.), p. 154 n.
47. It comes as not altogether a shock to discover at least one writer who advanced a view precisely opposed to that of Amonn. A. Schor (in his dissertation *Die rein ökonomische Kategorie in der Wirtschaft* [Königsberg, 1903]) can find the purely economic aspect of affairs only by abstracting completely from the social element.
48. R. T. Bye, "The Scope and Definition of Economics," *Journal of Political Economy*, October, 1939, p. 625; J. F. Hayford, "The Relation of Engineering to Economics," *Journal of Political Economy*, January, 1917, p. 59.
49. See above n. 42. See also B. M. Anderson, *Social Value* (Cambridge, 1911); L. H. Haney, "The Social Point of View in Economics," *Quarterly Journal of Economics*, 1913; T. Parsons, "Some Reflections on 'The Nature and Significance of Economics,'" *Quarterly Journal of Economics*, May, 1934, pp. 518 f.; Alec L. Macfie, *Economic Efficiency and Social Welfare* (London, 1943). The justification for what might seem the perfunctory treatment of the matters touched on in this paragraph must be that, important as they are in other connections, they have far less relevance—and that of a chiefly negative character—for our own discussion.
50. On this, see Talcott Parsons and Neil J. Smelser, *Economy and Society* (Glencoe, 1956), p. 6.
51. *Ibid.* Parsons and Smelser ascribe the original suggestion to Professor W. W. Rostow. See also P. A. Sorokin, *Society, Culture and Personality* (New York, 1947), pp. 7 f.

NOTES TO CHAPTER V

1. See, e.g., E. Cannan, *A History of the Theories of Production and Distribution in English Political Economy from 1776-1848*, ch. I.
2. J. Dupuit, "On the Measurement of Utility of Public Works" (translated in *International Economic Papers*, No. 2, p. 89).
3. W. Bagehot, *Works* (Hartford, 1889), V, 324.
4. R. Lowe, "Recent Attacks on Political Economy," *Nineteenth Century*, November, 1878, p. 864.
5. For passages in which Bagehot consistently refers to economics as the "science of business," see his *Works* (Hartford, 1889), III, 269; V, 243, 259, 324. See III, 44 for a passage in which Bagehot writes of Cairnes that he defined "the exact sort of science which political economy is" better than any previous writer.
6. The use of money as the criterion for defining the nature of economic activity, on the grounds that human action directed towards consumer goods is first channeled into a search for general purchasing power in the form of money, bears a close similarity to a distinction used later by Robbins and Hayek. In the following chapter we shall notice the identification by these writers of the economic motive with the desire for *general* opportunity, the ability to achieve unspecified ends. On this point see also L. Robbins, *Nature and Significance* (2nd ed.), pp. 30-31.
7. For examples of writers who have fairly recently sought for a defining criterion in this division between man's money-getting actions and his other actions, see K. Rivett, "The Definition of Economics," *Economic Record*, November, 1955, pp. 221, 229; E. Heimann, "Comparative Economic Systems," in *Goals of Economic Life*, ed. A. D. Ward (New York, 1953), pp. 122 f.
8. Parsons has minimized the importance to Marshall of his criterion of measurability (*Structure of Social Action*, p. 134). Robbins consistently associates the criterion of money as a measuring rod with Pigou rather than with Marshall. See also J. N. Tewari, "What Is Economics?" *Indian Journal of Economics*, April, 1947, for a similar implication of a difference between Marshall and Pigou with regard to the idea of money as a measuring rod.
9. A. Marshall, *The Present Position of Economics* (London, 1885). Passages from this lecture appear again in the *Principles;* in particular, several passages having reference to this chapter reappear verbatim in Appendix D (in the 8th edition).
10. A. Marshall, *Principles of Economics* (8th ed.; Macmillan & Co.), p. 1.
11. A. Marshall, *The Present Position of Economics*, pp. 22 f.
12. *Ibid.*, p. 28.
13. *Ibid.*, pp. 22-25.
14. *Ibid.*, p. 29.
15. *Ibid.*, p. 31.

16. A. Marshall, *Principles,* p. 38. Similar passages are to be found on pp. 15, 27, 57.
17. A. C. Pigou, *Wealth and Welfare* (London: Macmillan & Co., 1912), p. 3.
18. *Ibid.,* p. 8. See also Pigou's inaugural Cambridge lecture, published as *Economic Science in Relation to Practice* (London, 1908).
19. A. C. Pigou, *The Economics of Welfare* (4th ed.; London: Macmillan & Co., 1932), p. 11.
20. See G. Tarde, *Psychologie économique* (Paris, 1902), p. 77.
21. B. Croce, "On the Economic Principle II," in *International Economic Papers,* No. 3, p. 197.
22. A. Marshall, *The Present Position of Economics,* p. 27.
23. See the article by L. Mises in *Studium Generale,* VI, No. 2, 1953.
24. F. H. Knight, "The Nature of Economic Science in Some Recent Discussion," *American Economic Review,* June, 1934, p. 236.
25. S. Patten, "The Scope of Political Economy," reprinted in S. Patten, *Essays in Economic Theory,* ed. R. Tugwell (New York: Alfred Knopf, 1924), p. 192.
26. *Ibid.,* p. 185.
27. *Ibid.* For other passages on economics and measurable motives, see O. R. Trowbridge, *Bisocialism* (1903), p. 106; R. Scoon, "Professor Robbins' Definition of Economics," *Journal of Political Economy,* August, 1943, p. 321.
28. On the possibility of infinite utility, see P. H. Wicksteed, "On Certain Passages in Jevons' *Theory of Political Economy,*" *Quarterly Journal of Economics,* 1889, reprinted in *Common Sense,* II, 736.
29. L. Mises, *Socialism* (London: Jonathan Cape, 1936), p. 116.
30. Writers who have criticized the criterion of money as a measuring rod include J. A. Hobson, *Free Thought in the Social Sciences* (New York, 1926), pp. 97 f.; R. G. Hawtrey, *The Economic Problem* (London, 1925), p. 184; F. A. Fetter, "Price Economics Versus Welfare Economics," *American Economic Review,* 1920, pp. 721, 736; A. L. Macfie, *An Essay on Economy and Value* (London, 1936), pp. 72-73.
31. See, e.g., V. Pareto, "On the Economic Phenomenon," *International Economic Papers,* No. 3, p. 190; H. J. Davenport, "Fetter's 'Economic Principles,'" *Journal of Political Economy,* March, 1916; W. Mitchell, *The Backward Art of Spending Money,* pp. 232-233, 256-257; J. Viner, "The Utility Concept in Value Theory and Its Critics," *Journal of Political Economy,* 1925, p. 659.
32. At least one writer explicitly identified the position of the "price-economists" as the "catallactic point of view" (Carl Parry, "A Revaluation of Traditional Economic Theory," *American Economic Review* [Supplement, 1921], p. 123.)
33. For a discussion of the restriction of price-economics to monetary phenomena see F. A. Fetter, "Davenport's Competitive Economics," *Journal of Political Economy,* June, 1914, pp. 554 ff.
34. See above, ch. I, n. 4.

35. L. Mises, *Nation, Staat und Wirtschaft* (1919), p. 133. See also L. Mises, *Human Action* (1949), p. 232 on the same point.
36. W. C. Mitchell, "The Role of Money in Economic Theory," *American Economic Review* (Supplement, 1916), reprinted in *The Backward Art of Spending Money*, p. 171.
37. *The Backward Art of Spending Money*, pp. 256-257.
38. W. C. Mitchell, "Thorstein Veblen," in *The Backward Art of Spending Money*, pp. 304-305.
39. *Op. cit.*, p. 256.
40. C. H. Cooley, especially, expanded on the pecuniary influences on society in a number of papers in the second decade of this century. See also A. A. Young, "Some Limitations of the Value Concept," *Quarterly Journal of Economics*, May, 1911, p. 415.
41. L. Robbins, "Live and Dead Issues in the Methodology of Economics," *Economica*, August, 1938, p. 344.

NOTES TO CHAPTER VI

1. L. Robbins, *The Nature and Significance of Economic Science* (2nd ed.; Macmillan & Co.), p. 16.
2. *Ibid.*, pp. 12-14.
3. L. Robbins, *The Economic Causes of War* (London: Jonathan Cape, 1939), pp. 117-118. This point is discussed further in a later section of this chapter.
4. Earl of Lauderdale, *Inquiry into the Nature and Origin of Public Wealth* (Edinburgh, 1804), pp. 56-57.
5. See, e.g., N. Senior, *An Outline of the Science of Political Economy*, pp. 14 f.
6. On this point see Hayek's essay "Carl Menger," *Economica*, 1934, printed as the Introduction to the edition of Menger's *Collected Works* of the London School of Economics, p. xiii. See also Knight's critical comment on this in his Introduction to the English edition of Menger's *Grundsätze* (Glencoe, 1950), p. 13, n. 5.
7. C. Menger, *Principles of Economics* (trans. Dingwall and Hoselitz, Glencoe, 1950), p. 96.
8. H. Dietzel, *Theoretische Sozialökonomik*, p. 160.
9. See A. Schäffle, *Das gesellschaftliche System der menschlichen Wirthschaft* (Tübingen, 1873), p. 2; G. Cohn, *Grundlegung der Nationalökonomie* (Stuttgart, 1885), p. 4 (see, however, an earlier passage by Cohn cited in Menger's *Untersuchungen*, p. 254).
10. F. J. Neumann, *Grundlagen der Volkswirtschaftslehre* (Tübingen, 1889), p. 16.
11. L. Haney, *History of Economic Thought* (New York: Macmillan & Co., 1949), p. 600; see also K. Wicksell, *Lectures on Political Economy* (London, 1934), I, 32, for the same point.
12. For these references to precursors of Robbins' definition, see *Nature and Significance*, pp. 15, 16; L. Robbins, "Live and Dead Issues in the

Methodology of Economics," *Economica*, August, 1938, p. 344; A. Lowe, *Economics and Sociology* (London, 1935), p. 42; A. Emery, "The Totalitarian Economics of Othmar Spann," *Journal of Social Philosophy*, April, 1936, pp. 270-271; F. Oppenheimer, "Alfred Amonn's 'Objekt und Grundbegriffe,'" *Weltwirtschaftliches Archiv*, Bd. 27 (1928), I, 174-175. A. Voigt, "Die Unterscheidung von Wirtschaft und Technik, Erwiderung," *Zeitschrift für Sozialwissenschaft*, 1915, p. 395; Shils and Finch, eds., *Max Weber on the Methodology of the Social Sciences* (Glencoe: Free Press, 1949), pp. 63 f.; *Gesammelte Aufsätze zur Wissenschaftslehre von Max Weber* (Tübingen, 1922), p. 365. See, however, Weber's comment on Voigt's position, in *Verhandlung des ersten Deutschen Soziologentages* (*Schriften der Deutschen Gesellschaft für Soziologie*, 1911), pp. 265 f.

13. See D. H. MacGregor, *Economic Thought and Policy* (London, 1949), pp. 1-6; see also O. F. Boucke, *A Critique of Economics* (New York, 1922), p. 249.

14. See H. Myint, *Theories of Welfare Economics* (Harvard, 1948), pp. 2 f., for a discussion of the position of the classical economists towards the scarcity view of economics.

15. L. Robbins, *Nature and Significance*, p. 15 n.; for examples of writers who seem to view the act of economizing as being essentially identical with that of maximizing, see F. H. Knight, "The Nature of Economic Science in Some Recent Discussion," *American Economic Review*, June, 1934, p. 228; F. Machlup, "Marginal Analysis and Empirical Research," *American Economic Review*, September, 1946, p. 519.

16. L. Robbins, *Nature and Significance*, pp. 16-17; see also Robbins' Introduction to his edition of Wicksteed's *Common Sense of Political Economy*, p. xxii.

17. Among the writers who have hailed Robbins' stress on the concern of economics with an aspect of action are A. L. Macfie, *An Essay on Economy and Value*, pp. 2-6; G. Tagliacozzo, "Croce and the Nature of Economic Science," *Quarterly Journal of Economics*, May, 1945, pp. 308 f; W. H. Hutt, *Economists and the Public* (London, 1936), pp. 308-309.

18. L. M. Fraser, *Economic Thought and Language*, p. 32.

19. These writers include E. Heimann, "Comparative Economic Systems," in *Goals of Economic Life*, ed. by A. D. Ward (New York, 1953), p. 122; J. S. Early, "The Growth and Breadth of Theoretical Economics," in *Economic Theory in Review*, ed. by C. L. Christenson (1949), pp. 12-13; see also S. Schoeffler, *The Failures of Economics: a Diagnostic Study* (Harvard, 1955), pp. 11 f.

20. For examples see B. Higgins, *What Do Economists Know?* (Melbourne, 1951), pp. 2-3; L. M. Fraser, *Economic Thought and Language*, p. 32; L. Robbins, *Nature and Significance*, p. 22. See also G. J. Stigler, *The Theory of Price* (revised ed., 1952), p. 1 n.

21. *Nature and Significance*, pp. 19 f.

22. R. W. Souter, "'The Nature and Significance of Economic Science' in Recent Discussion," *Quarterly Journal of Economics*, May, 1933, p. 384.

23. *Ibid.,* p. 386.
24. *Ibid.,* p. 399.
25. *Ibid.,* p. 390.
26. *Ibid.,* p. 395 n.
27. *Ibid.,* p. 400.
28. T. Parsons, "Some Reflections on 'The Nature and Significance of Economics,' " *Quarterly Journal of Economics,* May, 1934, pp. 536-537, 530-531.
29. J. S. Early, "The Growth and Breadth of Theoretical Economics," in *Economic Theory in Review,* p. 13.
30. On these matters see G. Myrdal, *Value in Social Theory* (London, 1958), pp. 206 ff. See also the Introduction by P. Streeten, pp. xxi f.
31. R. W. Souter, *op. cit.,* p. 379; T. Parsons, *op. cit.,* pp. 513-516; A. L. Macfie, *An Essay on Economy and Value,* p. 16; see also F. H. Knight's review of Robbins' *Nature and Significance* in the *International Journal of Ethics,* April, 1934, p. 359.
32. T. Parsons, *op. cit.,* pp. 514 f.
33. For Robbins' views on the purposive element in economic activity, see *Nature and Significance,* p. 93.
34. F. Kaufmann, "On the Subject Matter and Method of Economic Science," *Economica,* November, 1933, p. 383.
35. See F. Zweig, *Economics and Technology* (London, 1936), p. 20.
36. T. Parsons, *op. cit.,* pp. 523 f.
37. Cited in L. Robbins, *Nature and Significance,* p. 35. See also E. Fossati, *The Theory of General Static Equilibrium,* ed. G. L. Shackle (1957), p. 9.
38. K. Rivett, "The Definition of Economics," *Economic Record,* Vol. XXXI, No. 61 (November, 1955), pp. 217-219.
39. G. Tagliacozzo, "Croce and the Nature of Economic Science," *Quarterly Journal of Economics,* May, 1945.
40. Cf. Parsons, *The Structure of Social Action,* ch. IV, for a discussion of the degree in which Marshall refused to consider wants as data for economics.
41. On this see, e.g., F. H. Knight, "Professor Parsons on Economic Motivation," *Canadian Journal of Economics and Political Science,* 1940, p. 464.
42. The fact that means as well as ends are data for the economist is made clear by a number of writers; see A. Lowe, *Economics and Sociology,* p. 43: F. H. Knight, "The Nature of Economic Science in Some Recent Discussion," *American Economic Review,* 1934, p. 229. Among the writers apparently not admitting this, see W. C. Mitchell, *Backward Art of Spending Money,* p. 224.
43. Max Weber, *The Theory of Social and Economic Organization* (translated by A. M. Henderson and T. Parsons, New York, 1947), pp. 162, 209. For passages in which Weber discusses the distinction between economics and technology, see Shils and Finch, eds., *Max Weber on the Methodology of the Social Sciences* (Glencoe: Free Press, 1949), pp. 34-35; and "R. Stammler's 'Ueberwindung' der materialistischen

Geschichtsauffassung," *Archiv für Sozialwissenschaft und Sozialpolitik,* 1907, reprinted in *Gesammelte Aufsätze zur Wissenschaftslehre von Max Weber,* p. 328.

44. See, e.g., F. Zweig, *Economics and Technology* (London, 1936), pp. 20 f.
45. For an example of the use of this kind of distinction, see Dorfman, Samuelson, and Solow, *Linear Programming and Economic Analysis* (1958), p. 202.
46. F. H. Knight, "The Nature of Economic Science in Recent Discussion," *American Economic Review,* June, 1934, p. 228; see also Knight's review of Robbins' *Nature and Significance* in the *International Journal of Ethics,* April, 1934, p. 359; and his "Professor Parsons on Economic Motivation," *Canadian Journal of Economics and Political Science,* 1940, p. 463.
47. See especially T. Parsons, *Quarterly Journal of Economics,* May, 1934, pp. 516-518.
48. F. Hayek, *The Road to Serfdom* (University of Chicago Press, copyright 1956 by the University of Chicago), p. 89, and footnote. See also above, ch. V, n. 6.
49. P. Plough (pseud.), *Letters on the Rudiments of . . . Catallactics* (London, 1842), p. 15.
50. For such criticism see K. Rivett, "The Definition of Economics," *Economic Record,* November, 1955, pp. 227 f.
51. G. Myrdal, *Value in Social Theory* (London: Routledge & Kegan Paul, 1958), p. 237; see also Myrdal's *Political Element in the Development of Economic Theory.*
52. J. A. Schumpeter, *History of Economic Analysis* (1954), p. 805.
53. *Nature and Significance,* pp. 147 ff.
54. For the claim to have discovered an inconsistency in Robbins' position on this point, see L. M. Fraser, "How Do We Want Economists to Behave?" *Economic Journal,* December, 1932, p. 557 n.; A. L. Macfie, *An Essay on Economy and Value,* p. 27.
55. L. Robbins, "Mr. Hawtrey on the Scope of Economics," *Economica,* 1927, p. 174.
56. On Knight's position in the positive-normative controversy, see his article: "Professor Parsons on Economic Motivation," *Canadian Journal of Economics and Political Science* (1940), p. 461; see, however, below n. 65.
57. R. Souter, *Quarterly Journal of Economics,* May, 1933, pp. 402 ff.
58. Cf. T. W. Hutchison, *Significance and Basic Postulates of Economic Theory* (London, 1938), pp. 153-155.
59. See T. Parsons, *Quarterly Journal of Economics,* May, 1934, p. 520.
60. A. L. Macfie, *An Essay on Economy and Value* (Macmillan & Co.), p. 69.
61. *Ibid.,* pp. vii-viii. See also Macfie's article "What Kind of Experience Is Economizing?" *Ethics,* 1949, pp. 19 ff.
62. See also the discussion concerning Macfie's position above in ch. III of this essay.
63. A. L. Macfie, *Economy and Value,* p. 34.

64. *Ibid.,* pp. 69-70.
65. See Knight's preface to Macfie, *Economic Efficiency and Social Welfare* (London, 1943), p. v; see also F. H. Knight, " 'What Is Truth' in Economics?" *Journal of Political Economy,* February, 1940, reprinted in his *On the History and Method of Economics* (Chicago, 1956), p. 172; F. Kaufmann, "On the Postulates of Economic Theory," *Social Research,* September, 1942, p. 393.
66. T. Veblen, *Theory of the Leisure Class* (Modern Library, 1934), p. 15.
67. T. Veblen, *Essays in Our Changing Order* (New York: Viking Press, 1943), pp. 80-81; see also R. B. Perry, "Economic Value and Moral Value," *Quarterly Journal of Economics,* May, 1916, pp. 444 f.
68. R. T. Bye, "The Scope and Definition of Economics," *Journal of Political Economy,* October, 1939 (Copyright 1939 by the University of Chicago), p. 645.
69. T. Scitovsky, *Welfare and Competition* (London, 1952), p. 9.
70. R. T. Bye, *op. cit.,* p. 646.
71. B. Wootton, *Lament for Economics* (New York, 1938), p. 106.
72. See Wootton, *op. cit.,* p. 96; cf. also T. W. Hutchison, *Significance and Basic Postulates,* p. 135.
73. K. Rivett, "The Definition of Economics," *Economic Record,* Vol. XXXI, No. 61 (November, 1955), p. 217.

NOTES TO CHAPTER VII

1. On the term "praxeology," see A. Espinas, "Les origines de la technologie," *Revue philosophique de la France et de l'étranger,* 15th Year, July-December, 1890; L. Mises, *Human Action* (1949), p. 3; F. A. Hayek, *The Counter-Revolution of Science,* p. 209, note 20.
2. For such early glimpses of the possibility of a science of human action, see H. Storch, *Cours d'économie politique* (St. Petersburg, 1815), I, ii; R. Jennings, *Natural Elements of Political Economy* (London, 1855), p. 41, where political economy is described as "a science of human actions"; W. E. Hearn, *Plutology: or the Theory of the Efforts to Satisfy Human Wants* (London and Melbourne, 1864).
3. Sidney Sherwood, "The Philosophical Basis of Economics, A Word to Sociologists," *Publications of the American Academy of Political and Social Science,* October 5, 1897.
4. See further above, ch. II, in the section entitled "The Science of Subsistence."
5. See, however, T. Parsons, "Economics and Sociology: Marshall in Relation to the Thought of His Time," *Quarterly Journal of Economics,* February, 1932, p. 340, for the emphasis on that aspect of Pareto's thinking which cuts him off from economic behaviorism.
6. See *International Economic Papers,* No. 3, pp. 190, 204.
7. For a similar charge of implicit metaphysical bias in the position of those denying the concept of human action, see L. Mises, *Theory and History* (Yale, 1957), pp. 3 f.

8. The writings of R. G. Collingwood reveal some similarity to Croce's views. See, e.g., his "Human Nature and Human History," *Proceedings of the British Academy*, Vol. XXII (1936): "The self-knowledge of reason is not an accident; it belongs to its essence." See also his "Economics as a Philosophical Science," *Ethics*, Vol. XXXVI (1926).

9. B. Croce, *Philosophy of the Practical* (English ed.; London: Macmillan & Co., 1913), pp. 365-371. For a brief exposition of the position which Croce's views on economy occupy within his complete system of philosophy, see G. Tagliacozzo, "Croce and the Nature of Economic Science," *Quarterly Journal of Economics*, May, 1945.

10. M. Weber, "Die Objektivität sozialwissenschaftlicher und sozialpolitischer Erkenntnis," *Archiv für Sozialwissenschaft und Sozialpolitik*, 1904; translated in Shils and Finch, eds., *Max Weber on the Methodology of the Social Sciences* (Glencoe: Free Press, 1949), p. 83.

11. See, e.g., M. Weber, "Die Grenznutzlehre und das 'psychophysische' Grundgesetz," *Archiv für Sozialwissenschaft und Sozialpolitik*, 1908; reprinted in *Gesammelte Aufsätze zur Wissenschaftslehre von Max Weber* (Tübingen, 1922), pp. 364-365.

12. For criticism of Weber's conception of economics, see L. Mises, "Soziologie und Geschichte, Epilog zum Methodenstreit in der Nationalökonomie," *Archiv für Sozialwissenschaft und Sozialpolitik*, 1929, pp. 465 ff. See further T. Parsons, *The Structure of Social Action*, ch. XVI, and *Essays in Sociological Theory, Pure and Applied* (Glencoe, 1949), pp. 67-147.

13. Cf. F. A. Hayek, *The Counter-Revolution of Science*, p. 209, n. 24.

14. See also L. Mises, *Socialism* (English ed.; London, 1936), pp. 111 ff.; L. Mises, "Vom Weg der subjektivistichen Wertlehre," *Schriften des Vereins für Sozialpolitik*, 183/1, pp. 76-93; L. Mises, "Begreifen und Verstehen," *Schmollers Jahrbuch*, 1930.

15. See, e.g., L. Robbins, *Nature and Significance* (1930); also his "Live and Dead Issues in the Methodology of Economics," *Economica*, August, 1938; F. Kaufmann, *Methodology of the Social Sciences* (English ed.; New York, 1944), ch. XVI; M. Bowley, *Nassau Senior and Classical Political Economy* (1937), p. 64; T. W. Hutchison, *The Significance and Basic Postulates of Economic Theory* (1938); O. Morgenstern, *The Limits of Economics* (English ed.; 1937), p. 154.

16. See, e.g., L. M. Lachmann, "The Science of Human Action," *Economica*, November, 1951, p. 413.

17. See, e.g., G. H. Schmidt, "Rapports de l'économie politique avec la morale et le droit," *Revue d'économie politique*, 1900, p. 334; G. Tarde, *Psychologie économique* (Paris, 1902), p. 151.

18. On the use of teleology for the recognition of causation as running from the future back to the present, see W. C. Mitchell, "Commons on Institutional Economics," *American Economic Review*, December, 1935, reprinted in *The Backward Art of Spending Money*, p. 334; Z. C. Dickinson, "The Relations of Recent Psychological Developments to Economic Theory," *Quarterly Journal of Economics*, May, 1919, p. 388; see also the reference to Weber's writing above in note 10. Cf., how-

ever, M. J. Plotnick, *Werner Sombart and His Type of Economics* (New York, 1937), pp. 88-89.

19. K. Engliš, *Grundlagen des wirtschaftlichen Denkens* (Brunn, 1925).
20. See J. N. Tewari, "What Is Economics?" *Indian Journal of Economics*, April, 1947, pp. 421 ff., for the identification of rationality with purposefulness.
21. For an example of this kind of criticism, see J. Robinson, *Economics Is a Serious Subject* (Cambridge, 1932), p. 10.
22. For this type of objection, see L. M. Fraser, *Economic Thought and Language*, p. 37 n.; T. W. Hutchison, *Significance and Basic Postulates of Economic Theory*, pp. 115 ff.
23. Croce's characterization of the action of a man yielding to temptation as placing himself in contradiction to himself finds a recent echo in a passage in Little's *Critique of Welfare Economics*, p. 23. Little makes it clear that what is meant by a man's maximization of his utility is simply his behaving in the way in which he said he would behave. "Roughly speaking, maximizing utility means telling the truth."
24. *International Economic Papers*, No. 3, p. 201. For an appraisal of Croce's position, see A. L. Macfie, *An Essay on Economy and Value*, Appendix B, pp. 143 ff.
25. *International Economic Papers*, No. 3, p. 177.
26. Professor Mises has not recognized the close similarity to his own position which is evidenced in Croce's writing (see L. Mises, *Theory and History*, p. 308). What appears to be the principal point of difference between their positions has little relevance to the conception of the character of economic science. Both writers emphasize the rationality of *all* human action; both recognize that a chosen program may fail to be adhered to either because of a technical error (an error of knowledge) or because of the choice of a new program of ends with respect to which action will be "rational." Where the two writers disagree is that the discarding of a chosen program in favor of one chosen in response to a "temptation of the moment" is, for Croce, itself a special kind of error—an economic error, an error of will. For Mises, there is room for only one kind of error, an error of knowledge (see *Theory and History*, p. 268). The conscious abandonment of a chosen program under the influence of a fleeting temptation is considered "positively" as merely the adoption of a new set of ends instead of the old, and that is all.
27. G. Tagliacozzo, "Croce and the Nature of Economic Science," *Quarterly Journal of Economics*, May, 1945, pp. 319-320.
28. Especially relevant to the considerations of this section are Mises' strictures on Weber's "ideal type" of rational economic behavior. See above, note 10.
29. The proposition that the notion of purpose implies a constraint that one select the most suitable means for the fulfilment of the purpose is not a proposition *about* that purpose. The proposition as such cannot, for example, be "explained" (as Macfie does) by the postulation of a moral urge to fulfil one's purposes. Rather, the proposition, on the praxeo-

logical view, sets forth the nature of purpose itself. The statement that man's actions are purposeful is thus only another way of saying that man feels constrained to match means to ends.

30. F. H. Knight, "Professor Parsons on Economic Motivation," *Canadian Journal of Economics and Political Science*, 1940, p. 463. In this connection it is of interest to notice that the position of economic science in the face of changing hierarchies of chosen programs has been set forth with exceptional clarity by F. S. C. Northrop in his article "The Impossibility of a Theoretical Science of Economic Dynamics," *Quarterly Journal of Economics*, November, 1941, reprinted as ch. XIII in his *The Logic of the Sciences and the Humanities* (New York: Macmillan & Co., 1947). Northrop demonstrates the impossibility of theoretical economic dynamics (on the assumptions and with the method of contemporary economic theory) by pointing out the lack, in economic affairs, of the conditions for such a theory. The data of economics (human wants) are, for its theorems, purely formal entities, whose specific properties are necessarily not to be considered. Moreover, there is no way of deducing the structure of future wants from present wants because wants obey no "conservation law." Nor, Northrop adds, is there any a priori reason why the subject matter of economics should be conceived in terms of concepts obeying such a law. The quest for an economic dynamics may well "have its basis in a dogmatic assumption, with respect to which our empirical knowledge already gives the lie." Northrop takes two groups of critics to task: those who mistakenly demand of economics that it take account of changes in the basic data— the relevant chosen ends; and those who, despairing of such an achievement, conclude that economics is of no use whatsoever. Both extremes err in their assessment of the nature of the scientific contribution that it is in the power of economic theory to make.

31. See, e.g., L. Mises, *Theory and History*, ch. XII; F. H. Knight, "Professor Parsons on Economic Motivation," *Canadian Journal of Economics and Political Science*, 1940, pp. 463 ff.; F. H. Knight, " 'What Is Truth' in Economics?" *On the History and Method of Economics* (Chicago, 1956), pp. 171-173.

32. For passages in which the a priori view has been compared to scholasticism, see R. F. Harrod, *The Trade Cycle*, pp. 38-39; E. C. Harwood, *Reconstruction of Economics*, p. 39.

33. See, e.g., T. W. Hutchison, *Significance and Basic Postulates of Economic Theory*, p. 116; P. A. Samuelson, *Foundations of Economic Analysis* (Cambridge, 1948), p. 91.

34. On this see the references in the previous note; see also A. G. Papandreou, *Economics as a Science* (1958). For a criticism of this position, see F. Machlup, "The Inferiority Complex of the Social Sciences" in *On Freedom and Free Enterprise, Essays in Honor of Ludwig von Mises*, ed. M. Sennholz (1956).

35. L. Robbins, "Live and Dead Issues in the Methodology of Economics," *Economica*, August, 1938, p. 348.

36. See, e.g., L. Mises, *Theory and History*, pp. 283 ff.; F. H. Knight, " 'What

Is Truth' in Economics?" *On the History and Method of Economics,* p. 160; F. A. Hayek, *Counter-Revolution of Science,* Part I, ch. III; cf. also P. A. Sorokin, *Socio-cultural Causality, Space, Time* (Durham, 1943), ch. I. See also F. S. C. Northrop, *Logic of the Sciences and the Humanities,* p. 247, for the recognition of the "empirical verification" of economic theory in the confirmation of its logical derivation from the immediately confirmed postulates. On this see also M. Rothbard, "Mises' 'Human Action': Comment," *American Economic Review,* March, 1951, p. 181; M. Rothbard, "Towards a Reconstruction of Utility and Welfare Economics" in *On Freedom and Free Enterprise, Essays in Honor of Ludwig von Mises,* ed. M. Sennholz (1956), pp. 225-228.

37. L. Mises, *Human Action* (Yale, 1949), p. 65; cf. M. Pantaleoni, *Pure Economics* (English ed.; London, 1898), p. 8.

38. L. Mises, *Human Action,* p. 66. See also F. A. Hayek, "Economics and Knowledge," *Economica,* 1937; reprinted in *Individualism and Economic Order* (1948), pp. 47-48.

39. See especially the remarks on Mises' "apriorism" by H. Bernadelli in his "What Has Philosophy to Contribute to the Social Sciences, and to Economics in Particular?" *Economica,* November, 1936, p. 449. For an analysis of propositions concerning land rent which displays the a priori nature of the pure economic theory involved as well as its relation to the empirical finding that makes the theory applicable to specific situations, see Hayek, *Counter-Revolution of Science,* p. 32.

40. For a systematic table of the possible praxeological sciences and the place that economics occupies within the system, see M. Rothbard, "Praxeology: Reply to Mr. Schuller," *American Economic Review,* December, 1951, pp. 945-946.

41. F. H. Knight, "The Common Sense of Political Economy," *Journal of Political Economy,* October, 1934, reprinted in *On the History and Method of Economics* (University of Chicago Press, copyright 1956 by the University of Chicago), p. 110.

42. L. Mises, *Human Action,* p. 235.

43. C. L. Robbins, *Nature and Significance,* p. 22.

44. E. Cannan, *Wealth* (1st ed.), ch. I.

45. L. Robbins, *Nature and Significance,* p. 22.

Indices prepared by Vernelia A. Crawford

Note: The subject index to *The Economic Point of View* includes titles of chapters and selections, each listed under the appropriate subject classification. With the exception of these specific page references, which are hyphenated, the numbers in each instance refer to the *first* page of a discussion. A page number followed by a figure in parentheses indicates the number of a footnote reference. Author entries follow in a separate index.

Index of Subjects

217

Index of Authors

223